T0311784

Overtourism and Tourism Education

Since 2017, the term 'overtourism' has become the buzzword for destinations suffering the strain of tourism. It is a critical issue for the 21st century and beyond, and to date has only been examined from a tourism industry perspective. This book takes a different stand by investigating overtourism from a tourism education perspective.

The recent global COVID-19 pandemic was expected to halt travel and, arguably, overtourism. However, industry experts and researchers share the opinion that instead of declining, overtourism is simply experiencing a shift, with a swarm of 'second home' and domestic travel that is likely to engulf many tourism destinations. Against this backdrop, the issue of overtourism remains relevant and studies on ways to cultivate responsible consumer mindsets to deal with overtourism and other sustainability issues in the tourism industry are called for. This book focuses on education as a transformative and strategic tool to tackle overtourism and related negative impacts. It presents original research on the topics of overtourism, education, and sustainability, and puts forward a range of practical and transformative tourism education strategies to mitigate overtourism and to promote the sustainable development of destinations.

This book will be of great interest to upper-level students, researchers, and academics in tourism, development studies, cultural studies, and sustainability, as well as professionals in the field of tourism management.

Hugues Séraphin is Senior Lecturer in Event and Tourism Management Studies at the University of Winchester, UK. Prior to his career in academia, he worked in various roles in the tourism and hospitality sector in the Caribbean and in Europe.

Anca C. Yallop is a Senior Lecturer in Business Strategy at Auckland University of Technology, Auckland, New Zealand. She previously worked at the University of Winchester, UK. Her research has been published in book chapters and peer-reviewed international journals.

Contemporary Geographies of Leisure, Tourism and Mobility

Series Editor: C. Michael Hall, Professor at the Department of Management, College of Business and Economics, University of Canterbury, Christchurch, New Zealand

The aim of this series is to explore and communicate the intersections and relationships between leisure, tourism and human mobility within the social sciences.

It will incorporate both traditional and new perspectives on leisure and tourism from contemporary geography, e.g. notions of identity, representation and culture, while also providing for perspectives from cognate areas such as anthropology, cultural studies, gastronomy and food studies, marketing, policy studies and political economy, regional and urban planning, and sociology, within the development of an integrated field of leisure and tourism studies.

Also, increasingly, tourism and leisure are regarded as steps in a continuum of human mobility. Inclusion of mobility in the series offers the prospect to examine the relationship between tourism and migration, the sojourner, educational travel, and second home and retirement travel phenomena.

The series comprises two strands:

Contemporary Geographies of Leisure, Tourism and Mobility aims to address the needs of students and academics, and the titles will be published in hardback and paperback. Titles include:

Tourism Development in Japan
Themes, Issues and Challenges
Edited by Richard Sharpley and Kumi Kato

Overtourism and Tourism Education
A Strategy for Sustainable Tourism Futures
Edited by Hugues Séraphin and Anca C. Yallop

Tourism in Asian Cities
Edited by Saurabh Kumar Dixit

For more information about this series, please visit: www.routledge.com/
Contemporary-Geographies-of-Leisure-Tourism-and-Mobility/book-series/
SE0522

Overtourism and Tourism Education

A Strategy for Sustainable Tourism Futures

Edited by
Hugues Séraphin and
Anca C. Yallop

LONDON AND NEW YORK

First published 2021
by Routledge
2 Park Square, Milton Park, Abingdon, Oxon OX14 4RN

and by Routledge
52 Vanderbilt Avenue, New York, NY 10017

Routledge is an imprint of the Taylor & Francis Group, an informa business

British Library Cataloguing-in-Publication Data
A catalogue record for this book is available from the British Library

Library of Congress Cataloging-in-Publication Data
Names: Séraphin, Hugues, editor. | Yallop, Anca C., editor.
Title: Overtourism and tourism education : a strategy for sustainable
tourism futures / edited by Hugues Séraphin and Anca C. Yallop.
Description: Abingdon, Oxon ; New York, NY : Routledge, 2021. |
Series: Contemporary geographies of leisure, tourism and mobility |
Includes bibliographical references and index.
Subjects: LCSH: Overtourism—Study and teaching (Higher) |
Tourism—Study and teaching (Higher)
Classification: LCC G156.5.O94 O95 2021 (print) |
LCC G156.5.O94 (ebook) | DDC 338.4/79100711—dc23
LC record available at https://lccn.loc.gov/2020026354
LC ebook record available at https://lccn.loc.gov/2020026355

ISBN: 978-0-367-46884-2 (hbk)
ISBN: 978-1-003-03176-5 (ebk)

Typeset in Times New Roman
by codeMantra

Contents

Figures

Tables

Contributors

Kathleen M. Adams is Professor of anthropology at Loyola University Chicago. She is the author of several books and has also published articles on the politics of tourism, the genesis of tourism imagery, tourist arts, tourism and resilience, public interest anthropology in heritage sites, and tourism's cultural ramifications for hinterland groups in Indonesia.

Richard W. Butler is Emeritus Professor at Strathclyde University, Glasgow, having taught also at the University of Western Ontario, the University of Surrey, James Cook University (Australia), CISET, Venice and NHTV University (Breda, Holland). Trained as a geographer, he is a past president of the International Academy for the Study of Tourism and of the Canadian Association for Leisure Studies. In 2016 he was named UNWTO Ulysses Laureate. He has been advisor to UNWTO and Canadian, Australian, and UK governments. He has published over 100 articles and 20 books on tourism. His main research interests are tourism development cycles and tourism on islands and in remote areas. He is a lapsed bird-watcher and poor golfer.

María M. Carballo has a PhD from the University of Las Palmas de Gran Canaria. She is currently a professor of economics at the University of Las Palmas de Gran Canaria. She is a researcher at the University Institute of Tourism and Sustainable Economic Development (TIDES). She specialises in destination image, tourist behaviour, safety and security, and environment issues in tourism and in analysing tourist preferences.

Rita R. Carballo has a PhD from the University of Las Palmas de Gran Canaria. She is currently a professor of tourism and business at the University of Las Palmas de Gran Canaria and a researcher at the University Institute of Tourism and Sustainable Economic Development (TIDES). She specialises in cultural, tourism experience, tourist behaviour, destination image, and safety and security issues in tourism, and their management and marketing implications.

Nimit R. Chowdhary is a professor of tourism. He heads the Department of Tourism and Hospitality Management at Jamia Millia Islamia, a top ranked university in India. He has more than 25 years of teaching, training, consulting, and research experience. He has authored nine books, published around 115 papers and chapters. He has supervised 15 PhDs. His research interests are in tourism marketing, destination management, rural tourism, and tour guiding and leadership. He has significant experience of teaching in different regions of India and around the world. He has successfully administered academic programmes and institutions.

Monica M. Coroş is Associate Professor in travel agency management, international tourism operations, cultural tourism, entrepreneurship, and purchasing management in the Department of Hospitality Services, Faculty of Business, Babeş-Bolyai University of Cluj-Napoca (Romania). She completed her doctoral degree in management at the Babeş-Bolyai University of Cluj-Napoca (Romania) with a thesis on tourism demand and supply management. Her research covers topics related to destination management organisations, sustainable tourism, rural tourism, entrepreneurship, and SMEs.

Dr Naomi F Dale is an associate professor of management in the Faculty of Business, Government and Law at the University of Canberra. She was the recipient of an Australian Postgraduate Award scholarship and completed her PhD in 2013 investigating destination choice by school excursion groups in Australia. Naomi's research includes educational tourism, policy impacts of curriculum, and visitor research at national capital and cultural attractions. Other emerging research interests include the application of social media, education strategies for engagement through e-platforms (tourism and events). Other key areas are around sustainability, service channels, consumer behavior, and marketing.

Patrick J.N. L'Espoir Decosta is a senior lecturer in the College of Business and Economics at the Australian National University, Canberra, Australia. He completed his PhD in 2011 at the Hong Kong Polytechnic University on the legacy of colonialism in the tourism development of former island colonies. His research interests span the areas of curriculum development in higher education, evidence-based management of education, tourism marketing and promotion, and critical studies of tourism. Other key areas of research include the sharing economy, the commercial relevance of place and space.

Frédéric Dosquet obtained his PhD in marketing from Pau University (France). Professor at ESC PAU Business School, he has published more than 40 contributions mainly in tourism, public management, and political marketing. He is a visiting professor at University Saint Joseph de Beirut (Lebanon) and Lagune University (Ivory Coast); he is a columnist in the French newspapers, radios, and TV.

Babu George achieved his PhD in management studies from Goa University, Doctor of Business Administration from Swiss Management Center University, Master of Tourism Administration from Pondicherry University, and BSc in Electronics from Mahatma Gandhi University. George has more than 15 years of advanced business research, university teaching and administrative service experience in the United States and internationally. Before joining Fort Hays State University in 2015, Dr George worked for Swiss Management Center University, University of Liverpool, University of Nevada Las Vegas, Alaska Pacific University, and the University of Southern Mississippi, among others. He is a visiting professor at various higher education institutions around the world. He is the editor of *International Journal of Qualitative Research in Services.* Until recently he was the managing editor of *Journal of Tourism.* He has more than a hundred peer reviewed and well-cited research publications. He has authored and edited more than seven books. He is a passionate observer of the complex dynamics of creative destruction that makes idea innovations possible. In his free time, he offers free consulting for the budding grassroots level entrepreneurs.

Oana A. Gică is Associate Professor in the Department of Hospitality Services, Faculty of Business at Babeș-Bolyai University of Cluj-Napoca (Romania). She holds a doctoral degree in management. Her main research topics are entrepreneurship and SME management, strategic planning, sustainable tourism, and rural tourism.

Nichole C. Hugo is an Assistant Professor at Eastern Illinois University in the Hospitality and Tourism Department. She holds a PhD in community resources and development, an MS in tourism and recreation management, and a BS in tourism development and management from Arizona State University, USA. Her research and teaching focus on international tourism management, marketing developing countries, and sustainable practices in the tourism industry. Previous publications include research on sustainable practices in the bed and breakfast industry, the impact of the Zika virus on tourism in Jamaica, and the role of culture and heritage in community festivals.

Snigdha Kainthola is a research scholar of tourism in Jamia Millia Islamia, a top ranked university in India. She is a graduate in history and has completed her master's in business administration (tourism) with specialisation in Travel and Tourism. She has worked in the tourism industry for two years as a tour guide and is experienced in handling tourist groups, particularly solo women travelling outside India. Her research interests are management, tourism marketing, spiritual and experiential tourism.

Carmelo J. León has a PhD from the University of Las Palmas de Gran Canaria and an MSc in economics from the University of Manchester, UK. He is the Director of the Management Board of the University Institute of Tourism and Sustainable Economic Development (TIDES) at the University of Las Palmas. He specialises in environmental and socio-economic aspects of tourism and the environment, and in developing the marketing implications of analysing tourist preferences.

Seleni Matus is a PhD candidate at Rovira I Virgili University, Tarragona, Spain. Her research interest is in tourism governance and the role of networks in destination management. Seleni is the director of the International Institute of Tourism Studies (IITS) and teaches sustainable tourism destination management at the George Washington University in Washington DC. She is the faculty member of the global tourism practicum of the GW School of Business. Other key areas of interest include tourism education and adventure tourism.

Maximiliano Korstanje is a leading global cultural theorist specialising in terrorism, mobilities, and tourism. Korstanje serves as a senior researcher at the University of Palermo, Buenos Aires, Argentina, (economics department) and as an Editor in Chief of *International Journal of Safety and Security in Tourism and Hospitality* (University of Palermo, Argentina). He has acted as a visiting professor at CERS (Centre for Ethnicity and Racism Studies) at the University of Leeds (United Kingdom), TIDES in the University of Las Palmas de Gran Canarias, Spain and the University of La Habana, Cuba. In 2016, he was included as Scientific Editor for Studies and Perspective in Tourism (CIET) and as an honorary member of the Scientific Council of Research and Investigation hosted by UDET (University of Tourist Specialities, Quito Ecuador). With more than 1,200 publications and 30 books, Korstanje is an editor of the book series *Advances in Hospitality, Tourism and Service Industries* (IGI Global, US) and *Tourism Security-Safety and Post Conflict Destinations* (Emerald Group Publishing, UK). He is elected as a foreign faculty member of the Mexican Academy of Tourism Research (Mexico) as well as a foreign member of The Tourism Crisis Management Institute (University of Florida, US). In 2018, his biography was selected to be part of the roster of Alfred Nelson Marquis Lifetime Achievement Award (Marquis Who's Who). Korstanje has been awarded as Editor in Chief Emeritus for the *International Journal of Cyber-warfare and Terrorism*. Currently he works as an active advisor and reviewer of different editorial projects at the leading academic publishers such as Elsevier, Routledge, Emerald Group Publishing, Palgrave Macmillan, Cambridge Scholar Publishing, Edward Elgar, CABI, Nova Science Publishers, and IGI global among others. His latest book is *The Challenges of Democracy in the War on Terror* (Routledge UK).

Ovidiu I. Moisescu is Associate Professor in branding, public relations, marketing places and tourism economics at Babeş-Bolyai University of Cluj-Napoca, Romania. He completed his PhD in marketing at the West University of Timişoara (Romania), as well as a postdoctoral research post at Babeş-Bolyai University of Cluj-Napoca (Romania) and Corvinus University of Budapest (Hungary). His research focuses on brand equity, CSR, tourism marketing, and place branding.

Peter M. Sanchez is Professor of political science at Loyola University Chicago. He earned his PhD in government from the University of Texas at Austin. He has authored two books and numerous book chapters and articles published in academic journals, such as *Journal of Latin American Studies, International Politics, The Latin Americanist, Annals of Tourism Research, Harvard Journal of Hispanic Policy,* and *Journal of Developing Areas.*

Hugues Séraphin, PhD, is a senior lecturer in event and tourism management studies. He is also an associate researcher at La Rochelle Business School (France). Hugues Seraphin holds a PhD from the Université de Perpignan Via Domitia (France) and joined The University of Winchester Business School in 2012. He was the programme leader of the event management programme between 2015 and 2018. Dr Hugues Seraphin has expertise and interests in tourism development and management in post-colonial, post-conflict and post-disaster destinations. He has recently published in *International Journal of Culture, Tourism, and Hospitality Research*; *Current Issues in Tourism*; *Journal of Policy Research in Tourism, Leisure and Events*; *Journal of Business Research*; *Worldwide Hospitality and Tourism Themes*; *Tourism Analysis*; and *Journal of Destination Marketing & Management.*

Tammi J. Sinha has over 20 years' experience as a lean practitioner, academic, and change agent working across sectors and universities, taking a communities of practice approach to build capability in change, innovation, sustainability, and improvement. Research interests include climate action through systems thinking, circular design, operations, and supply chains. Currently she is Director of the Centre for Climate Action.

Svetla Stoyanova-Bozhkova is Senior Lecturer in the Faculty of Management at Bournemouth University in the UK. She is Chartered Manager and Senior Fellow of the HEA. Svetla graduated from the University of Birmingham, Centre for Urban and Regional Studies and holds a doctoral degree in tourism development in transition economies from Bournemouth University. Her teaching experience in the UK and abroad is complemented by a 20-year experience at senior management positions in the industry and academia. Svetla has a wide range of academic and research interests including economic development, sustainability, destination management, customer experience management, and emotional intelligence.

Pinaz Tiwari is a research scholar of tourism in Jamia Millia Islamia, a top ranked university in India. She is a graduate in commerce and has

completed her master's in business administration (Tourism) with specialisation in international tourism business. She has worked in the tourism industry for a short span of two years. She has experience in customer
relationship management and has worked closely with destination management companies and travel agents. She enjoys teaching, travelling,
and reading books. Her research interests are over-tourism, destination
management, sustainable tourism, and tourism marketing.

Beverley Wilson-Wünsch obtained her PhD at the School of Business of the
University of Maastricht, the Netherlands. She is a full-time professor
in the Department Hospitality, Tourism and Events at the International
University of Bad Honnef, Germany (IUBH Campus Studies). She held a
visiting professorship in the Department of Hospitality Management, at
the University of Missouri, Columbia, USA for some time. Before that,
she worked as a lecturer of hospitality management at the Stenden University, the Netherlands for over seven years. Beverley's research spans
tourism and hospitality as well as education, training, and development
in these areas.

Anca C. Yallop, PhD, is a senior lecturer in business strategy at Auckland
University of Technology (AUT), New Zealand. She holds a PhD in
Marketing (Romania) and has completed her second PhD in marketing
research ethics (Auckland University of Technology, New Zealand). Dr
Anca C. Yallop specialises in strategy, responsible management and eth-
ics, insight management, and business research methods. Her research
has appeared in journals such as the *International Journal of Market
Research, Leisure Studies, Journal of Information, Communication and
Ethics in Society, World Leisure Journal, International Journal of Culture, Tourism and Hospitality Research, Journal of Tourism Futures,* and
Worldwide Hospitality and Tourism Themes. She serves on the editorial
review board of the *International Journal of Market Research.*

COVID-19 and the mutation of overtourism

The case of France

Hugues Séraphin and Frédéric Dosquet

Introduction

COVID-19, as a global pandemic, has led to a travel ban in and out destinations, which is severely impacting the tourism industry and cognate sectors (Jamal & Budke, 2020). However, in France, the outbreak of COVID-19 has not stopped individuals from moving in and out of cities (INSEE, 2020). Instead, the outbreak of the virus has led to an exodus from major cities to the countryside or coastal areas (INSEE, 2020). As of 17 March 2020, Paris had lost 11% of its residents (INSEE, 2020). Moving from one place (permanent residency) to another (second home) for safety and health reasons could be assimilated to tourism, since Jaakson (1986) associated second home tourism with terms such as surety, and time and distance (what perfectly fits the context of this study). In addition, from an historic perspective, one of the very first forms of tourism was health related (Lickorish & Jenkins, 1997). Nowadays, this form of special interest tourism is known as wellness tourism, defined as 'The act of travelling for the purpose of physical or psychological wellbeing' (Stainton, 2020 [Online]). COVID-19, as a pandemic, was expected to stop tourism (Getz, 2012; Jamal & Budke, 2020); instead, it has shed light on second home tourism in some areas in France, way before the start of the tourism season, and for non-tourism–related reasons.

The research question (RQ) of this study is as follows: can the exodus of Parisians to the countryside and coastal areas in France be considered as a form of overtourism?

For this study, France is chosen because it is the world's leading destination (Gouv.fr [Online]).

Methodology

Theoretical foundation of the study

This study adopts the following definition of overtourism, which is a combination of two existing definitions of the term (Capocchi et al., 2019; Singh, 2018): overtourism describes destinations where hosts or locals feel that there are too many visitors, whose interests conflict with theirs, which subsequently leads to a decrease in the quality of life of both parties.

Theoretical framework of this study

Based on a deductive approach, which is defined as a method that seeks to draw valid conclusions from initial premises (Hammond & Wellington, 2013), the starting point of this study is the following syllogism: overtourism is assimilated with an excess of visitors to a destination; COVID-19 has led to an exodus of Parisians to the countryside and coastal areas; therefore, COVID-19 is contributing to overtourism.

Stages of the study

- Stage 1
  The study provides evidence that the exodus of Parisians presents the same characteristics as overtourism. This stage is essentially based on literature review, therefore theory-based.
- Stage 2
  This stage has the same purpose as stage 1 but uses a different approach. Indeed, this stage is based on a news media narrative approach, therefore based on practice (or real life case).
- Stage 3
  The findings from stage 1 (theory) and 2 (practice) will be combined, and a conclusion drawn.

Overall, this study could be said to have adopted bricolage as the overarching methodological approach. Indeed, for this approach the researcher or bricoleur is 'moving between different disciplines and uses different tools, methods and techniques, whatever is at hand, in order to construct meaning out of data' (Hammond & Wellington, 2013: 15). This research method is also a way to avoid commitment to traditional research steps, and as a result bricolage, as a research method, is also referred to as 'trial of error' (Hammond & Wellington, 2013). For Cardno et al. (2017), bricolage is all about daring to be different. That said, this method of research is also said to offer a new form of rigour to social research (Kincheloe, 2005), and in some cases a necessary step towards developing theory (Fincher et al., 2011). The steps followed by this study have been influenced by Cardno et al. (2017).

Pilot study

The purpose of the study is not to rely on an exhaustive literature review. The limited number of articles used could be explained by the fact this research note is first and foremost a pilot study, which is a small scale version of a full study (Van Teijlingen & Hundley, 2001). "Pilot studies are particularly valuable in situations where little is known about the research topic" (Persaud, 2012: 2).

Application of the methodology

Application of stage 1

The first column of Table 1 lists some randomly selected characteristics of overtourism. The second column (characteristics of the exodus of Parisians triggered by COVID-19) provides evidence of matches with the first column. When no information is provided it is because evidence is not supporting evidence. As for the last one, it provides the different sources of information.

Table 1 Similarities between overtourism and exodus triggered by COVID-19

Some characteristics of overtourism	Characteristics of exodus triggered by COVID-19	Sources
Leisure purpose (either built/ natural heritage or tangible/intangible heritage)		Adie et al. (2019)
Poor destination planning/ management	Limited effort by the French government to stop the exodus at the beginning of the breakout of the pandemic	Panayiotopoulos and Pisano (2019); (*Le Télégramme* [Online]; *Nouvel Obs* [Online]); Seraphin and Ivanov (2020); Phi (2019); Adie et al. (2019)
Poor revenue management		
Aggressive marketing strategy		Seraphin et al. (2019)
Destination overrun by tourists	As of 17 March 2020, Paris has lost 11% of its residents, who have all moved to their second home (countryside/coastal areas)	INSEE (2020); (*Le Télégramme* [Online]; *Libération* [Online])
Tourist numbers are impacting on the life of locals	As a form of tourism, second homes also remain a challenge for municipalities, due to the fact that they trigger an increase in property price, increase in crime rate, accidents, need to increase public transport provision, and so on, which subsequently lead to a need for municipalities to increase their assignment of resources in terms of police, health care, and so on In the COVID-19 context, second home tourism is pointed out for causing a substantial increase in the population in rural areas	Phi (2019); Hoogendoorn and Visser (2015); Visser (2008); Larsson and Muller (2017); Marjavaara (2007); Hiltunen (2008); Blazquez-Salom et al. (2019); (*Le Télégramme* [Online]; *Libération* [Online])
Overtourism leads to tourismphobia	The exodus to the countryside/coastal areas as a result of COVID-19 is causing distress and anger among locals due to the fear that visitors are spreading the virus	Phi (2017); (*Le Télégramme* [Online]; *Nouvel Obs* [Online]); Séraphin et al., 2020)

Source: The authors.

Table 1 reveals that there are similarities between some of the characteristics of overtourism, and the exodus of Parisians triggered by COVID-19. The level of correlation could be said to be moderate to strong based on the correlation coefficient and strength of association (Table 2), adapted from the Pearson product-moment correlation (Silver et al., 2013).

Application of stage 2

Similar to Phi (2019) who used news media to frame overtourism, this study also adopts a news media narrative approach as its analytical framework, as it 'can produce important insight into emerging wicked problems' (Phi, 2019: 1). The use of news media can also be justified by the fact that 61% of sources used in the very first paper on COVID-19 and tourism, by Jamal and Budke (2020), are current media sources. This type of source is particularly relevant and accepted for unfolding situations such as the current pandemic (Jamal & Budke, 2019).

Documentary analysis (Table 3), using an adaptation of a framework (Figure 1), developed by Hammond and Wellington (2013), was performed on 23 French news articles (Appendix 1) published in leading national newspaper outlets (such as 'Liberation', 'Le Nouvel Observateur', and 'Le Parisien').

Once again, the limited number of articles used can be explained by the fact that this research note is first and foremost a pilot study. In addition, in a study attempting to define the pedigree of overtourism, Capocchi et al. (2019) analysed 22 journal articles.

Table 2 Level of match between overtourism and exodus triggered by COVID-19

Range of correlation coefficient	*Strength of association*
6/7 or more characteristics in Table 1 are matching	Perfect match
5/7 characteristics in Table 1 are matching	Very strong
4/7 characteristics in Table 1 are matching	Moderate to strong
3/7 characteristics in Table 1 are matching	Weak to moderate
2/7 characteristics in Table 1 are matching	Weak
1/7 characteristics in Table 1 are matching	Very weak
None of the characteristics in Table 1 is matching	Nonexistent to very weak

Source: The authors (adapted from Silver et al., 2013).

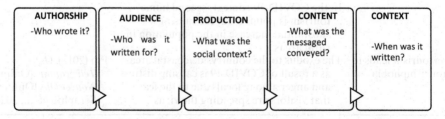

Figure 1 Documentary analysis framework.

Table 3 Analysis of French news media on exodus related to COVID-19

Item No.	Authorship/source	Date released/date published	Production Context/Frame	Audience	Centring on	Content (summary/key points)
1	*Le Parisien*	16.03.20	COVID-19	General public	Crisis tourists	Before the strict lockdown Parisians are leaving Paris for safer environments (generally second home in the countryside).
2	*Marianne*	16.03.20			Crisis tourists	Before the strict lockdown Parisians are leaving Paris for safer environments (generally second home in the countryside)
3	*Libération*	16.03.20			Travelling issues	Parisians travelling to second homes in the countryside are spreading the virus
4	*Le Télégramme*	17.03.20			Locals Crisis tourists Destination management	Locals consider that Parisians are putting them in danger by coming with the virus, as Paris was the starting point of the pandemic in France, and the leading city in France in terms of number of people affected. Parisians are told they are not welcome in Belle-ile-en-mer as a destination for Parisians May: Parisians have a second home (countryside/coastal areas) Some destinations can't cope with the flux of visitors from Paris (supply)
5	*HuffPost*	17.03.20			Crisis tourists Destination management	Parisians are leaving Paris for safer environments (generally second home in the countryside) The countryside is the favourite destination of the Parisians for a lockdown period

(Continued)

Item No.	Authorship/source	Date released/date published	Production/ Context/Frame	Audience	Centring on	Content (summary/key points)
6	L'Express	17.03.20			Crisis tourists Destination management	Parisians are leaving Paris for safer environments (generally second home in the countryside)
7	Sud Ouest	17.03.20			Destination management	The countryside is associated with well-being and cities with diseases
						Local authority/government to put in place safety measures and limit exodus towards the countryside
						Locals are renting their countryside houses to Parisians
8	Nouvel Obs	17.03.20			Destination management	Countryside/coastal destinations can't cope with the flux of Parisians (water issues/ health and safety issues)
9	Nouvel Obs	18.03.20			Crisis tourists	Parisians are leaving Paris for safer environments (seaside/coastal areas)
10	Egora	18.03.20			Travelling issues	Parisians travelling to the countryside are spreading the virus
11	Le Progres.fr	18.03.20			Locals	Parisians are told they are not welcome
12	20 minutes	18.03.20			Travelling issues	Parisians travelling to the countryside are spreading the virus
13	DNA	18.03.20			Travelling issues	Parisians travelling to the countryside are spreading the virus
14	DNA	20.03.20			Destination management	Some destinations can't cope with the flux of visitors from Paris (supply)
15	Europresse	20.03.20			Destination management	Brittany as a destination for Parisians

No.	Source	Date	Category	Description
16	*Ouest-France*	24.03.20	Locals	Locals consider that Parisians are putting them in danger by coming with the virus, as Paris was the starting point of the pandemic in France, and the leading city in France in terms of number of people affected
17	*Le Monde*	26.03.20	Crisis tourists	1 million Parisians left Paris within a week
18	*Ouest-France*	27.03.20	Crisis tourists	Between 1 and 2 million Parisians left Paris within a week
19	Actu.fr	30.03.20	Crisis tourists Destination management	The countryside is the favourite destination of Parisians
20	LCI	09.04.20	Crisis tourists	Sarthe as a destination for Parisians +1/10 Parisians are leaving to the countryside
21	France Info TV	10.04.20	Destinations management	Yvonne (+7% increase in the population) Gers (+ 6% increase in the population) Orne/Cotes d'Armor (+5% increase in the population)
22	France Bleu	11.04.20	Crisis tourists Destination management	The countryside is the favourite destination of Parisians Pays de la Loire as a destination for Parisians
23	Europresse	15.04.20	Locals	Locals consider that Parisians are putting them in danger by coming with the virus, as Paris was the starting point of the pandemic in France, and the leading city in France in terms of number of people affected Locals are getting violent against Parisians (tourismphobia)

Source: The author (adapted from Hammond & Wellington, 2013 + news media).

The exodus phenomenon triggered by COVID-19 centres on (Table 3):

1   'Crisis tourists', defined in this study as 'individuals or groups traveling from one place to another for the purpose of physical and/or psychological wellbeing during a crisis (global warming, energy crisis, war, terrorism or global pandemics)', is the most dominant theme, which highlights the tendency of these tourists to travel to their second home, generally located in so considered safer destinations (in the case of this study: countryside or coastal areas).
2   On locals, who are considered as victims. The highlights are (a) the negative impacts on local residents such as the spread of the virus and shortage of some supplies and (b) the development of tourismphobia towards Parisians (cars and other belongings are vandalised; Parisians are told they are not welcome).
3   Destination management, as rural areas are not able to cope with the influx of Parisians, who, because of their second home, have made those destinations their favourite destinations during the crisis.
4   Travel issues (mobility of 'crisis tourists'), which are contributing to the spread of the virus to non or less affected areas. The bad management of central government and local authorities is also pointed out (*Le Télégramme* [Online]).

The exodus triggered by COVID-19 centres on the same elements identified by Phi (2019); the slight difference is that the exodus triggered by the crisis is also focused on issues related to mobility from a life or death perspective, what could be assimilated to dark tourism, a form of tourism associated with terms such as 'death', 'macabre', and 'morbid' (Lenon & Foley, 2005), whereas for overtourism the focus is on impacts on the environment (Phi, 2019), the quality of life of locals (Blazquez-Salom et al., 2019), heritage (Adie, Falk and Savioli, 2019), and so on. The exodus triggered by the pandemic is endangering the life of locals, because of the spread of the virus (*Le Télégramme* [Online]; *Nouvel Obs* [Online]), which gives a new perspective to the relationship between locals and visitors, and to tourismphobia.

The level of correlation between the centring elements related to exodus triggered by COVID-19 and the centring elements related to overtourism could be said to be very strong based on the correlation coefficient and strength of association (Table 4).

Table 4 Level of match between centring overtourism and centring exodus triggered by COVID-19

Range of correlation coefficient	*Strength of association*
4/4 centring match	Perfect match
3/4 centring match	Very strong
2/4 centring match	Moderate to strong
1/4 centring match	Weak
None of the centring match	Nonexistent to very weak

Source: The authors (adapted from Silver et al., 2013).

Overall results and discussion

Application of stage 3

The more conceptual focus analysis aspect of the study reveals a moderate to strong correlation between characteristics of overtourism and exodus triggered by COVID-19. As for the more practical focus analysis aspect of the study based on news media, it reveals a very strong correlation between the elements overtourism is centring on and the elements the exodus caused by the pandemic is centring on. Based on both findings, it could therefore be said that there is a correlation between overtourism and the exodus of Parisians. However, because of the differences, this research note is referring to the term 'mutation' of overtourism.

Mutation

In tourism, Fournier (2010) explains that a mutation is the shift from one stage to another, and the shift can be the result of a change of a variable (environment, context, and social). The term 'mutation' is also associated with the terms 'evolution' (Girard, 2010) or 'transformation' (Breton, 2004). This definition perfectly suits the context of this study, since:

- The exodus triggered by the pandemic is mainly triggered by the fact that many Parisians own a second home (INSEE, 2020); *Le Télégramme* [Online]; *Libération* [Online]), and not by the popularity of the destination (Singh, 2018), the heritage (Adie et al., 2019), an aggressive marketing strategy (Séraphin et al., 2019), and so on, as it is usually the case for overtourism.
- Overtourism which has so far only been presented in literature as sensu stricto, tourism related (Dodds & Butler, 2019; Milano, Cheer & Novelli, 2019; Séraphin et al., 2020), as centring exclusively on (1) tourists, and the fact that they travel massively to popular destinations at the same time; (2) locals, who are presented as victims; (3) cities, which witness sometimes the destruction of their heritage; and (4) and the industry, accused of bad management (Adie et al., 2019; Phi, 2019). This study adds survival as a centring element that overtourism does not have. This additional element has therefore shed light on second home tourism as a placebo to COVID-19.

Second home tourism

Second home is associated with terms such as routine and novelty, inversion, back-to-nature, identity, surety, continuity, work, elitism, aspiration, time and distance (Jaakson, 1986), vacation home, holiday home, and leisure home (Roca, 2013). As a form of tourism, second homes also remain a challenge for municipalities, due to the fact that they trigger an increase in property price (Hoogendoorn & Visser, 2015; Visser, 2008), an increase in crime rate, accidents, the need to increase public transport provision, and so on, which subsequently lead to a need for municipalities to increase their assignment of resources in terms of police, health care, and so on (Larsson & Muller, 2017).

The characteristics of second home tourism are quite related to the characteristics of overtourism covered in Table 1. As COVID-19 has led Parisians to move to their second home, it gives more ground to the evidence so far provided in this study to argue that COVID-19 has led to a mutation or transformation of overtourism, supported this time by second home tourism.

Equally important is mentioning the fact that this exodus to second home (countryside areas or coastal areas) triggered by COVID-19 is not indigenous to France, as it happens in other parts of the world such as the United States, Turkey, Spain, Italy, Germany, Greece, and Norway (Appendix 2).

Conclusion

This study has connected COVID-19 with three forms of tourism, namely, second home tourism, overtourism, and dark tourism. In addition, three main findings have drawn from this study:

- First, there is a correlation between overtourism and the exodus of Parisians to their second home.
- Second, whether triggered by crisis or tourism, an exodus is centred on the same four core elements, namely, tourists, locals, destinations, and destination management.
- Third, the exodus created by crisis is a mutation of overtourism generated by leisure purposes, marketing, low cost of tourism products and service, poor planning, and so on (Adie et al., 2019; Panayiotopoulos & Pisano, 2019; Seraphin et al., 2019; Seraphin & Ivanov, 2020) because (1) the motivation is survival in a pleasant and safe environment, (2) the destination is chosen according to the location of the second home, (3) tourismphobia is not towards foreigners but towards fellow citizens, and (4) this new form of overtourism suggests a return to nature away from cities (Lickorish & Jenkins, 1997).

The results of this study could potentially be generalised, as the exodus phenomenon experienced by Paris is also experienced by other major cities of the world.

References

Adie, B.A., Falk, M., and Savioli, M. (2019). Overtourism as a perceived threat to cultural heritage in Europe. *Current Issues in Tourism*, pp. 1–5, doi:10.1080/13683 500.2019.1687661.

Blazquez-Salom, M., Blanco-Romero, A., Carbonell, J.C. and Murray, I. (2019). "Tourist gentrification of retail shops in Plama (Majorca)," In Milano, C., Cheer, J.M., and Novelli, M. (Ed.), *Overtourism: Excesses, discontents and measures in travel and tourism*, CABI, Wallingford, pp. 190–204.

Breton, J.M. (2004). Paradigme d' ecotourisme et societies traditionelles en mutation: Le cas de l' Outre-mer français, *Teoros*, 23(2), 54–60.

Canosa, A., Graham, A. and Wilson, E. (2019). "My overloved town: The challenges of growing up in a small coastal tourist destination (Byron Bay, Australia)," In Milano, C., Cheer, J.M., and Novelli, M. (Ed.), *Overtourism: Excesses, discontents and measures in travel and tourism*, CABI, Wallingford, pp. 190–205.

Capocchi, A., Vallone, C., Amaduzzi, A. and Pierotti, M. (2019). Is 'overtourism' a new issue in tourism development or just a new term for an already known phenomenon? *Current Issues in Tourism*, doi: 10.1080/13683500.2019.1638353.

Cardno, C., Rosales-Anderson, N. and McDonald, M. (2017). Documentary analysis hui: An emergent bricolage method for culturally responsive qualitative research. *MAI Journal*, 6(2), 143–152.

Dodds, R. and Butler, R. (Ed.), *Overtourism*, De Gruyter, Berlin.

Fincher, S., Tenenberg, J. and Robins. A. (2011). *Research design: Necessary bricolage*. https://dl.acm.org/doi/abs/10.1145/2016911.2016919.

Fournier, L.S. (2010). Mise en tourisme des produits du terroir, evenements festifs et mutations du Patrimoine ethnologique en Provence (France). *Ethnologies*, 32(2), 103–144.

Getz, D. (2012). *Event studies, theory, research, policies for planned events*, Routledge, New York.

Girard, M. (2010). Recompositions du monde artisanal et mutations urbaines au regard des mises en Patrimoine et en tourisme au Maghreb et au Moyen-Orient (FES, Istanbul, Alep). *Les Cahiers d EMAM*, 20, 103–105.Hammond, M. and Wellington, J. (2013). *Research methods. The key concepts*, Routledge, Abingdon.

Hiltunen, M.J. (2008). Environmental impacts of rural second home tourism. Case Lake District in Finland. *Scandinavian Journal of Hospitality and Tourism*, 7(3), 243–265.

Hoogendoorn, G. and Visser, G. (2015). The economic impact of second home development in small-town south Africa. *Tourism Recreation Research*, 35(1), 55–66.

INSEE (2020). "Population présente sur le territoire avant et après le début du confinement – Premiers résultats," 24 April. https://www.insee.fr/fr/information/4477356.

Jaakson, R. (1986). Second-home domestic tourism. *Annals of Tourism Research*, 13(3), 367–391.

Jamal, T. and Budke, C. (2020). Tourism in a world with pandemics: Local-global responsibility and action. *Journal of Tourism Futures*, doi:10.1108/JTF-02-2020-0014.

Kincheloe, J.L. (2005). On to the next level: Continuing the conceptualisation of the bricolage. *Qualitative Inquiry*, 11(3), 323–350.

Larsson, L., and Muller, D.K. (2017). Coping with second home tourism: Responses and strategies of private and public service providers in western Sweden. *Current Issues in Tourism*, 22(16), 1958–1974.

Lennon, J. and Foley, M. (2005). *Dark tourism: The attraction of death and disaster*. Thomson, London.

Le Nouvel Observateur (L'Obs) (2020). "Les Parisiens se réfugient à Belle-Ile-en-Mer : « Personne n'a pensé qu'ils seraient aussi cons." https://www.nouvelobs.com/

coronavirus-dewuhan/20200318.OBS26261/les-parisiens-se-refugient-a-belle-ile-en-mer-personne-n-a-pense-qu-ils-seraient-aussi-cons.html?utm_term=Autofeed&utm_medium=Social&utm_source=Twitter#Echobox=1584558864

Le Télégramme (2020). "Coronavirus: Tension sur Belle-Ile-en-Mer avec les résidents secondaires," 17 March. https://www.letelegramme.fr/dossiers/confrontes-au-corona virus-des-bretons-temoignent/coronavirus-tension-sur-belle-ile-en-mer-avec-les-residents-secondaires-17-03-2020-12528216.php?utm_term=Autofeed&utm_medium=Social&utm_source=Twitter#Echobox=1584472161.

Libération. (2020). "En quittant Paris, on accélère la propagation du coronavirus," 16 March, https://www.liberation.fr/france/2020/03/16/en-quittant-paris-on-accelere-la-propagation-du-coronavirus_1781946.

Lickorish, L.J. and Jenkins, C.L. (1997). *An introduction to tourism*, Butterworth Heinemann, London.

Marjavaara, R. (2007). The displacement myth: Second home tourism in the Stockholm archipelago. *Tourism Geographies*, 9(3), 296–317.

Milano, C., Cheer, J.M. and Novelli, M. (Ed.). (2019) *Overtourism: Excesses, discontents and measures in travel and tourism*, CABI, Wallingford.

Ministère de l'Economie et des Finances (2018). "Chiffres clés du tourisme." https://www.entreprises.gouv.fr/etudes-et-statistiques/statistiques-du-tourisme/donnees-cles/memento-du-tourisme.

Panayiotopoulos, A. and Pisano, C. (2019). Overtourism dystopias and socialist utopias: Towards an urban armature for Dubrovnik. *Tourism Planning & Development*, doi:10.1080/21568316.2019.1569123.

Persaud, N. (2012). "Pilot study," In Salkind, N.J. (Ed.), *Encyclopaedia of research design,* Sage, London, pp. 12–18.

Phi, G.T. (2019). Framing overtourism: A critical news media analysis. *Current Issues in Tourism,* doi: 10.1080/13683500.2019.1618249.

Roca, Z. (2013). *Second home tourism in Europe: Lifestyle issues and policy responses*, Ashgate, Farnham.

Sanchez, P.M. and Adams, K.M. (2008). The Janus-faced character of tourism in Cuba. *Annals of Tourism Research*, 35(1), 27–46.

Seraphin, H. and Ivanov, S. (2020). Overtourism: A revenue management perspective. *Journal of Revenue and Pricing Management,* doi: 10.1057/s41272-020-00241-7.

Séraphin, H., Ivanov, S., Dosquet, F. and Bourliataux-Lajoinie, S. (2020). Archetype of visitors in Overtourism destinations. *Journal of Hospitality & Tourism Management,* doi: 10.1016/j.jhtm.2019.12.001.

Séraphin, H., Zaman, M., Olver, S., M., Bourliataux, S. and Dosquet, F. (2019). Destination branding and overtourism. *Journal of Hospitality and Tourism Management,* 38, 1–4, doi:10.1016/j.jhtm.2018.11.003.

Silver, L., Stevens, R., Wrenn, B., & Loudon, D. (2013). *The essentials of marketing research*, London: Routledge.

Stainton, H. (2020). "Types of tourism: A glossary," *Tourism Teacher.* https://tourism teacher.com/types-of-tourism-glossary/

Van Teijlingen, E. and Hundley, V. (2001). "The importance of pilot studies," *Social Research Update*, 35, University of Surrey, 1360–7898.

Visser, G. (2008). South Africa has second homes too! An exploration of the unexplored. *Current Issues in Tourism*, 3(4–5), 351–383.

Acknowledgements

As editors of this book, we would like to thank all contributors for their hard work and, particularly, for their quick turnaround of chapters, despite all the difficulties related to the COVID-19 pandemic and lockdown challenges. We would like to thank Routledge for supporting our idea to publish this topical book and for their guidance throughout the journey. The global phenomenon of overtourism has been addressed in this book from an education angle, but also from different national and cultural angles. This book's identity has been shaped by the editors working across the United Kingdom and New Zealand.

Finally, as the lead co-editor for this book, I would like to say a big thank you to Dr Anca C. Yallop for her efficiency in getting this book across the finish line during a challenging time such as this. Having a great co-editor makes a huge difference.

Introduction

Hugues Séraphin and Anca C. Yallop

Overtourism, education, and sustainability

Achieving sustainability requires finding a balance among three key elements: the needs of the people, preserving the planet, and having a performing economy. Reducing, reusing, and recycling are prerequisites in this endeavour (Seraphin, Gladkikh and Vo-Thanh, 2020). As a strategy, sustainability is fully imbedded in the tourism industry (and cognate sectors) because the industry is fully aware of its negative impacts, but also because customers are demanding products and services that are considerate of the environment and populations (Seraphin and Nolan, 2019; Seraphin, Gladkikh and Vo-Thanh, 2020). Despite the importance of making sustainability in the tourism industry an inclusive project, some members of the society such as children and young people have been labelled as passive and powerless; as a result, they are not involved in activities aiming at achieving these ultimate objectives (Seraphin and Yallop, 2019a, b). Seraphin and Vo-Thanh (2020) have suggested strategies (via empowerment fun activities in resort mini-clubs) that would enable resorts (more generally speaking, the hospitality sector) to empower children to be sustainable tourism actors. Within this line of thoughts, this book focuses on education as a strategic and transformative tool to tackle overtourism and related negative impacts. To date, no other existing research has focused on education as a transformative strategy. Indeed, all existing strategies have overlooked the fact that tourism is both an industry and a field of study (Seraphin, 2012). Because of the Janus-faced character of tourism (Sanchez and Adams, 2008), strategies used to address issues in the industry should also reflect the nature of the industry. Presently, this is not the case. This book is therefore filling this gap in the literature and illustrates that tourism education can be used successfully as a tool in cultivating a responsible consumer mindset to confront overtourism and other sustainability issues in the tourism industry.

COVID-19 and overtourism

With the breaking out of the COVID-19 pandemic, which is gravely threatening the tourism industry and cognate sectors (Gossling, Scott and Hall,

2020; Higgins-Desbiolles, 2020; Jamal and Budke, 2020; Lapointe, 2020; Renaud, 2020), some may assume that discussing and investigating over-tourism becomes somewhat irrelevant. However, Séraphin and Dosquet explain in the preface section of this book that the issue remains highly relevant. Indeed, the COVID-19 pandemic was expected to halt travel and tourism; instead, it has shed light on 'second home' tourism, which, in turn, has further highlighted the issue of overtourism. To substantiate this point, the preface uses France as a case study, and reveals that (1) there is a cor-relation between overtourism and the exodus of Parisians to their second home; (2) whether generated by crisis or tourism, exodus is centred on the same four core elements, namely, tourists, locals, destinations, and desti-nation management; and (3) exodus generated by crisis is a mutation of overtourism because: (a) the motivation is survival in a pleasant and safe environment, (b) the destination is chosen according to the location of the second home, (c) tourismphobia is not towards foreigners but towards fel-low citizens, and (d) this new form of overtourism is suggesting a return to nature away from cities.

The structure of the book

The book offers academics, students, and practitioners education-based al-ternatives to existing strategies. In contrast with other existing books in the field (see Dodds and Butler, 2019; Milano, Cheer and Novelli, 2019; Seraphin, Gladkikh and Vo-Thanh, 2020) which suggest short-term strategies that are immediately implementable, but with potentially short-term outcomes that might not last very long, the key point of difference that makes this book stand out is offering strategies which are long term in terms of their imple-mentations and expected (positive outcomes).

Part I of the book (*Conceptual framework*) is structured around three chapters. Chapter 1 examines the potential application of education to the problem of overtourism in the context of a single model, the tourism area life cycle (TALC). This focus raises at least two questions: first, why should the TALC model be singled out for attention and discussion as distinct from other models? Second, who or what should be educated if the problems stem-ming from overtourism are to be mitigated? Chapter 2 provides an overview of how the United Nations Principles for Responsible Management Educa-tion (PRME) can be used as an educational tool in business schools to help achieve the United Nations Sustainable Development Goals (SDGs). The purpose is to gain an understanding of how effective these principles are in guiding sustainable curriculum and practices for future business leaders. This chapter discusses the creation of PRME, how the principles have been applied and an analysis of their results. The final chapter of Part I, Chapter 3, has three main purposes: (1) to highlight the dual, Janus-faced nature of the study of tourism as an industry and field of study, (2) to discuss how education is used to promote sustainable tourism and prevent overtourism, both in the academia as well as where tourism occurs, and (3) to offer suggestions concerning the value of education as an avenue for harmonising the Janus-faced character of tourism in order to foster a tourism industry that can better achieve global sustainability.

Part II of the book (*Practical strategies and impacts*) consists of four chapters. Chapter 4 discusses the expansion of the tourism industry in the past few decades, expansion that resulted in a rise of negative connotations such as overtourism, gentrification, and anti-tourism movements globally. Earlier studies have highlighted the importance of tourism education as a measure to handle the mismanagement occurring at famous destinations. This chapter proposes ways to empower tourism education among the various groups of stakeholders and intends to give an insight into channelling and empowering tourism education in such a way that it contributes towards managing a destination affected by overtourism more responsibly. Chapter 5 examines the role of education as a change agent in redeeming destinations from the ill effects of overtourism. The concept of 'undertourism' or 'degrowth tourism' is discussed to provide the much-needed contrast to the debate. Chapter 6 investigates how tourism training at university and industry levels contributes to the sustainability of the destination and mitigates overtourism. This chapter is based on a Structural Equations Model approach to empirically demonstrate that there is a general acceptance that changes have to occur via the provision of training in the tourism industry. Main results show that tourism training in universities has a positive significant influence on the sustainability of a destination. Finally, Chapter 7 aims to assess the relationship between tourism education and tourism destination development, as well as to emphasise the importance of tourism education for the competitiveness and sustainability of tourism destinations. In order to assess the relationship between tourism education and tourism destination performance, this study took into account four essential indicators: the number of graduates in the 'Personal services' field of education (in which tourism education is a core component), the number of nights spent at tourist accommodation establishments, the turnover in the accommodation industry, and the added value in the industry, respectively.

The third and final part of the book, Part III (*Transformative strategies*), includes Chapter 8, which addresses the debate on strategic and transformative education as a tool for achieving sustainable development, a tool that is increasingly attracting the attention of scholars and policy-makers at international, national, and institutional levels in many counties. The purpose of this chapter is to provide an overview of the key concepts of transformative learning and education for sustainable development, and how these have evolved into a leading approach to teaching and learning in higher education. Chapter 9 addresses the need for educational change in the face of uncertainties posed by overtourism. It is underpinned by a critical discussion of the challenges to liberal education to connect with the broader PRME higher education goals in order to develop future leaders with the knowledge, skills, and capabilities to address the United Nations SDGs. Finally, Chapter 10 brings together the disciplines of transformative education, strategy development, performance, and the role of tourism education to enrich and embed sustainability in future tourism leaders. Educating for sustainable development (ESD) is a crucial part of the UN Sustainable Development Goals, as SDG4 (Quality Education) and SDG 13 (Climate action) are intrinsically linked. Bringing in the dimensions of transformative tourism education will ensure that all we leave behind as travellers/tourists are 'footprints'. Treading lightly on the earth is a winning formula for tourism, tourism education, and transformative tourism education.

References

Dodds. R., & Butler, R.W. (2019). *Overtourism: Issues, realities and solutions*. Berlin: De Gruyter.

Gossling, S., Scott, D., & Hall, C.M. (2020). Pandemics, tourism and global change: A rapid assessment of COVID-19, *Journal of Sustainable Tourism*, doi:10.1080/09 669582.2020.1758708.

Hall, C.M., Scott, D., & Gossling, S. (2020). Pandemics, transformations and tourism: Be careful what you wish for, *Tourism Geographies*, doi:10.1080/14616688.20 20.1759131?scroll=top.

Higgins-Desbiolles, F. (2020). Socialising tourism for social and ecological justice after COVID-19, *Tourism Geographies*, doi:10.1080/14616688.2020.1757748.

Jamal, T., & Budke, C. (2020). Tourism in a world with pandemics: Local-global responsibility and action, *Journal of Tourism Futures*, doi:10.1108/JTF-02-2020-0014.

Lapointe, D. (2020). Reconnecting tourism after COVID-19: The paradox of alterity in tourism areas, *Tourism Geographies*, doi:10.1080/14616688.2020.1762115.

Milano, C., Cheer, J.M., & Novelli, M. (2019). *Overtourism: Excesses, discontents and measures in travel and tourism*. Wallingford: CABI.

Renaud, L. (2020). Reconsidering global mobility – Distancing from mass cruise tourism in the aftermath of COVID-19, *Tourism Geographies*, doi:10.1080/146166 88.2020.1762116.

Sanchez, P.M., & Adams, K.M. (2008). The Janus-faced character of tourism in Cuba, *Annals of Tourism Research*, 35(1), 27–46.

Séraphin, H. (2012). *L'enseignement du tourisme en France et au Royaume-Uni*. Paris: Publibook.

Séraphin, H., Gladkikh, T., & Vothanh, T. (eds.). (2020). *Overtourism: Causes, implications and solutions*. London: Palgrave Macmillan.

Séraphin, H., & Nolan, E. (eds.) (2019). *Green events and green tourism: An international guide to good practice*. London: Routledge.

Séraphin, H., & Vo-Than, T. (2020). Investigating the application of the principles for responsible management education to resort mini-clubs, *The International Journal of Management Education*, doi: org/10.1016/j.ijme.2020.100377.

Séraphin, H., & Yallop, A. (2019a). An analysis of children' play in resort mini-clubs. Strategic implications for the hospitality and tourism industry, *World Leisure Journal*, doi:10.1080/16078055.2019.1669216.

Séraphin, H., & Yallop, A. (2019b). Proposed framework for the management of resorts mini clubs: An ambidextrous approach, *Leisure Studies*, 38(4), 535–547.

Part I

Conceptual framework

1 Overtourism, education, and the tourism area life cycle model

Richard W. Butler

Introduction

This chapter examines the potential application of education to the problem of overtourism in the context of a single model, the tourism area life cycle (TALC) (Butler, 1980). That focus raises at least two questions: why should the TALC model be singled out for attention and discussion as distinct from other models, and in the context of education relating to this model, who or what should be educated if the problems stemming from overtourism are to be mitigated?

This chapter progresses by discussing briefly the history and nature of the TALC model and its relationship to overtourism, and then examines the issue of education relating to that model and its application. This is followed by a brief review of the issues of overtourism and overdevelopment in specific destinations in comparison with the TALC model. The final section of the chapter reviews potential lessons and implications that could be learned from the model in attempting to mitigate the negative results of overtourism.

The tourism area life cycle model

This writer is assuming that the TALC model was singled out because it specifically deals with the issue of overdevelopment (and perhaps by implication, overtourism) and the potential negative effects on tourist destinations if appropriate management actions are not taken. Hall (2006, p. XV) noted that 'The TALC is one of the most cited and contentious areas of tourist knowledge (and) has gone on to become one of the best known theories of destination growth and change within the field of tourism studies'. It is also the most frequently cited paper in the context of destination development and therefore something which many students of tourism have been informed about (Wang et al., 2016). The model itself does not deal specifically with the term overtourism (which did not appear in the literature until almost four decades after the original model), although it does discuss the potential for, and implications of, overdevelopment of tourist destinations. The model was first introduced in its original form in 1980 and has been referenced and used in academic study since shortly after that date. As a great deal has been written on the model, including its origins and related literature, and its applications (see for example the contributors in Butler, 2006a, b), a short summary of the model should suffice here.

Stages of development

The model is descriptive rather than analytic in focus, and lists a series of stages through which, it is argued, most tourist destinations progress as they develop through time. These stages are exploration, involvement, development, consolidation, stagnation, followed by either or both of decline and rejuvenation. The TALC model is based on the well-known business model the Product Life Cycle, and it is argued that destinations/resorts can be thought of as products, in that they are produced, developed, marketed, promoted, modified, and exploited in much the same way as other products such as cars and computers. Like these latter products, tourist destinations are dynamic, sometimes in a positive sense and sometimes, particular in the later stages of their life cycle, in a negative sense. The TALC model did not claim that any or all destinations would inevitably progress through all of the earlier stages, although it did suggest that if there was not appropriate modification and management of a destination and its resources, it would be likely to follow the pattern illustrated by the model and progress through overdevelopment to decline. The absence of the element of inevitability in the TALC was, in contrast to that element in other models, relating to resident attitudes to tourism (Doxey, 1975) and to the changing nature of the market being attracted (Plog, 1973).

Key elements of the model

The major points of the TALC are that destinations are dynamic, and that there are identifiable stages of development through which most progress; that without appropriate management, there would likely be overdevelopment of destinations relative to their carrying capacity (considered in terms of natural resources, infrastructure, cultural features, and societal attitudes to tourism); and that there would then be a subsequent decline in the attractiveness of destinations to the overall tourism market as their attributes and facilities became dated and unappealing to changing markets. The likely result of such changes in destinations would be an overall decline in the numbers of visitors and resulting expenditure, and the possibility of an irreversible negative downward spiral process of declining yields, declining investments, and declining visitor numbers (Coelho and Butler, 2012), leading in some cases to an exit stage (Baum, 1998). The origins of the TALC (Butler, 2006) lay in the mostly European examples of destinations that were established and boomed in the railway era and had begun to decline as newer destinations became accessible, primarily as a result of vastly improved and lower costing transportation, particularly air transport (Butler, 2014).

Similar patterns could be observed in the north eastern USA (Stansfield, 1978), Canada (Wolfe, 1952), and Australia (Butler and McDonnell, 2011). It is appropriate to evaluate the model now some four decades on to ascertain if its relevance still exists, as different forms of destinations, reflecting different patterns of transportation and political development may make the generalisations of the original model less applicable. That task has been examined by a considerable number of other authors and while some argue for its continued relevance, others make valid criticisms about specific elements of the model and have put forward variations and alternatives (again as discussed by contributors in Butler, 2006a, b).

The TALC model and overtourism

The relationship between the TALC model and overtourism is neither a simple nor a direct one, and, as noted elsewhere (Butler, 2019), part of the problem is that what is called overtourism may well be what has previously been described as overdevelopment, i.e. a destination has continued to develop and grow in terms of accessibility, infrastructure, and visitor numbers beyond the level that neither local residents nor visitors find acceptable or attractive. In such cases it may be that physical development has outstripped the perceptual limits of the destination, so it simply is, or appears to be, too busy to many potential visitors and local residents, or, the development of infrastructure may have caused major changes in the appearance and ambience of the destination such that it no longer resembles its earlier form and has lost some of its appeal to the market. This is not to suggest that there should be no development or change in destinations. To do so would most likely condemn such destinations to become ever more out of date with the changing market and tastes of potential visitors (Plog, 1973). There is dynamism in both the supply and the demand sides of tourism and responsible resort operators need to ensure that their destination remains attractive to existing and potential customers, but that does not mean that resorts should automatically respond to every slight shift in market preferences, nor should resorts change a successful operation simply in order to appear 'modern'. It is possible to retain traditional appearance and level of customer service, and most importantly, perhaps, quality of experience, in older destinations and still be financially successful and in line with resident preferences, as destinations such as St Moritz and some Mediterranean destinations demonstrate.

It is also important to be aware that overtourism can occur at any point in a destination's life cycle and not only in its later stages. Overtourism occurs when a destination has excessive numbers of tourists compared to its carrying capacity, however that may be measured. This could be in terms of visitor attitudes (as Doxey (1975) forecast), in terms of physical space (manifesting itself in crowding and congestion), in terms of infrastructure (including transportation to and within the destination), and in terms of the natural environment (witnessed in pollution, scarcity of resources such as water, and loss of biodiversity). If visitation exceeds capacity in the early stages of development, overtourism could then take place even though tourist numbers might be less than experienced later in the destination's life cycle, when its capacity has been increased through development. It is key to appreciate, however, that not all elements can be increased in terms of their carrying capacity, most beaches are finite in dimensions, water resources are often limited by natural processes, and biodiversity may be incompatible with intensive use. It is necessary therefore not only to take into account tourist numbers and stage of development, and the carrying capacity of a destination but also to appreciate that all of these factors are dynamic and change throughout a destination's life cycle.

Education on tourism destination life cycles: for whom and why?

The second question relates as to whom education (about the TALC model and other aspects of tourism development, including the sustainable development of tourism) might or should be extended. The charge is often laid that tourists need to be better educated about what they should enjoy, to where they should travel, and particularly how they should behave, but in reality, the situation is much more complicated than simply better educated tourists. There is little doubt that many tourists are poorly educated in some, perhaps even many, aspects of tourism, including the culture and mores of some of their destinations, and certainly the issue of appropriate behaviour when away from home, but tourists being better educated would, at best, only solve a part of the problem of overtourism as it is generally framed. It needs to be understood that all players and stakeholders in tourism, in both the demand and supply sectors, would benefit from being better educated, or at least being better informed, about the issues and implications of overdevelopment, and in the context of the TALC model, in terms of inappropriate development and implications of development on local natural and cultural environments in destinations. However, such education and information are not easily delivered and may be even harder to implement for the reasons noted below. In terms of the education sector itself, the teaching of tourism now begins in the school curriculum in some countries, and the teaching of tourism at universities and colleges has expanded massively at the global level. There is a full range of modules, courses, and degree programmes offered at undergraduate and postgraduate levels in many countries, both developed and undeveloped. The principles of sustainable development in the context of tourism are included in many of these programmes and the TALC model is universally cited in those dealing with tourism destination development.

Education of tourists

There are many calls that tourists should be educated in order to prevent what may be considered 'inappropriate' behaviour, frequently related to hedonistic displays such as drunkenness (Iamsterdam, 2018) but such education would not necessarily prevent crowding or overdevelopment per se. Such calls are often put in the context of what the writers feel is undesirable 'mass tourism' (Hanley and Walton, 2010). In reality, many such views are insulting to the type of tourism that very large numbers of tourists throughout the world regard as both normal and attractive, in part at least because of economics. Such tourism is generally more moderately priced and thus within the financial capability of large numbers of people, than the more academically acceptable forms of tourism such as sustainable tourism, ecotourism, or cultural tourism. Few destinations now like to promote themselves as mass tourist destinations because of critical attitudes, even though the per capita impact of tourists to those destinations may be less in environmental terms, if not also cultural issues, than tourists engaged in more 'responsible' forms of tourism, which can result in heavy individual demands on environments and resources as well as often high carbon costs in terms of travel. Thus, in the context of educating tourists, what is often meant in reality is changing their choice of either or both destinations and activities. Well intentioned though such education may be, it smacks of elitism and is often impractical, as suggested alternative destinations are often incapable of handling what would be vastly increased numbers of visitors.

Education and the tourist industry

If education is intended to be focused on the tourist industry, change is unlikely to occur at any significant level. The tourist industry is generally focused, like most capitalist enterprises, on its own financial well-being, mostly embodied as profits for owners. There is nothing inappropriate in such a viewpoint, but when that viewpoint is focused on the short-term financial outlook, problems are easy to envisage. Many tourist enterprises, particularly small and medium sized ones, have limited financial capital and for reasons of survival, can only act in the short-term. They are concerned with performance from season to season, if not even week to week, and for them, taking a longer-term view, while being understood as more desirable, may prove impractical in reality. Thus reducing prices immediately in response to what may be short-term problems such as weather, infections, civil disturbance, or political events is often necessary to continue to attract customers and survive in the immediate future, even if such lower prices threaten their long-term viability. When intermediaries such as tour companies and airlines demand such reductions in order to maintain their own economic links and provide customers, the pressure on small individual tourist enterprises is almost unavoidable (Buhalis et al., 2004) Education alone will not help such businesses nor change their manner of operation at an individual level. Education and resulting behaviour change at the enterprise level will only come about if such inputs are coordinated and integrated at the destination level at least, and in most cases, at regional or even national levels, since policies at 'higher' levels can easily override those instituted at local levels

(Dodds and Butler, 2010). Many tourist companies, particularly larger ones, have learned that 'going green' or becoming 'sustainable' at least in name can be not only beneficial in marketing but also result in reduced expenditure on resources such as energy, water, and food. However, considerable initial financial and human investment may be needed to achieve such gains, investment which may be beyond the means of many small operators, and the costs involved, rather than ignorance, are often the reason for inaction. Education would need to be supported by financial incentives and assistance to produce a permanent shift in design and operation for the majority of tourist businesses, most of which are small scale.

Education of the public sector

Education at the public sector level is equally complex and difficult. Many tourist sector public officials are often well-educated in terms of tourism practice and sometimes theory, but face the problem of proposing and implementing policies that could prevent over-development and improve sustainability which are likely to be unpopular with the electorate and thus unacceptable to their political masters. Many jurisdictions have tourist plans which read sensibly and would appear to be capable of preventing over- or inappropriate development but which are not implemented (Dodds and Butler, 2010) because of political concerns. The Ecotax of Calvia in Mallorca is an excellent example of political response to a rational policy to limit the extent and nature of development but which was cancelled after the political proponents were rejected in subsequent local elections (Dodds, 2007). Another example is that noted by Martin (2006) at Hilton Head in South Carolina, where limiting development was supported by local residents in one local election and then rejected in quick succession in the next election. There is no doubt that ignorance can be, and almost certainly is, a factor in the overdevelopment or inappropriate development of some destinations, but many other factors, including the political reality, can be as, or more, important a problem in terms of failing to prevent the decline of established destinations. Part of the political problem with overtourism is what are often inconsistent goals between different levels of the political power structure. In a majority of cases, national level governments are in favour of increasing tourism to their countries; it improves the balance of payments, serves as an export industry, and provides a powerful tool for regional development, particularly in rural and remote areas and islands where resources may be scarce, unemployment high, and workforce skill levels low. Overcrowding is not generally experienced at a national level and thus issues of overcrowding become a local issue to be resolved locally while higher levels of government can continue to promote international and domestic tourism. At a regional/state/provincial level, similar arguments mitigate against action to reduce tourism numbers, particularly if pressure is being exerted from higher levels of power to continue to allow or encourage tourism to grow. Only at the local level, where costs and problems are experienced directly and the local electorate may be turning against increased tourism, is any action against overtourism likely to be found, and even at that level, there will be proponents of greater tourism because of the economic benefits. If education is to play an effective role in mitigating overtourism, it is important that the lessons from the TALC model and others are addressed at all levels of government and that consistency in goals, objectives, and actions are coordinated and integrated so that effective long-term planning and management of tourism can be undertaken.

Overtourism and common features in specific destinations

Much of the attention paid to overtourism has been focused on a few major destinations, Venice and Barcelona in particular, with other urban centres including Edinburgh, Paris, Prague, and Dubrovnik, while much less attention has been given to tourism in small centres or even isolated communities and regions. This situation may have arisen because of the disproportionate coverage given to major urban centres in all forms of the popular media, and the presence in those places of what are often highly articulate and influential groups of individuals skilled at presenting their opinions to the media. Some of these locations, perhaps Venice is the most indicative, have been destinations for tourists for centuries, and have long had a contradictory relationship with tourism, as noted by the art critic John Ruskin who was horrified by the impact of tourists on Venice in the 1870s (Hewison, 2000). In other cases, such as Dubrovnik, a steady increase in tourist numbers was accelerated beyond what was viewed as acceptable by a combination of its increased popularity as a cruise ship destination, and most recently, its role as a setting for the *Game of Thrones* television series. While the TALC model suggested a long-term evolutionary cycle of increasing development, a number of destinations have experienced sudden rises and falls in popularity as a result of external factors. On the negative side these include conflict, particularly war, although war and its artefacts often stimulate tourism once actual conflict has ceased (Butler and Suntikul, 2013) and most recently, disease as the Coronavirus has shown. On the positive side, in terms of increased numbers of visitors, media coverage (television, film, and blogs) has become a major stimulant to tourism, along with literary and artistic portrayal of locations, as have low cost air services and cruise ship visitation.

Venice

Venice, through its architecture and artistic connections, has attracted tourists for several hundred years, and they have been a source of criticism for almost as long a period. Ruskin, noted earlier as a critic of tourism, was one of the first to argue that tourists should be charged to visit Venice, an idea finding an echo in the Venice Card proposal (Russo, 2006). Venice illustrates several of the points of the TALC model. Its limited physical area makes overcrowding and congestion almost inevitable and improvements in transport technology make increased numbers equally inevitable through decreased costs and ease of accessibility. Venice, with its unique physical form, has barely changed its appeal since it first attracted tourists, and it is its ambience that has been most directly damaged by overtourism. It also faces, as do many destinations, the loss of facilities and services for residents, with these being replaced by services for tourists, and increased congestion for all services, including those shared by residents and visitors (Nolan and Seraphin, 2019). The oft-cited decline in residential population of Venice is a reflection of increased demand for properties for tourist purposes and loss of local amenities. Perhaps of all the elements of the TALC model, it is the lack of appropriate management of resources that has bedevilled Venice and allowed tourism there to become overtourism in the classic sense. Despite years of discussion and many proposals to resolve the tourism problems, little has been done in Venice to limit or effectively manage tourist numbers and behaviour. Limiting additional hotel development resulted in generally low budget hotels being constructed in Mestre at the mainland end of the causeway, accentuating the day visitor problem with few benefits to the city and other proposals appear to have come to naught. As yet, however, and contrary to the TALC model, the loss of amenity, crowding, increased prices, and even resident resentment have not led to a decline in tourism to Venice, although development in terms of facilities and infrastructure in the city has been minimal for a number of years. It is, perhaps, the true uniqueness and iconic nature of Venice that have enabled it to not follow the TALC to its suggested final stages despite the lack of management of its resources.

Barcelona

The case of Barcelona is somewhat different. While it has tourist attractions, it was hosting the Olympic Games in 1992 which established it as a tourist destination, followed by its selection as a cruise ship port, and the presence of attractions such as Sagrada Familia, neighbouring beaches and small towns such as Sitges (Barcelona Field Studies Centre, 2020). As Goodwin (2019) has noted problems with tourist numbers have been noted in Barcelona for almost two decades and there have been a number of management and policy innovations to attempt to resolve the problems. Overall, however, these attempts have not proven successful in resolving major crowding and behavioural issues in at least Las Ramblas and to a lesser extent, other areas of the city. Part of the problem in Barcelona is that it is a major port city and commercial hub as well as a political centre, and thus attracts many visitors other than conventional tourists. Of equal significance is the fact that, as in Venice, the airport is not under the control of the city government and thus can continue to expand and attract more flights, and the port like-wise, can continue to attract cruise ships despite the city's concerns. The neighbouring small towns of Sitges and Calafall have progressed through the traditional life cycle (Barcelona Field Studies Centre, 2020) and experienced rejuvenation in part as a result of increased numbers of tourists to Barcelona and new investment, while also increasing pressure on the larger city, again being out-with its control. In the case of Barcelona then, it might be argued that what is being experienced is essentially overcrowding in a small part of the city, reflecting that Barcelona is much more than a tourist destination and not experiencing 'true' overtourism, despite some resident opposition to tourists and tourism. In that sense it is quite different to the situation in Venice or Dubrovnik, or even Prague and Edinburgh, where more than a localised area is experiencing severe negative effects of excessive numbers. Regardless, in the context of the TALC model, it is the lack of effective overall coordinated management of tourism that is at the root of the problem in all of these destinations.

Summary

In the majority of other tourist destinations experiencing overtourism, including rural areas, the situation has arisen because of a traditional focus on developing and growing tourism rather than on managing tourism. The subtitle of the original TALC article was 'implications for management of resources', and the absence of such management particularly proactive management is what has allowed tourism to exceed the ability or capacity of destinations to withstand the numbers of tourists they are now experiencing. In rural areas this may be a question in relative terms, small number of tourists in absolute terms, but far more than even fewer residents can accommodate. Thus the greatest lesson which can be drawn from the TALC literature and research is that because of the dynamic nature of all aspects of tourism, anticipatory and adaptive management to control tourism is essential for the well-being of all destinations.

Overtourism and the TALC model: implications

So how could greater awareness of and education about models such as the TALC assist destinations that are experiencing overtourism? As noted earlier, the TALC model has been a feature of many tourism development and management courses and modules at a large number of universities and colleges worldwide, and is also included in at least some high school programmes that include tourism in their content; thus its existence is reasonably well known in education circles (Wang et al., 2016) and not confined to senior academic levels. Based on this writer's personal experience in many countries there is a reasonably high level of awareness of the model among those working in destination management organisations (DMOs), private consulting firms, and public agencies involved with tourism and regional development. Some of the destinations at the forefront of overtourism publicity, Venice and Barcelona for example, also have education programmes that feature tourism development models including the TALC (e.g. Barcelona Field Studies Centre, 2020, CISET in Venice), so lack of awareness of the model is perhaps not a factor in the appearance of overtourism in such places. It may well be that those actually in control or exercising control over development are unaware of the model and others like it, but one might suggest that even if they were aware of and receptive to the arguments in the model, they might not accept that this should mean that development in their destination should be limited or even halted. There tends to be a belief that tourists will always come to a destination as long as it is continually being updated and developed because that is what has happened previously, despite the fact that warnings about such fallacies have existed for more than half a century as shown by the writings of such as Krippendorf (1987) and Christaller (1968). To persuade or educate decision makers who have traditionally seen success primarily, if not exclusively, in terms of growth, to understand fully the concept of sustainable development and the issues raised in the TALC is a major task. It is understandably difficult for any person in a position of power and responsibility to argue for reduced growth ('degrowth') let alone no growth, although such a policy may be essential to maintain the quality and attractiveness (marketability) of a destination, to say nothing of its sustainability (Iamsterdam, 2018).

Examples

Education could begin with providing examples of those destinations which have maintained their appeal and still attract acceptable numbers of tourists after a long life cycle. In that context acceptable should be taken as being acceptable to local residents in social and cultural sense, as being financially viable for the destination, and as being compatible with the destination's natural environmental systems. The fallacy of short-term booms resulting from chasing a dynamic and ever-changing market can be illustrated by examples such as Atlantic City, which, while successfully reversing a long-term decline brought on by lack of investment and a rapidly reducing market for its offerings by legalising gambling and experiencing an economic boom from casino development, saw its new life cycle last less than two decades before it began to falter against newer competition and ever newer attractions in other destinations. Macau may follow the same path, although the enormous Chinese market on its doorstep may delay the process for some time. Places which have retained their markets and appeal include older small towns in Europe, the havens of the rich such as Davos, St Moritz, Monaco, and other Mediterranean resorts at a relatively small scale. There the factors in common have been limited communities operating on a small scale, offering quality experiences, and retaining a limited and consistent market through focused image creation and maintenance. While many destinations cannot hope to replicate the success in affluent markets like the destinations noted earlier, education about why they have remained successful is vitally necessary and some if not all of the key elements can be developed and appropriate actions taken to keep destinations attractive, which is the ultimate message from the TALC model.

Education about tourism characteristics and growth

Perhaps the first item of education about tourism for those in positions of power and influence should be about the nature and dimension of tourism itself, before there is discussion of development and overdevelopment. If people are not aware of the potential scale of tourism, the full and varied nature of its potential impacts, and the effects on resident populations and their environments, then they are not likely to make properly and fully informed decisions on the nature, scale, and rate of tourism development. Even those bodies with particular responsibilities for tourism such as the UNWTO should be well aware of the issues involved in tourism development, but appear to be unaware of and unconcerned by the effects of excessive growth. In 2018 the UNWTO was still arguing that 'Growing numbers are not the enemy [...] The sector needs regulations and clear guidelines, but not ones which would curb growth' (Rifal, 2017). There clearly needs to be education that growing numbers of tourists in destinations which are not capable of handling those numbers successfully are, indeed, 'the enemy' and that curbs on such growth are necessary, and that if such action is not taken, then serious consequences, including declines of tourism in the long term as places become less attractive, will ensue. To argue that 'while local communities must be consulted and fully engaged in tourism planning, "tourism-phobia" on the part of the citizens is largely a result of the failure manage the growth in a sustainable manner' (op. cit.) is to mislead and ignore reality. Complaints and protests against excessive numbers of tourists, some of whom behave in an inappropriate manner, is not tourism-phobia but a justified and understandable reaction to unacceptable conditions and loss of quality of life by residents in tourist destinations. It has to be accepted that in some destinations there are limits to the numbers of tourists who can be successfully received. Even if tourists behave appropriately, even if infrastructure is capable of dealing with the numbers of visitors, and even if there is strong support for tourism, it is still possible for there to be too many tourists for the comfort and perceptual well-being of local residents.

At the time of writing this chapter the Coronavirus was beginning to profoundly affect the global economy and it was dawning on many people, including politicians, that tourism was also being seriously damaged by the effects of the virus and critically that tourism was a major global economic factor. Ignorance of the dimension of tourism, its complexity, and its relationships to other economic activities and to communities involved means that concerns about overtourism and overdevelopment of tourism were always likely to be underestimated in most people's minds. It is rare for decision makers and developers to be worried about over-success in almost any endeavour, particularly one which employs large numbers of people, and generates large amounts of income, often in areas that have little alternative sources of employment and income.

Coordination and integration

Another implication might be that rather than simply endorsing education and improved awareness of academic research and models such as the TALC, what is needed is greater coordination and integration between the different stakeholders and parties involved in tourist destinations. If the different elements that are responsible for the development, protection, and maintenance of the attributes and overall attractiveness of destinations were to share knowledge and perceptions more than at present in most places, the development path might be more appropriate to the overall goals and desires of those different elements. Agreement on a common pathway, whether it be preservation, sustainability, development, growth, de-growth, or some other direction is not likely to be achieved without the sharing of views. The lack of such agreement almost inevitably leads to discord and opposition to one or more of the differing viewpoints which can lead to any or all of undesired and inappropriate development, lack of necessary development of infrastructure or other improvements and innovations, antagonism towards developments and tourists, abandonment of destinations by tourism companies and potential developers, and over-riding decisions being made by higher levels of government that may not fit with local preferences.

Future patterns

Although the TALC is not a predictive tool but a scenario argued to be common to many destinations, particularly older ones that entered tourism in a different era, it has been used as a predictor of potential decline (Manente and Pechlaner, 2006) and in many studies is often cited as an example of what will happen to a variety of destinations. Its real role, however, in education, is to alert destination decision makers that without appropriate action, its scenario may well come to pass. To do nothing is often as harmful as over-development, as without proactive management, most destinations will be overtaken by changing tastes and markets and potentially enter decline, or at least reduced attractiveness, from under-, rather than over-, development and visitation.

Mitigation management and control

One action to mitigate overtourism that is often stated is to educate DMOs to relocate tourists to underused or under-visited parts of communities, thus spreading the load and reducing pressure in specific locations. While such action may be appropriate in theory, in reality tourists concentrate in specific locations because of the presence of specific attractions (the Eiffel Tower, the Louvre in Paris, Big Ben and Buckingham Palace in London, Times Square and the Statue of Liberty in New York, for example) and will willingly avoid these iconic sites (Weidenfeld, 2010) in order to visit less crowded parts of those cities. This is particularly true of tourists who are visiting a destination for the first time, and even more so for long haul first-time visitors who may not intend to return and thus are particularly keen to see 'the sights' of specific destinations. In an era when showing proof of one's travels in the social media (Gretzel, 2017) is important, not visiting such sights is highly unlikely and also unattractive to potential visitors. Having to pre-book visit times, or wait in long line-ups may be annoying to visitors but such behaviour is becoming increasingly normal as places become busier as tourist numbers increase. Preventing visitation at all is problematic because of the image of the destination becoming known as unwelcoming to tourists, with potential long-term negative economic costs. The response to the Coronavirus shows how quickly a negative image can result in loss of tourism, and when this is accompanied by government action to restrict or halt tourism, the economic effect can be catastrophic for destinations so affected. How fast and how completely destinations will recover remains to be seen, although previous crises tend to pass and be ignored within one or two years unless they are regularly repeated. The loss of tourism through the virus crisis, however, shows why many destinations and countries are fearful of reducing or limiting tourism for any reason, let alone local issues like overtourism.

Sustainability in tourism development

It would be a mistake to think that the TALC model is yet another call for sustainability in tourist destinations, although applying the principles of the model may well result in a more sustainable form of destination, if that involves limiting the scale (and rate) of tourism development to a level that is compatible with the resources and attributes of the destination. The nature of the form of tourism being promoted and accepted can also be an issue, for as others have noted (e.g. Plog, 1973; Christaller, 1968), as the characteristics of visitors change, so too do the characteristics of the destination in order to remain attractive to a new type of visitor with different tastes and preferences. A key issue in this context is whether the destination leads the changes in the directions in which it desires to proceed or whether it responds to changing wishes of the changing market, in other words, playing catch-up with the market, but inevitably being behind ongoing changes in preferences and thus becoming increasingly vulnerable to newer destinations purpose built for current market trends. DMOs have to be educated to the fact that in some situations older established destinations may be ill-equipped to make the changes necessary to compete for new markets, for example, northern European resorts could not compete effectively with more southern destinations suddenly accessible to northern populations because of transportation innovations which offered better weather and lower costs than their northern counterparts. In such situations, decisions have to be made on what pathways are to be followed to ensure continued viability. Such decision may result in abandonment of certain existing traditional attractions which appeal only to a diminishing market, and the institution of new attractions, as long as they are compatible with both the inherent attributes of the destinations involved and the wishes of the local residents.

All too often, the response of destinations that feel that they are becoming uncompetitive has been to reduce prices and attempt to capture a lower income sector of the market. This pattern can be seen in some older UK resorts (Butler, 2014), and in Malta, Greece, and Spain, including the Balearic Islands, with resorts such as Magaluf gaining an undesired reputation as catering to the very lowest end of the market in terms of economic expenditure, inappropriate behaviour, and resulting negative image development. The TALC is a call to take appropriate measures to avoid entering the downward negative spiral of decreasing numbers, decreasing income, and decreasing investment and upgrading noted by Russo (2002) and others. Perhaps ironically, in chasing the lowest end of the market, these destinations are not avoiding overtourism, as they may well find themselves overcrowded with large numbers of inappropriately behaving tourists and a ruined reputation as far as their formerly traditional market segments are concerned.

Conclusions and implications

In the overall context of education implications stemming from the TALC model, one of the most important issues is the site-specific nature of destinations and their development. While the TALC proposes a universal pattern of development, it is clear that the detailed nature of development at any destination will vary from one destination to another, reflecting a number of site specific factors, including environmental conditions, characteristics of the population of the host community, the range of forms of tourism participated in at that destination, its history and culture, and its political composition. This latter factor is one that is often ignored in the study of tourism development and yet has tremendous influence on how tourism is developed (its rate, scale, and form) and how a community will be able to respond to such problems as overtourism and its implications.

Another important aspect of development is the political one. The few studies which have been made on the political influence on tourism have mostly been at national levels and reflected political change (Butler and Suntikul, 2010, 2017) rather than the influence of political ideology or policy at lower levels such as individual destinations. The fact remains, however,

that political viewpoints have tremendous influence on tourism development, and the nature of national politics in particular can determine overall
tourism development policy at a national, and thus inevitably a community
level. Tourism development under Franco in Spain and in China and Vietnam (Suntikul et al., 2010) under liberalising communist regimes provides
convincing evidence of this. Thus, while the TALC shows the general theoretical pattern of destination growth and possible decline, each individual
destination will have a unique pattern, even if most follow the broad as-
ymptotic curve of the original model. Decision makers and DMOs need to
identify and recognise the inherent attributes and limitations of their own
community and determine to what degree it might or might not follow the
general pattern provided by the model.

It has to be recognised that there is a major role for individuals in the development of tourism at a range of scales and for different types of tourism,
and that some personalities, the 'Giants' of tourism (Butler and Russell,
2010), have shaped both the locations of tourism and the way the industry
has been developed in terms of elements such as attractions, accommodation, transportation, and image. The establishment of destinations can owe
much to single individuals as well, as Butler and McDonnell (2011) showed in
the case of Manley in Australia, in the United Kingdom, and Russell (2010)
also demonstrated how individual entrepreneurs can significantly alter the
pattern of development of a destination and even, as in the case of the Gold
Coast in Australia, a major tourist region. Such individual efforts can not
only result in the creation of a destination but may continue to influence and
shape the nature and scale of destinations long after their establishment.
The founding influence of Walt Disney (Shani and Logan, 2010), for example, has continued long after the establishment of the first Magic Kingdom
and the corporation he founded has successfully developed and redeveloped
subsequent destinations in several locations. The Disney operations reveal
the importance of total control over development, a situation that is lacking
in most tourist destinations, where a multitude of actors, both private and
public, often with widely varying goals and objectives, may fail to produce
a clear vision and development path for a destination, resulting in a reactive
pattern of development and the potential to follow the TALC pattern of
likely stagnation and decline when development is not coordinated and not
following an agreed direction of development.

References

Barcelona Field Studies Centre. (2020) *Applying the Butler Model to Tourism in
Sitges and Calafell*, Geography Fieldwork.com.

Baum, T.G. (1998) Taking the exit route: Extending the tourism area life cycle model,
Current Issues in Tourism, 1(2), 167–175.

Buhalis, D., Butler, R.W. and Bastakis, C. (2004) The perception of small and medium sized tourism accommodation providers on the impacts of tour operators'
power in Eastern Mediterranean, *Tourism Management*, 25, 151–170.

Butler, R.W. (1980) The concept of a tourist area cycle of evolution and implications for management of resources, *The Canadian Geographer*, XXIV(1), 512.

Butler, R.W. (2006) The Origins of the Tourism Area Life Cycle, in Butler, R.W. (ed.) *The Tourism Area Life Cycle: Applications and Modifications*, Channelview Publications: Clevedon, pp. 13–26.

Butler, R.W. (2006a) *The Tourism Area Life Cycle: Applications and Modifications*, Channelview Publications: Clevedon.

Butler, R.W. (2006b) *The Tourism Area Life Cycle Conceptual and Theoretical Issues*, Channelview Publications: Clevedon.

Butler, R.W. (2014) Coastal tourist resorts: History, development and models, *Architecture, City and Environment*, 9(25), 203–228.

Butler, R.W. (2018) Sustainable tourism in sensitive environments: A wolf in sheep's clothing? *Sustainability*, 10(6), 1789.

Butler, R.W. (2019) Overtourism and the Tourism Area Life Cycle, in Dodds, R. and Butler, R.W. (eds.) *Overtourism Issues, Realities and Solutions*, De Gruyter: Berlin, pp. 76–89.

Butler, R.W. and McDonnell, I. (2011) One man and his boat (and hotel and pier...) Henry Gilbert Smith and the establishment of Manly, Australia, *Tourism Geographies*, 13(3), 343–359.

Butler, R.W. and Russell, R. (2010) *Giants of Tourism Key Individuals in the Development of Tourism*, CABI: Wallingford.

Butler R.W. and Suntikul, W. (2010) *Tourism and Political Change*, Goodfellow: Oxford.

Butler, R.W. and Suntikul, W. (2013) *Tourism and War*, London: Routledge.

Butler, R.W. and Suntikul, W. (2017) *Tourism and Political Change: Issue and Implications*, Goodfellow: Oxford.

Christaller, W. (1968) Some considerations of tourism location in Europe: The peripheral regions – Underdeveloped countries – Recreation areas, *Regional Science Association Papers XII*, Lund Congress, 95–105.

Coelho, J. and Butler, R. (2012) A quantitative approach of the tourism area life cycle, *European Journal of Tourism, Hospitality and Recreation*, 3(1), 9–32.

Dodds, R. (2007) Sustainable tourism and policy implementation: Lessons from the case of Calvia, Spain, *Current Issues in Tourism*, 10(4), 296–322.

Dodds, R. and Butler, R.W. (2010) Barriers to implementing sustainable tourism policy in mass tourism destinations, *Tourismos*, 5(1), 35–52.

Doxey, G.V. (1975) A causation theory of visitor-resident irritants Methodology and research inferences, *Proceedings of the Travel Research Association 6th Annual Conference*, Travel Research Association: San Diego, pp. 195–198.

Goodwin, H. (2019) Barcelona-crowding Out the Locals-a Model for Tourism Management? in Dodds, R. and Butler, R.W. (eds.) *Overtourism Issues, Realities and Solutions*, De Gruyter: Berlin, pp. 125–138.

Gretzel, U. (2017) Social media activism in tourism, *Journal of Hospitality and Tourism*, 15(2), 1–14.

Hall, C.M. (2006) Introduction, in Butler, R.W. (ed.) *The Tourism Area Life Cycle Conceptual and Theoretical Issues*, Channelview Publications: Clevedon, pp. XV–XIX.

Hanley, K. and Walton. J. K. (2010) *Constructing Cultural Tourism: John Ruskin and the Tourist Gaze*, Bristol: Channel View Publications.

Hewison, R. (2000) *Ruskin's Venice,* Pilkington Press: Guildford.

Iamsterdam (2018) Amsterdam launches a campaign to stop offensive behaviour, 29 May, Iamsterdam.org (Accessed 18 November 2018).

Krippendorf, J. (1987) *The Holiday Makers,* Heineman: London.

Manente, M. and Pechlaner, H. (2006) How to Define, Identify and Monitor the Decline of Tourist Destinations: Towards an Early Warning System, in Butler, R.W. (ed.) *The Tourism Area Life Cycle Conceptual and Theoretical Issues*, Channelview Publications: Clevedon, pp. 235–253.

Martin, B. (2006) The TALC and Politics, in Butler, R.W. (ed.) *The Tourism Area Life Cycle: Applications and Modifications*, Channelview Publications: Clevedon, pp. 227–249.

Nolan, E. and Seraphin, H. (2019) Venice: Capacity and Tourism, in Dodds, R. and Butler, R.W. (eds.) *Overtourism Issues, Realities and Solutions*, De Gruyter: Berlin, pp. 139–151.

Plog, S. (1973) Why destinations rise and fall in popularity, *Cornell Hotel and Restaurant Quarterly*, 13, 6–13.

Rifal, T. (2017) Tourism: Growth is not the enemy; it's how we manage it that counts, UNWTO Press Release August 15, Madrid.

Russell, R. (2010) Keith Williams: Chaos Maker on the Gold Coast, in Butler, R.W. and Russell, R. (eds.) *Giants of Tourism Key Individuals in the Development of Tourism*, CABI: Wallingford, pp. 243–254.

Russo, A.P. (2002) The vicious circle of tourism development in heritage cities, *Annals of Tourism Research*, 29(1), 165–182.

Russo, A.P. (2006) A Re-foundation of the TALC for Heritage Cities, in Butler, R.W. (ed.) *The Tourism Area Life Cycle: Applications and Modifications*, Channelview Publications: Clevedon, pp. 139–162.

Shani, A. and Logan, R. (2010) Walt Disney's World of Entertainment Attractions, in Butler, R.W. and Russell, R. (eds.) *Giants of Tourism Key Individuals in the Development of Tourism*, CABI: Wallingford, pp. 155–169.

Stansfield, C.A. (1978) Atlantic city and the resort cycle, Background to the legalization of gambling, *Annals of Tourism Research*, 5(2), 238–251.

Suntikul, W. Butler, R.W. and Airey, D. (2010) The influence of foreign direct investment on accommodation patterns in Vietnam as a result of the open-door policy, *Current Issues in Tourism*, 13(3), 261–275.

Wang, X.X., Weaver, D.B., Xiang, L. and Zhang, Y. (2016) In Butler (1980) we trust? Typology of citer motivations, *Annals of Tourism Research*, 61(1), 216–218.

Weidenfeld, A. (2010) Iconicity and 'flagshipness' of tourist attractions, *Annals of Tourism Research*, 37(4), 851–854.

Wolfe, R.I. (1952) Wasaga Beach – The divorce from the geographic environment, *The Canadian Geographer*, 2, 57–66.

2 The PRME framework in tourism education

Nichole C. Hugo

Introduction

With increasing demands facing society and businesses related to sustainable development, many organisations have started focusing on education to achieve the goals of sustainability. The United Nations Decade of Education for Sustainable Development (UNDEFSD) was declared for 2005–2014 in order to refocus attention on sustainability education (Moscardo, 2015). With business schools being at the forefront of training future leaders, having them incorporate curriculum focusing on sustainable efforts can be used as a tool to help educate these individuals who have the opportunity to transform the way businesses operate. This not only impacts the students in the business school but the employees they will one day lead and the clients they will work with. This is particularly important in regards to the issue of overtourism, where proper management and sustainable practices are necessary in order to maintain and protect these destinations from the destruction caused by visitors.

As global organisations have become more involved in working with the tourism industry on sustainable initiatives, it has become evident that this industry has the capability to impact change at the local and global scale, both in positive and negative ways (Saarinen, 2014). The World Bank has highlighted the role tourism can play with improving local economies, particularly in developing countries, as it provides job opportunities for people with limited skills or formal education (World Bank, 2012). Support for the tourism industry to play a major role in achieving the United Nations Millennium Development Goals, and subsequently the United Nations Sustainable Development Goals (SDGs), has also led to a stronger connection between tourism and sustainability (UNWTO, 2006). Education in business schools that focuses on sustainable initiatives is imperative to assist with a wide range of sustainable challenges, including overtourism. To address this need the United Nations Principles for Responsible Management Education (PRME) were developed by the UN Global Compact to improve these educational efforts. These principles serve as a guide to provide structure for sustainable areas to focus on, as well as ensuring accountability through assessment and reports. This chapter will discuss the creation of these principles, their implementation at business schools around the world, and how they can deal with issues related to sustainability.

UN Global Compact and PRME

The UN Global Compact works to advance societal goals, such as the UN SDGs, through the mobilisation of global companies and stakeholders (UN Global Compact, 2019). While many global organisations focus on motivating governments to incorporate sustainable practices, businesses tend to have little direction in this area. With demands from investors and stakeholders taking the focus of many business decisions, it can be challenging to be guided into altering tactics that may require more upfront costs for the sake of positive, sustainable changes. However, as more consumers are being diligent about ethical practices, fair trade, and other sustainable initiatives, businesses are starting to see the value of corporate social responsibility as a way to stay competitive. A survey of over 3,000 executives found that 43% seek to align sustainability with their overall business goals, mission or values, which was up from 30% from two years before (Bonini and Bové, 2014). While implementing policies related to sustainability was previously linked to cost cutting or reputation management, an alignment with the core beliefs of the company demonstrates a shift in the mindset of managers. However, managers may not have the knowledge to implement the best strategies to be able to achieve their sustainability goals. In addition, businesses, as well as government organisations and universities, may strive to incorporate sustainable practices within their own agencies, but collaboration and partnerships have been found to be critically important to the success of their initiatives (Todeschini, Cortimiglia, Callegaro-de-Menezes and Ghezzi, 2017). The UN Global Compact strives to unite business and with more than 6,000 voluntary participants, it's the world's largest corporate citizenship initiative (Rasche, 2009).

PRME originated as a result of the efforts of the UN Global Compact. In 2006 the Head of the Global Compact Networks, Manuel Escudero, developed a concept paper to strengthen the idea of sustainable learning in higher education institutions, which highlighted a new vision of education in which sustainable practices and global corporate citizenship were essential (Escudero, 2006; Haertle, Parkes, Murray and Hayes, 2017). This paper, *Global Corporate Citizenship and Academia: A Global Convergence*, outlined the issues with the traditional educational structure and how institutions are lacking in preparing graduates to face current demands and challenges. The next year, PRME was developed and launched at the 2007 UN Global Compact Leaders Summit in Geneva, Switzerland to highlight 6 principles for sustainable development (Table 2.1). The UN Global Compact was developed to revolve around ten principles which focus on the core values of

Table 2.1 UN Global Compact Principles

UN Global Compact Principles:

Human Rights
Principle 1
Businesses should support and respect the protection of internationally
    proclaimed human rights within their sphere of influence.
Principle 2
Businesses should also make sure that they are not complicit in human rights
    abuses.

Labour
Principle 3
Businesses should uphold the freedom of association and the effective recognition
    of the right to collective bargaining.
Principle 4
Businesses should uphold the elimination of all forms of forced and compulsory
    labour.
Principle 5
Businesses should uphold the effective abolition of child labour.
Principle 6
Businesses should uphold elimination of discrimination in respect of employment
    and occupation.

Environment
Principle 7
Businesses should support a precautionary approach to environmental challenges.
Principle 8
Businesses should undertake initiatives to promote greater environmental
    responsibility.
Principle 9
Businesses should encourage the development and diffusion of environmentally
    friendly technologies.

Corruption
Principle 10
Business should work against corruption in all its forms including extortion and
    bribery.

Source: United Nations Global Compact, 2007.

human rights, labour, environment, and anti-corruption (United Nations
Global Compact, 2007).

While the UN Global Compact does not serve as a certification instrument, it is used to encourage participating companies to be transparent
about their sustainable engagement through reporting their progress and
implementation efforts (Rasche, 2009). Similarly, PRME endeavours to
do the same by encouraging sustainable initiatives to be implemented and
reported on. However, the focus of PRME is on education and practices
through business schools, instead of through corporations. The purpose

of developing the PRME was to assist with a globalised effort to work towards achieving the UN SDGs (UNPRME, 2019). PRME was meant to be used as a tool to motivate business schools to incorporate sustainable principles and work towards educating potential managers and leaders of their responsibility to assist with global issues of poverty, health and commerce (Tyran, 2017). The idea of increasing sustainability education in schools, which will help to equip today's business students with the knowledge and skills to deliver needed change for the future, is the central focus of this initiative (UNPRME, 2019). PRME defines six principles that are used to guide the educational and community outreach objectives for these schools.

PRME

Principle 1 – Purpose: We will develop the capabilities of students to be future generators of sustainable value for business and society at large and to work for an inclusive and sustainable global economy.

    Principle 2 – Values: We will incorporate into our academic activities and curricula the values of global social responsibility as portrayed in international initiatives such as the United Nations Global Compact.

    Principle 3 – Method: We will create educational frameworks, materials, processes, and environments that enable effective learning experiences for responsible leadership.

    Principle 4 – Research: We will engage in conceptual and empirical research that advances our understanding about the role, dynamics, and impact of corporations in the creation of sustainable social, environmental and economic value.

    Principle 5 – Partnership: We will interact with managers of business corporations to extend our knowledge of their challenges in meeting social and environmental responsibilities and to explore jointly effective approaches to meeting these challenges.

    Principle 6 – Dialogue: We will facilitate and support dialogue and debate among educators, business, government, consumers, media, civil society organisations and other interested groups and stakeholders on critical issues related to global social responsibility and sustainability (United Nations Global Compact, 2007).

    Overall, these principles work towards interdisciplinary and multilevel collaboration in a wide range of areas. From the classroom to the community, aspects of sustainability are incorporated into the curriculum and demonstrated through practice. Social, environmental and economic principles of sustainability are encouraged through this framework. An emphasis on networking with managers, businesses and community stakeholders allows for real world educational experiences, but this also gives students the opportunity to support these areas with their own innovative ideas and newly obtained knowledge.

PRME connection to Sustainable Development Goals

The vision of the PRME 'is to realize the Sustainable Development Goals through responsible management education' (UNPRME, 2019, p. 1). During the 2015 Global Forum for Responsible Management Education in New York, a rejuvenated call for governments, corporate leaders, and academic institutions to support instructors in educating future business leaders on these initiatives and strive towards achieving the SDGs was demonstrated through signatories reaffirming their support for PRME (Parkes, Buono and Howaidy, 2017). With over 800 signatories, it is evident that PRME is becoming a global guide to the advancement of sustainable initiatives.

The SDGs were created by the UN as a follow-up to the Sustainable Millennium Goals in 2015. This initial programme was used to develop eight measurable goals, starting in 2000 and aiming to be achieved in 2015. While this initiative made strong strides to improve on each of its targets, it was apparent that further action was needed to address these goals, as they were not achieved by their target date. As a result, 17 goals were created to be achieved by 2030 (United Nations, 2020).

Sustainable Development Goals

Goal 1. End poverty in all its forms everywhere

Goal 2. End hunger, achieve food security and improved nutrition and promote sustainable agriculture

Goal 3. Ensure healthy lives and promote well-being for all at all ages

Goal 4. Ensure inclusive and equitable quality education and promote lifelong learning opportunities for all

Goal 5. Achieve gender equality and empower all women and girls

Goal 6. Ensure availability and sustainable management of water and sanitation for all

Goal 7. Ensure access to affordable, reliable, sustainable and modern energy for all

Goal 8. Promote sustained, inclusive and sustainable economic growth, full and productive employment and decent work for all

Goal 9. Build resilient infrastructure, promote inclusive and sustainable industrialisation and foster innovation

Goal 10. Reduce inequality within and among countries

Goal 11. Make cities and human settlements inclusive, safe, resilient and sustainable

Goal 12. Ensure sustainable consumption and production patterns

Goal 13. Take urgent action to combat climate change and its impacts

Goal 14. Conserve and sustainably use the oceans, seas and marine resources for sustainable development

Goal 15. Protect, restore and promote sustainable use of terrestrial ecosystems, sustainably manage forests, combat desertification, and halt and reverse land degradation and halt biodiversity loss

Goal 16. Promote peaceful and inclusive societies for sustainable development, provide access to justice for all and build effective, accountable and inclusive institutions at all levels

Goal 17. Strengthen the means of implementation and revitalise the global partnership for sustainable development

Source: (United Nations, 2020)

Within each of these goals are multiple target objectives that are utilised to measure the progress made towards achieving these goals. PRME have the potential to be implemented in business schools to educate future leaders of professional environments in order to raise awareness of SDGs by adopting a holistic interdisciplinary approach of education (Annan-Diab and Molinari, 2017; Haertle, Parkes, Murray and Hayes, 2017).

Business schools and PRME

Business schools are deeply immersed in a variety of global issues, which is why targeting them to carry out and develop evolving solutions to future sustainable initiatives is of such strong importance. Its graduates deal with issues in a global society, including climate change, inequality of wealth, loss of cultural heritage, a drastically increasing population, human rights issues and natural disasters (Araç and Madran, 2014).

There is increased pressure for business leaders to be socially and environmentally responsible, as sustainable practices and policies become less trendy and more normalised in the business world. PRME was considered to be the world's largest corporate sustainability initiative at its 10th anniversary and it continues to gain support from the academic community (Parkes, Buono and Howaidy, 2017). Roughly 180 business schools around the world signed up to the PRME in its introduction, but grew to roughly 650 signatories just over ten years later (Pomering, Johnson and Noble, 2010; UNPRME, 2019). In early 2020, PRME had 821 signatories (UNPRME, 2020). The issue is that the schools are not implementing the principles in the same way. Some business schools have been incorporating PRME through studying general ideas for improving their relationship with sustainability, instead of integrating the specific framework into their programme with more depth. Even when PRME is implemented with a strong focus on the framework, differences still occur since schools stress different aspects of the principles (Godemann, Herzig and Moon, 2013). One school may focus more as societal problems, while another stresses global citizenship and others value traditional management knowledge. A survey of the first 100 business schools to sign on to PRME showed a willingness to embed sustainability into the curriculum, in addition to research or communities projects such as greening their campus or receiving certification for the environmental management system (Godemann, Herzig, Moon and Powell, 2011). However, since they all do it in different ways it is difficult to determine how effective the principles are.

Examples of business schools implementing PRME

Progress of business schools and their implementation of PRME have been evaluated by the universities themselves and by researchers analysing their advancement as a group. Results of the achievement of the business schools are conveyed through SIP (Sharing Information on Progress) reports (Haertle, Parkes, Murray and Hayes, 2017).

An analysis of the first 100 UN PRME signatories was undertaken by using content analysis schools of the SIP reports and telephone interviews of the deans and MBA programme directors of the business schools (Godemann, Herzig, Moon and Powell, 2011). Overall, the results found that while the majority of business schools strive to include sustainable practices within research, teaching, and operations, the principles are mostly emphasised in teaching. However, within this area most schools have created new courses or focused on revising individual modules instead of embedding sustainability issues holistically throughout the curriculum. Examples provided were chosen due to being recently published and represent diverse regions of the world, in order to provide a sample of the various ways business schools have implemented and evaluated their success in their PRME Reports.

Sheffield business school

Sheffield Business School in the United Kingdom has over 300 staff and 8,000 students, with one third of them being international students. This school is working towards integrating PRME into its curriculum and research activities by defining their goals for implementing the six principles and evaluating their progress by surveying their staff. Their results show that the first three principles, which are related to developing students, embedding concepts and creating experiences, had the highest levels of active engagement. An example of this engagement included the revision of courses, assessments and educational experiences, in which 80% of the staff reported active engagement with. The last three principles, which involve research, creating partnerships and facilitating critical debate, have some engagement, but could be focused on for improvement in the future. Leadership positions, such as in professional bodies and charities, were taken up by 40% of the staff (Gilligan and Ridley-Duff, 2018).

College of business at James Madison University

The College of Business at James Madison University is located in Virginia, US and became a signatory in 2016. The matching of the PRME to the goals and values of the college was highlighted throughout the SIP, but the strongest action related information communicated in the report focused on community outreach. While education provided through courses and student projects was highlighted in the report, the strength of the practices of sustainable initiatives was demonstrated through its service learning activities, including community service in the nearby area, as well as on study abroad trips. Other ways of implementing sustainable practices were through building social capital through community partnerships, teaching students about other cultures through diversity days, and the hosting of at least one Town Hall meeting by the college. While there were some publications of sustainability reported, the college primarily demonstrated their impact through service projects and sustainability related courses (Busing, 2020).

Acharya Bangalore business school

In India, the Acharya Bangalore Business School not only reports on including sustainability in their curriculum and describes how they engage with the community on social projects but actively uses sustainable energy practices to operate their campus. With a solar power plant, water harvesting and recycling practices, and waste management system, the campus strives to implement the practices they teach. Social improvements, such as providing resources to orphanages, creating a 'Women Cell' with an aim for females on campus to feel uplifted by being able to discuss issues in a safe place, and gender awareness week events, are also a strong focus of the school. The report demonstrated strong initiatives being undertaken through community outreach projects, as well as robust themes being included in the curriculum (Basani, 2020).

Analysis of PRME annual reports

While the communication of information through the PRME reports allows for accountability, as well as sharing information for other schools to utilise effective methods, there are some critiques of the reports. With the growing popularity of PRME among business schools, it is important to recognise efforts to improve on these reports in order to allow for innovative ideas to be shared, while minimising bloating of programme initiatives that have been exaggerated for the sake of appearance.

Benefits of PRME reporting

An encouraging result of PRME being utilised to motivate universities to incorporate it in creating ways to facilitate hands-on learning and global citizenship. Creative and innovative collaborations have been developed by universities to focus on innovative ways of teaching PRME. International Service Learning (ISL), which provides international experience for students and opportunities to demonstrate responsible leadership and ethical global citizenship, has been used in correlation with PRME (Tyran, 2017). This allows students to learn more about other cultures, while creating partnerships, and engaging in service to those in need.

Other creative initiatives include bringing programmes together through shared course content. In order to diversify the way content is taught to students, three universities came together to create ten, one credit hour courses that organised 45 learning outcomes from PRME into these mini courses (Dickson, Eckman, Loker and Jirousek, 2013). Industry experts were brought in to evaluate the syllabi and course activities in order to ensure the material not only met academic expectations but that they were also relevant to real world problems in the business realm. Grant opportunities were credited with giving the universities the ability to travel in order to research and acquire materials related to real world experiences, which might be a limitation for some universities.

Critique of data collection

While these results from the SIP reports give us an idea of how well the principles are viewed as being implemented by the school, these self-reports are susceptible to inaccurate results. The issue is that while the schools themselves indicated aspects of PRME being implemented, they do not measure how effectively it is applied or the outcome of the attempt. This also aligns with criticism that the UN Global Compact (where PRME stems from) has vague principles that are hard to implement and a verification mechanism to measure results is lacking (Rasche, 2009). For corporations that are a part of the UN Global Compact, reports are meant to be submitted in order to accent the moral purpose of business (Williams, 2004). However, with a lack of uniformed measurement it is hard to tell if a company is making real progress or simply exaggerating its accomplishments in order to improve its image. Since reports are left to the mercy of the skill of the staff member organising and communicating the information in the report, a company that is actually being more progressive in applying sustainable practices may not shine as brightly compared to businesses that are more accomplished in writing. The same goes for PRME – without clear goals and uniform measurement tools, evaluating each school and what it is truly achieving is inconsistent. Even if more detailed information was provided in the reports, such as course syllabi, how effective the instructor is at educating students on the wide variety of issues for these themes is difficult to determine. In addition to PRME being measured by an annual report that is measured by how effectively the writer of the report can articulate the curriculum, research, and outreach programmes of the schools, each university is focusing on different aspects of sustainability. While one school might be working towards community improvement through planting trees, another one might be doing outreach at a women's shelter. Is one spending too much attention on the environment, while the other is preoccupied with societal impacts – both of which ignores other important aspects of sustainability that are needed to obtain the balance required to truly enhance community development?

Providing evaluation information, such as test results, might allow for more information to be obtained related to how well they are grasping the information, but there are issues with this method as well. Universities may focus on different aspects of sustainability, so the knowledge levels of students will be different from school to school, with some students having knowledge on different areas within the industry. Creating a standardised test might seem like a solution to this problem, but often time's professors just teach for the test, and the students miss out on other ways of gaining and applying the information in more creative and meaningful ways. In addition, different regions of the world may have a different issue in sustainability that plagues them more, and standardisation may cause them to miss out on putting in the additional effort into the most important problems they face. However, including testing as one of multiple measurements may allow for. The Sustainability Literacy Test is already being used by some schools, but it is not a requirement in reporting information. Questions through this assessment cover basic foundational terms in sustainability, key information related to the three pillars of sustainability (economic, social and environmental), and general knowledge of environmental challenges (Carteron, Haynes and Murray, 2014).

Not only have the SIP reports been critiqued by other scholars, but the idea that 'the PRME discourse assumes and promotes a problematic understanding of management education that includes of positioning of business schools as servants of the corporate sector' (Louw, 2015, p. 184) also raises the question of the effectiveness of this route of stimulating sustainability.

PRME and the tourism industry

While PRME focuses on improving sustainable practices in general, it may not be clear how it relates to the tourism industry, as it does not specify this field in its initiative. However, a strong connection can be made between sustainability and the tourism industry, as these practices are necessary to maintain the destinations for long-term prosperity. The United Nations World Tourism Organization highlights that sustainable development is 'tourism that takes full account of its current and future economic, social and environmental impacts, addressing the needs of visitors, the industry, the environment and host communities' (UNWTO, 2019, p. 1). It goes on to note that sustainable tourism development incorporates these values, but it requires constant monitoring, with preventive or corrective measures needed to maintain the area. UNWTO actively includes the UN SDGs as a focus for its research and implementation strategies, with its own web page 'Tourism for SDGs' (UNWTO, 2020).

Negative impacts of tourism

As mentioned previously, business students are learning to deal with issues related to global society dealing with climate change, inequality of wealth, loss of cultural heritage, a drastically increasing population, human rights issues, and natural disasters, all of which are issues related to sustainability (Araç and Madran, 2014). Each of these issues can also be linked to the tourism industry. With the rise in population, humans are generating more carbon dioxide and other greenhouse gases, causing a warming of the Earth. The changes in weather is causing more natural disasters and extending pollen seasons, which means that people with allergies, asthma or respiratory issues are experiencing greater health issues. With the melting of glaciers, resulting in rising sea levels, we are seeing loss of habitat and changes in our ecosystem. Coastal areas are particularly vulnerable to damage caused by climate change (Thinh, Thanh, Tuyen and Hens, 2019). With over 1 billion people travelling internationally since 2012, and with that number increasing each year (UNWTO, 2019), it is evident that the excessive production of carbon dioxide from the tourism area of transportation alone is impacting the environment.

Foreign owned companies are pricing local businesses, particularly in developing countries, which creates a barrier for them to be able to generate revenue and support local development. Locals in the tourism industry are typically employed with entry-level work, but are not given the knowledge, skills, or opportunity to be promoted to high paying positions. In addition, when tourism starts to boom in an area, a transition of jobs may occur, which means that a loss of traditional livelihoods may occur as the development of tourism shifts jobs into that sector (Su, Wall and Xu, 2016). This can leave residents without the stable occupations they previously relied on. This not only hinders the ability for the price gap between the wealthy and low-income to be filled but may make it worse if jobs are given away to foreigners. In order to meet the desire of tourists that are looking for familiarity when they travel abroad, the westernisation of cultures is also a prevalent issue. From the commodification of cultural symbols and goods, to the alteration of local cuisine, and the commercialisation of dance, art and local traditions, the desecration of cultural heritage is staggering in the tourism industry (Kaosa-ard, 1994; Coronado, 2014). Societal norms may also change as locals take on behaviours and customs of visitors, whether it is to appease the tourists or through heavy numbers of foreign cultural influence. An example would be taking on a more exacting and rushed lifestyle, in order to keep up with the fast-paced tourism industry (Iverson, 2010). As social rights, gender rights, and human rights in general have come under attack as mass migrations of people have been met with pushback from local residents (Jamal and Camargo, 2018), the tourism industry gives people the opportunity to learn about other cultures in order to create more tolerance and understanding between diverse groups of people. A strong connection between SDG 5 (gender equality) and 8 (sustainable economic growth and decent work) has been made to the tourism industry to illustrate the ways it can assist with human rights issues (Alarcón and Cole, 2019). The idea that the tourism industry provides job opportunities, particularly for women when they may not be given formal education or employment opportunities, helps to highlight the specific ways that tourism can help improve human rights globally. Roughly 55% of employees in the tourism industry are women, with some countries like Peru and Lithuania seeing over 70%, it is evident that rights for employment and the ability to earn wages for women is improved in this field (Baum, 2013; Alarcón and Cole, 2019). Additional issues caused by the tourism industry include the waste of water and electricity of tourists while they are away from home. A study on the Big Island of Hawaii found that the tourism industry accounted for 21.7% of the island's total energy usage, 44.7% of its water consumption, and 10.7% of its waste generation (Saito, 2013). Air and water pollution from transportation or poorly managed disposal practices is also taking its toll. While these issues encompass negative impacts in the tourism industry as a whole that are related to what business students are learning through their university, overtourism incorporates additional problems. These issues may even have a stronger need for immediate action from sustainable initiatives, as the exaggerated stress on a destination may lead to irreparable damage.

Negative sustainability impacts

The importance of sustainability in the tourism industry continues to rise as the population grows, as well as an increase in international tourism. In 2018 the tourism industry saw a 6% increase in international tourist arrivals from the previous year, with 1.4 billion people travelling abroad (World Bank, 2019). In particular, areas that are suffering from overtourism are in need of greater urgency to implement sustainable practices, as the massive amount of visitors in a short period of time can cause degradation to the environment and culture quickly. Overtourism has some unique negative impacts, in addition to the general impacts to the tourism industry in general, which can be addressed through education provided through PRME. These impacts include degradation and erosion to natural and cultural sites, vandalism and litter, theft, and an inability to meet the staffing demands needed to deal with overcrowding. Proper management practices to combat overtourism is particularly important, not only to help the destination be successful in the short term but to also sustain itself and provide benefits for the community for the long term.

Overtourism has been linked to backlash of the tourism industry, including antitourism movements (Seraphin, Gowreesunkar, Zaman and Bourliataux-Lajoinie, 2019; Milano, Novelli and Cheer, 2019; Alexis, 2017) and workers simply walking out of the overcrowded Louvre when it becomes overwhelmed with tourists (Lowery, 2019). The unbalance of tourists versus the residents that live there not only fuels the animosity towards travellers but the disrespect of the people and community compounds the issue (Taş Gürsoy, 2019). This has led to looking at the rights of residents and determining how much say as stakeholders they have on tourism management policies (Perkumienė and Pranskūnienė, 2019). Stress on the physical landscape and buildings of a destination, particularly without continuous upkeep and maintenance, can lead to lasting damage. While degradation and erosion can happen at a site even when overtourism is not an issue, the overwhelming number of people to a site means that not only can more damage be caused in a shorter amount of time, but it can also be difficult to implement maintenance practices when a place is constantly packed with people. An additional issue with overtourism is that with the abundance of people, it can be difficult to monitor all of the visitors, so they may wander into areas they are not supposed to, potentially causing damage to sensitive areas (Goodwin, 2017).

Vandalism and litter are also more likely to occur at destinations that are experiencing overtourism (Singh, 2018). Even if a site implements fines for such acts, it can be difficult to catch the people responsible in order to ticket the visitor. Just as with the issue of degradation and erosion, the vast number of people needing to be monitored or educated on the negative impact of their action makes it difficult to control. Vandalism and litter make the destination look less desirable for future travellers, which may cause economic issues for the area. If an area is reliant on tourism for revenue and taxes, the loss of tourists can make it difficult for the area to sustain its current way of life and operations. Not only is there a potential for a loss of profits from potentially declining tourism, but there can be an increased cost to clean up the area as a result of vandalism and litter as well (Goodwin, 2017). Increased theft can also occur from overtourism, as crowds can make pickpocketing easier to carry out and get away with (Biagi and Detotto, 2014). Theft can also occur as artefacts are taken from cultural sites, or even natural resources removed from the environment.

Destinations may also struggle keeping up with staffing at hotels, restaurants, transportation services, and attractions. This could be due to a lack of skilled people needed to address the large numbers, as tourists can outnumber the residents when overtourism is experienced. Or it could be that temporary staff is needed during the high season and it is difficult to hire and train professionals needed for the period of time needed (Terry, 2016).

PRME and tourism research

PRME started being applied to tourism research roughly seven years after its conception, but overall research in this area is still lacking in general. With only a few studies being completed in the tourism industry, none of which focus on overtourism specifically, it is clear there is a wide gap needing to be filled (Araç and Madran, 2014; Heath, 2014; Seppelin, Blinnikka and Törn-Laapio, 2019; Gowreesunkar, Seraphin and Teare, 2019). However, researchers are starting to recommend more PRME research in the tourism industry, as they believe this can be a tool to combat issues in this field. PRME has been applied to tourism research by using the principles, combined with the 3C Model (context, complexity, and connectedness), in destination management and marketing organisations. In this study the idea that responsible leadership for these organisations is a critical factor for sustainable competitiveness of tourism destinations (Heath, 2014). The results indicated that PRME could form an integral part of the educational platform needed by future destination leaders.

PRME has also been applied to resort mini-clubs, or venues at resorts that provide activities and events for kids (Seraphin and Yallop, 2019), in order to educate children through educational play. Examples of activities included learning how to play a local instrument, learn a local language, learning about biodiversity or culture and how to preserve it, gardening, or attending local events. This was not only seen as a way to educate children on important life concepts but also gives resorts a competitive advantage by offering a unique service that is not cost intensive (Seraphin and Thanh, 2020). While initial research results have positively been related to PRME as a tool for tourism management and development, more research is needed as studies are very limited.

PRME as a tool to achieve sustainability in the tourism industry

With the critiques of the implementation and report of PRME, the effectiveness of these principles may be called into question. Can PRME be an effective tool to combat overtourism? Since PRME is just beginning its gradual movement into tourism research, there may be some scepticism as to whether or not these principles will be able to help educate future leaders to manage overtourism issues. However, the growth of the signatories in and of itself is already an indicator that PRME can assist the tourism industry. There have been many struggles within the field of sustainability, from generating awareness to changing wasteful behaviours that have been normalised for decades. The rapid spreading of PRME helps to emphasise the importance of education in sustainability, and subsequently the application in the business world. Sustainable practices may have large upfront costs or changing management practices might be met with resistance, but support demonstrating the growing popularity of the global adoption of these practices provides evidence that this is more than just a passing trend. As education on sustainability spreads, implementation of practices is more likely to follow.

As the implementation of PRME in business schools grows, so might the evaluation practices associated with it. When thinking about the evolution of successful sustainable management tools, such as LEED (Leadership in Energy and Environmental Design) certification, constant analysis and re-structuring of the evaluation system was undertaken and multiple versions of the programme have been produced. LEED uses a list of requirements and elective operations needed in order to earn points, with higher designations of certification available to those earning more points (USGBC, 2020). While it was not the first rating system for 'green' infrastructures, it has been the most widely adopted (Doan, Ghaffarianhoseini, Naismith, Zhang, Ghaffarianhoseini and Tookey, 2017), possibly because of its ability to accept criticism and improve its measurement system on those recommendations. Through the growth of implementing these principles, particularly with some universities already providing a strong foundation of significant advancement with their sustainable initiatives, PRME can be used as a tool to educate future leaders on fighting overtourism.

Conclusion

This chapter reviewed the background of the United Nations Global Compact and the creation of PRME. Connecting the principles of PRME with the SDGs, examples of what business schools are doing to learn about and implement sustainable initiatives was explored. Examples of issues within the tourism industry, particularly regarding overtourism, were given and ways PRME can assist with these issues were highlighted. The benefits and criticisms of PRME were addressed in relation to the ability of these principles to achieve success as a tool to combat overtourism, as a means of practical implementations. While there are recommendations for improvements to PRME, the popularity of the initiative and its ability to bring a spotlight on the issues of sustainability shows promise for tackling these issues. With ethical concerns brought on by corporate scandal and dishonesty, added on by traditional business school practice weakening the moral character of its students (Crane, 2004) the foundational ideas of corporate social responsibility are more important now than ever. Conceptually, PRME adds guidelines to encourage ethical practices and partnerships. If utilised within business schools with an aim at improving devolving practices that only focus on profits over people and the environment, other structured practices, measurements and evaluation procedures can occur over time, making sustainable practice the norm instead of the overachieving standard.

The idea that PRME has the potential to initiate change in sustainable policy in the tourism industry, as well as other areas of business, demonstrates the need for more research to be pursued on this topic. Future research regarding PRME may focus on how newly emerged leaders are applying these principles in the business world. Research has shown that there is a relationship between residents' perceived knowledge and empowerment in the tourism industry and their engagement levels (Joo, Woosnam, Strzelecka and Boley, 2020). Recommendations from this study address the idea of resident empowerment in other areas and it can be argued, with the connection to similar research, local empowerment can lead to engaging in political action (Rocha, 1997). Therefore, the idea that leaders who educate and empower their local residents in becoming active stakeholders in their community might also drive policy changes to enable sustainable management in the tourism industry. With a strong tie to the issues of overtourism, PRME can be used to bring awareness to the importance of sustainable practices and provide educational support to business schools evaluating these challenges.

References

Alarcón, D.M. and Cole, S. (2019). "No sustainability for tourism without gender equality," *Journal of Sustainable Tourism*, Vol. 22 No. 7, pp. 903–919.

Alexis, P. (2017). "Over-tourism and anti-tourist sentiment: An exploratory analysis and discussion," *Ovidius University Annals, Economic Sciences Series*, Vol. 17 No. 2, pp. 288–293.

Annan-Diab, F. and Molinari, C. (2017). "Interdisciplinary: Practical approach to advancing education for sustainability and for the Sustainable Development Goals," *The International Journal of Management Education*, Vol. 15 No. 2, pp. 73–83.

Araç, S.K. and Madran, C. (2014). "Business school as an initiator of the transformation to sustainability: A content analysis for business schools in PRME," *Social Business*, Vol. 4 No. 2, pp. 137–152.

Basani, A. (2020). PRME report. Bengaluru, India: Acharya Bangalore Business School.

Baum, T. (2013). "International perspectives on women and work in hotels, catering and tourism," Working paper, Bureau for Gender Equality and Sectoral Activities Department, Cornell University.

Biagi, B. and Detotto, C. (2014). "Crime as tourism externality," *Regional Studies*, Vol. 48 No. 4, pp. 693–709.

Bonini, S. and Bové, A. (2014) "Sustainability's strategic worth," available at: https://www.mckinsey.com/business-functions/sustainability/our-insights/sustainabilitys-strategic-worth-mckinsey-global-survey-results (accessed 23 February 2020).

Busing, M. (2020). Principles of Responsible Management Education (PRME): SIP Report SIP Report for 2018–2019.

Carteron, J.C., Haynes, K. and Murray, A. (2014). "Education for sustainable development, the UNGC PRME initiative, and the sustainability literacy test: Measuring and assessing success," *SAM Advanced Management Journal*, Vol. 79 No. 4, pp. 51–58.

Coronado, G. (2014). "Selling culture? Between commoditisation and cultural control in Indigenous alternative tourism," *Pasos. Revista de Turismo y Patrimonio Cultural*, Vol. 12 No. 1, pp. 11–28.

Crane, F.G. (2004). "The teaching of business ethics: An imperative at business schools," *Journal of Education for Business*, Vol. 79 No. 3, pp. 149–151.

Dickson, M.A., Eckman, M., Loker, S. and Jirousek, C. (2013). "A model for sustainability education in support of the PRME," *The Journal of Management Development*, Vol. 32 No. 3, pp. 309–318.

Doan, D.T., Ghaffarianhoseini, A., Naismith, N., Zhang, T., Ghaffarianhoseini, A. and Tookey, J. (2017). "A critical comparison of green building rating systems," *Building and Environment*, Vol. 123 No. 1, pp. 243–260.

Escudero, M. (2006). "Global corporate citizenship and academic: A global convergence," Concept paper, United Nations, New York.

Gilligan, C. and Ridley-Duff, R. (2018). Principles of Responsible Management Education (PRME): SIP Report SIP Report for Sheffield Business School.

Godemann, J., Herzig, C. and Moon, J. (2013). Integrating sustainability into business schools: Evidence from United Nations principles for responsible management education (UNPRME) sharing of information in progress (SIP) reports.

Godemann, J., Herzig, C., Moon, J. and Powell, A. (2011). Integrating sustainability into business schools–analysis of 100 UN PRME sharing information on progress (SIP) reports. Nottingham: International Centre for Corporate Social Responsibility, (58–2011).

Goodwin, H. (2017). "The challenge of overtourism," available at: https://harold goodwin.info/publications/ (accessed 30 October 2019).

Gowreesunkar, V., Seraphin, H. and Teare, R. (2019). Reflections on the theme issue outcomes: What smart and sustainable strategies could be used to reduce the impact of overtourism?, *Worldwide Hospitality and Tourism Themes*, Vol. 11 No. 5, pp. 634–640.

Haertle, J., Parkes, C., Murray, A. and Hayes, R. (2017). "PRME: Building a global movement on responsible management education," *The International Journal of Management Education*, Vol. 15 No. 2, pp. 66–72.

Heath, E. (2014, June). A key tourism education futures challenge: Facilitating responsible leadership learning for destination management and marketing organizations. In *8th Annual Conference-transformational learning: Activism, Empowerment and Political Agency in Tourism Education* (Vol. 3, pp. 142–163).

Iverson, T.J. (2010). "Cultural conflict: Tourists versus tourists in Bali, Indonesia," *International Journal of Culture, Tourism and Hospitality Research*, Vol. 4 No. 4, pp. 299–310.

Jamal, T. and Camargo, B.A. (2018). "Tourism governance and policy: Whither justice?" *Tourism Management Perspectives*, Vol. 25 No. 1, pp. 205–208.

Joo, D., Woosnam, K.M., Strzelecka, M. and Boley, B.B. (2020). "Knowledge, empowerment, and action: Testing the empowerment theory in a tourism context," *Journal of Sustainable Tourism*, Vol. 28 No. 1, pp. 69–85.

Kaosa-ard, M.S. (1994). "Thailand's tourism industry-What do we gain and lose," *TDRI Quarterly Review*, Vol. 9 No. 3, pp. 23–26.

Lowery, A., (2019). "Too many people want to travel," available at: https://www.theatlantic.com/ideas/archive/2019/06/crowds-tourists-are-ruining-popular-destinations/590767/ (accessed 12 April 2010).

Milano, C., Novelli, M. and Cheer, J.M. (2019). "Overtourism and tourismphobia: A journey through four decades of tourism development, planning and local concerns," *Tourism Planning and Development*, Vol. 16 No. 4, pp. 353–357.

Moscardo, G. (2015). The importance of education for sustainability in tourism. In G. Moscardo and P. Benckendorff, eds. *Education for Sustainability in Tourism*. Springer, Berlin, Heidelberg, pp. 1–21.

Parkes, C., Buono, A.F. and Howaidy, G. (2017). "The principles for responsible management education (PRME). The first decade–What has been achieved? The next decade–Responsible management education's challenge for the sustainable development goals (SDGs)," *The International Journal of Management Education*, Vol. 15 No. 2, pp. 61–65.

Perkumienė, D. and Pranskūnienė, R. (2019). "Overtourism: Between the right to travel and residents' rights," *Sustainability*, Vol. 11 No. 7, pp. 1–17.

Pomering, A., Johnson, L.W. and Noble, G. (2010). Conceptualising a contemporary marketing mix for sustainable tourism marketing. *Proceedings of the 20th Annual Conference of the Council for Australian University Tourism and Hospitality Education (CAUTHE)*, pp. 1–5.

Rasche, A., (2009). "'A necessary supplement' what the United Nations Global Compact is and is not," *Business and Society*, Vol. 48 No. 4, pp. 511–537.

Rocha, E.M. (1997). "A ladder of empowerment," *Journal of Planning Education and Research*, Vol. 17 No. 1, pp. 31–44.

Saarinen, J. (2014). "Critical sustainability: Setting the limits to growth and responsibility in tourism," *Sustainability*, Vol. 6 No. 1, pp. 1–17.

Saito, O. (2013). "Resource use and waste generation by the tourism industry on the Big Island of Hawaii," *Journal of Industrial Ecology*, Vol. 17 No. 4, pp. 578–589.

Seppelin, S., Blinnikka, P. and Törn-Laapio, A. (2019). *Special issues in responsible tourism.* Jyväskylä, Finland: JAMK University of Applied Sciences.

Seraphin, H., Gowreesunkar, V., Zaman, M. and Bourliataux-Lajoinie, S. (2019). "Community based festivals as a tool to tackle tourismphobia and antitourism movements," *Journal of Hospitality and Tourism Management*, Vol. 39 No. 1, pp. 219–223.

Seraphin, H. and Thanh, T.V. (2020). "Investigating the application of the principles for responsible management education to resort mini-clubs," *The International Journal of Management Education*, Vol. 18 No. 2, pp. 1–14.

Seraphin, H. and Yallop, A. (2019). "An analysis of children's play in resort mini-clubs: Potential strategic implications for the hospitality and tourism industry," *World Leisure Journal*, Vol. 62 No. 2, pp. 114–131.

Singh, T. (2018). "Is over-tourism the downside of mass tourism?" *Tourism Recreation Research* Vol. 43 No. 4, pp. 415–416.

Su, M.M., Wall, G. and Xu, K. (2016). "Heritage tourism and livelihood sustainability of a resettled rural community: Mount Sanqingshan World Heritage Site, China," *Journal of Sustainable Tourism*, Vol. 24 No. 5, pp. 735–757.

Taş Gürsoy, İ. (2019). "Beauty and the beast: A fairy tale of tourismphobia," *Tourism Planning & Development*, Vol. 16 No. 4, pp. 434–451.

Terry, W.C. (2016). "Solving seasonality in tourism? Labour shortages and guest worker programmes in the USA," *Area*, Vol. 48 No. 1, pp. 111–118.

Thinh, N.A., Thanh, N.N., Tuyen, L.T. and Hens, L. (2019). "Tourism and beach erosion: Valuing the damage of beach erosion for tourism in the Hoi an World Heritage site, Vietnam," *Environment, Development and Sustainability*, Vol. 21 No. 5, pp. 2113–2124.

Todeschini, B.V., Cortimiglia, M.N., Callegaro-de-Menezes, D. and Ghezzi, A. (2017). "Innovative and sustainable business models in the fashion industry: Entrepreneurial drivers, opportunities, and challenges," *Business Horizons*, Vol. 60 No. 6, pp. 759–770.

Tyran, K.L. (2017). "Transforming students into global citizens: International service learning and PRME," *The International Journal of Management Education*, Vol. 15 No. 2, pp. 162–171.

United Nations. (2020). "Sustainable development Goals: Knowledge platform," available at: https://sustainabledevelopment.un.org/?menu=1300 (accessed 30 October 2019).

United Nations Global Compact. (2007). *The Principles for Responsible Management Education.* New York: United Nations Global Compact.

United Nations Global Compact. (2019). "United Nations Global Compact: Who we are," available at: https://www.unglobalcompact.org/ (accessed 27 October 2019).

United Nations World Tourism Organization (UNWTO). (2006). UNWTO's declaration on tourism and the Millennium Goals: Harnessing tourism for the Millennium Development Goals. Madrid: UNWTO.

United Nations World Tourism Organization. (2019). "UNWTO: Sustainable development," available at: https://www.unwto.org/sustainable-development (accessed 27 October 2019).

United Nations World Tourism Organization. (2020). "UNWTO: Tourism 4 SDGs," available at: https://www.unwto.org/tourism4sdgs (accessed 27 October 2019).

UNPRME. (2019). "PRME: About us," available at: https://www.unprme.org/about-prme/ (accessed 27 January 2020).

UNPRME. (2020). "PRME: Reports," available at: https://www.unprme.org/reporting/participant-reports.php (accessed 27 January, 2020).

USGBC. (2020). "LEED rating system," available at: https://www.usgbc.org/leed (accessed 27 January 2020).

Williams, O.F. (2004). "The UN Global Compact: The challenge and the promise," *Business Ethics Quarterly*, Vol. 14 No. 4, pp. 755–774.

World Bank. (2012). *Transformation through Tourism: Development Dynamics Past, Present and Future*. Washington, DC: World Bank.

World Bank. (2019). "International tourism, number of arrivals," available at: https://data.worldbank.org/indicator/ST.INT.ARVL (accessed 11 April 2020).

3 Tourism as industry and field of study

Using research and education to address overtourism

Kathleen M. Adams and Peter M. Sanchez

Introduction

In the summer of 2015, after an absence of seven years, we returned to the Trastevere neighbourhood of Rome where we had lived for a year. When we resided there, the quarter was hailed in guidebooks as the 'most Roman' of Rome's neighbourhoods,[1] with its narrow cobblestone streets and photogenic grandmothers clustered on folding chairs outside their apartment buildings, chatting and catching rare breezes on balmy days. When we lived in that picturesque quarter, we learned to navigate the grandmothers, meandering walking tour groups, and tipsy foreign students who flocked to the neighbourhood's relatively cheap eateries, bars and clubs on weekend evenings. But by 2015, the zone had transformed: the narrow arteries leading to the neighbourhood's celebrated 1st-century basilica, Santa Maria de Trastevere, were now clogged with tourists. The scattered souvenir shops lining those lanes had multiplied, their displays of postcards and refrigerator magnets spilling out into the alleyways, further choking movements for residents and tourists alike. Many of the small, locally oriented shops we remembered had been replaced by trendy tourist-oriented restaurants, and Airbnb signs now adorned the entryways of many apartment complexes. While tourism was certainly lively when we resided in the neighbourhood, by 2015 the zone was in the throes of overtourism. Even though we were simply visitors on this return trip, the negative changes that had taken place were palpable. While catching up with a local grocer whose dry foods shop had been a fixture in the neighbourhood for decades, we heard about more of those transformations. As he lamented, 'None of us can afford to live here anymore – foreigners and investors are all buying up the apartments and making them into Airbnbs for the tourists'. He solemnly went on to observe that shop rents were escalating, and he was uncertain how much longer he could hold on. Other Trastevere friends had already moved away from the area, fleeing the climbing rents and unrelenting nightly ruckus of partying tourists and international students. Most of the grandmothers were now gone. For these Trastevere residents, overtourism was palpably challenging the sustainability of their livelihoods and neighbourhood quality of life.

The scenario above is one that is increasingly common throughout the world, in cities ranging from Hong Kong to Barcelona. Overtourism, however, affects all locations: cities, national parks, heritage sites, coastal areas, and islands. While recently the coronavirus has put overtourism on hiatus – a clear reminder that tourism as a monoculture is dangerous – the need for systematic research and education with an eye towards rendering tourism more sustainable is clear. In this chapter we argue that the study of tourism has a Janus-faced character where one face views tourism as a road towards development (focusing on job creation and capital accumulation), while the other face highlights the ills of the tourism industry (focusing on problems wrought by the overreliance on tourism, the leakage of capital, and the many issues associated with overtourism). Even though sustainable tourism has entered the lexicon of both faces of tourism, in our assessment, tourism as a path towards development still tends to eclipse the face that advocates limits to tourism growth. Our recommendation is that we continue to expand research on sustainable tourism – and overtourism – so that we can more fully educate all stakeholders about the benefits and costs of tourism. In recent years, the literature on sustainable tourism has mushroomed, but most of the work on overtourism to date has tended to concentrate more heavily on European destinations. In order to more effectively train tourism students in strategies for addressing overtourism in the locales where they will work, we need more case studies from additional parts of the world that are currently underrepresented in the literature. We also stress that for a holistic sustainable tourism approach to succeed, educational and policy efforts must take place at the local, regional, national, and global levels.

The classic Janus face of tourism education

Although the world's first tourism-oriented school was founded in 1893 on the shores of Lake Lemans in Lausanne, Switzerland, its focus was on training future hotel professionals and thus education emphasised pragmatic skills such as accounting, languages, and hospitality.[2] Such was also the case for what was purportedly the world's first four-year tourism-oriented university programme, established in 1922 at Cornell University, with the vision of training undergraduates to become professional hotel staff and hospitality managers.[3] It was not until many decades later, in the 1970s, that a few pioneering universities began offering courses emphasising the critical analysis of tourism dynamics. In this section we contrast the deeply entrenched educational objectives, values, and orientations that tend to dominate tourism management schools with the objectives, values, and orientations characteristic of tourism studies in theoretically focused academic disciplinary settings, such as cultural anthropology, sociology, political science, and geography. To illustrate possible pathways for resolving these tensions, this section also discusses the recent rise of new groups (such as critical tourism studies) attempting to bridge these divisions by fostering conversations between social justice-oriented tourism management scholars and critical theory-oriented scholars. Likewise, we also note the birth of new management models such as 'ambidextrous tourism management' that challenge the traditional monolithic focus on continued growth, regardless of its costs to local environments and communities. We believe the recent emergence of these groups and models offer new possibilities for the future of tourism education, particularly in relation to issues of overtourism and sustainability.

We have previously characterised this paradoxical divide between the economic, growth-driven approach to tourism and the critical analysis of its problematic dynamics and unintended consequences as the 'Janus-faced character of tourism' (Sanchez and Adams, 2008). In a similar vein, Aramberri (2010, pp. 9, 26–28) subsequently dubbed the clash between the management ('how to?') and the theoretical ('why?') realms of tourism research as the 'scissors crisis'. His use of this analogy is drawn from Trotsky's observations pertaining to 1920s Russia, when the dramatically varying rates of industrial and agrarian prices 'threatened to inevitably pit the two pillars of Soviet power ... [the industrial proletariat and the peasantry] against each other' (Aramberri, 2010, p. 9). In the 'scissors' analogy, the clash is inevitably an irreconcilably destructive one. We prefer to envision the contrast in less pessimistic terms, as tourism's dual faces, since we feel the current moment offers some possibilities for bringing these two distinctive approaches to tourism into more productive dialogue.[4]

Tourism and hospitality studies: growth still eclipsing sustainability?

Sustainability has entered the curriculum in most, if not all, tourism and hospitality programmes around the world. The hope is that students enrolled in these programmes will enter the tourism industry with a solid understanding of sustainable tourism so that tourist destinations will not experience the worst effects of tourism – overtourism. We note, however, that other negative effects of tourism include inequality, the leakage of tourism-generated revenues, and the unintended disruptive social and political consequences when tourism is used as a desperate attempt to rescue an economy, as the case of Cuba demonstrates (Sanchez and Adams, 2008). Ideally, sustainable tourism would eliminate or minimise these negative effects. Focusing on sustainability, however, can often clash with the goals of economic development – creating jobs and bringing in hard currency. Consequently, using education to promote sustainable tourism will require that hospitality and tourism programmes place much greater emphasis on sustainable tourism and the environmental, social, and cultural values they espouse.

However, as we all know, simply including sustainability as a menu item in the broader curriculum of tourism and hospitality programmes will not be enough to remedy the situation. First, there is the issue of how sustainability is presented in these programmes. After conducting a content analysis of course profiles from 60 top tourism and hospitality programmes, Cotterell et al. point out that evidence '... suggests that tourism students are graduating with narrow understandings of sustainability ... (2019, p. 882)'. The problem does not stop there. The authors conclude (Cotterell et al., 2019, p. 898),

> ... universities need to teach tourism students about much stronger and varied conceptualizations of sustainability that consider different perspectives including "very strong sustainability" rather than from a predominantly neo-liberal business viewpoint that can lead to over-tourism issues.

Tourism and hospitality programmes must therefore accomplish two difficult steps. First, they must enhance their focus on sustainability so that students acquire a richer, more nuanced understanding of both its importance and avenues for its implementation. That is, a programme's curriculum should enable students to develop skills necessary for effectively developing policies and practices that promote sustainable tourism. Many tourism and hospitality programmes remain hesitant to strengthen the focus on sustainable tourism, however (Wilson and von der Heidt, 2013). Second, these academic programmes need to more fully embrace sustainable tourism to ensure that the focus on development does not overshadow efforts at sustainability. These two steps will not come easily, in that most of the tourism and hospitality programmes are housed in business schools which favour employing the tourist industry for local and national growth and are thus less focused on sustainability, which would require some curtailment of tourist visits (Boyle, Wilson and Dimmock, 2015; Inui, Wheeler and Lankford, 2006). Bluntly stated, tourism and hospitality programmes are training students to go into careers in the tourism industry, an industry that relies on the continued expansion of tourism for its profits.

Undermining tourism growth and profits will be a hard sell unless the industry can be regulated, or governments and investors can be convinced that tourism's long-term survival depends on some degree of curtailment. Overtourism may be the phenomenon that launches this discussion, and the COVID-19 pandemic's (temporary?) decimation of tourism may prompt some further rethinking of continuing to rely on tourism's unchecked expansion as an economic panacea. It is essential, therefore, that hospitality programmes incorporate critical studies of tourism's ramifications into their curriculums, as a mechanism for moving away from the classic primary emphasis on tourism as a vehicle for economic advancement. Having looked at the business oriented 'face' of tourism education and its tendency to emphasise growth, we turn now to address the social science 'face' of tourism education, which has classically emphasised the critical analysis of tourism dynamics.

Critical approaches to teaching tourism in the academic realm

Pinpointing the beginnings of the academic study of tourism – particularly its relation to sustainability – is a difficult endeavour, as the topic emerged in different disciplines at different times. Butler (2015) observes that occasional studies of tourism's environmental and economic impacts appeared as early as the 1930s, but it was not until the 1950s and 1960s that a broader body of theoretically informed research on tourism began to emerge, mostly in geography and economics (Leite and Graburn, 2012). By the 1960s, most social science studies approached tourism in relatively uncritical terms, assuming continued tourism growth was a promising avenue for development. This is not surprising as this was the developmentalism decade with many scholars suggesting that economic 'take-off' was the only true path to national progress (Rostow, 1960). As Graburn and Jafari summed up, 'In the 1960s, the benefits of tourism were unquestioned. Research assumed that tourism was a labour-intensive growth industry, beneficial to both the Third World and the hinterlands of metropolitan countries' (Graburn and Jafari, 1991, p. 3). However, in the 1970s scholars from various disciplines began examining the negative consequences of excessive tourism (ibid, p. 4), and some of these early studies of national parks, island destinations, and resort towns addressed themes pertaining to 'recreational carrying capacity' or 'tourism saturation' address terrain we now label overtourism (e.g. Stankey and Lime, 1973; Wall and Wright, 1977; Hills and Lundgren, 1977; Singh, 1978; de Kadt, 1979). Most scholars point to the 1970s as the era when the social scientific study of tourism began taking shape (Cohen, 1984, p. 374; Crick, 1989). Coincidentally, this was also the decade in which the first theoretically oriented university-level social science courses on tourism appeared.

For instance, the earliest experimental class on the anthropology of tourism was introduced at the University of California Berkeley in 1976 by Nelson Graburn (1980, p. 56).[5] Graburn's pioneering tourism classes addressed tourism's history, cultural structures and impacts, and included works by Dean MacCannell's (1976) *The Tourist*, Erik Cohen's (1974) conceptual classification of tourists, and Valene Smith's (1977) edited volume *Hosts and Guests* (arguably the first anthropology 'text' on tourism and it's ramifications[6]). One half of Graburn's class content addressed tourism's economic, cultural, and social 'impacts' in various types of locales, ranging from islands, fragile environments (ecologically or structurally), to industrial settings (Graburn, 1980, p. 60). By the early 1990s, Graburn's template had taken root and those teaching tourism social sciences classes generally included theories directly related to sustainability and overtourism (although the term was not yet born). For instance, when one author of this chapter (Adams) first taught the Anthropology of Tourism in 1989, she included critical inquiries into the ramifications of excessive tourism for small communities, discussions of destination carrying capacities, and of geographer Richard Butler's (1980) classic model of a tourist area's life cycle (TALC), from discovery and development to decline.[7]

Today's tourism classes in various social science disciplines, generally continue to incorporate many of these classic works while adding new theoretical critiques of the tourism industry's overzealous neoliberal pursuit of growth, from the perspectives of political economy (i.e. Bianchi, 2012), political ecology (i.e. Mostafanezhad and Norum, 2019), social movements (i.e. Milano, Novelli and Cheer, 2019) and resilience (i.e. Cheer and Lew, 2017; Hall, Prayag and Amore, 2018). In sum, we can see the Janus-faced character of tourism studies in the bifurcated emphases of tourism education in hospitality schools and social science disciplines.

Bridging the educational divide: promising developments

Despite the historically Janus-faced character of tourism education, with its classic contrast between predominantly growth oriented ('how to') education in tourism management schools and more theoretically critical analyses in tourism social science classes, we find this a promising moment for productive exchanges between these two educational realms. Today, a growing number of scholars in both the social sciences and tourism schools are interested in uncovering avenues for rendering tourism more beneficial to local communities. More scholars in the social sciences are increasingly committed to public interest applications of their theoretical and field-based knowledge, turning their attention to the 'how to' and becoming actively engaged in ventures to develop sustainable tourism enterprises (i.e. Stronza, 2005, 2010, also see Adams, 2005) and to educate government officials and the public about the devastating effects of overtourism (i.e. Cole, 2012). Likewise, more scholars based in tourism management schools are trained in critical tourism theory and interested in fostering sustainable forms of tourism development (i.e. Dolezal, Trupp and Bui, 2020; Holdren and Novelli, 2011).

The recent rise of critical tourism studies (CTS) has fostered a new arena for collaboration and dialogue between scholars, practitioners and educators concerned with lassoing tourism for achieving the common good. CTS arose a little over a decade ago, and is gradually taking root, with biennial conferences in Europe, North America and the Asia-Pacific region. CTS is premised on the need for more systematic analyses of how both the practice of tourism and analyses of it are embedded in asymmetrical power relations and hegemonic discourses (Ateljevic, Morgan and Pritchard, 2007, 2012; Swain, 2009; Wijesinghe and Mura, 2018). This small but growing group of social-justice-oriented scholars from both tourism management schools and university social science departments are now working towards interdisciplinary approaches to tourism that embrace cultural plurality and empower local stakeholders (e.g. Coles, Hall and Duval, 2006; Hollinshead, 2016). Recent CTS conferences, such as the 2020 CTS-Asia Pacific conference in Japan, have been rich venues for presentations and discussions addressing the challenges posed by overtourism, COVID-19, and strategies for fostering resilience and empowerment for local stakeholders in tourism destinations.

In short, the work of CTS is gradually fostering new dialogues between tourism industry educators, social scientists, travel writers, and others, and we anticipate that a new body of educational materials will emerge from this work. We are hopeful that these intellectual exchanges and the long term partnerships that emerge from them will more effectively address some of the paradoxes embedded in the very fabric of tourism, particularly the fact that the ideals of sustainability (be it social, environmental, political, or cultural) are at loggerheads with neoliberal global capitalism.

In a similar vein, emergent business models such as 'ambidextrous tourism management' offer revolutionary new visions for tourism enterprises, potentially enabling them to better harmonise with environmental change (Mihalache and Mihalache, 2016). As outlined by various authors, ambidextrous tourism management entails simultaneously embracing two opposing inclinations: (1) market-focused 'exploitation' and (2) developing radical, proactive innovations and new capabilities that are attuned to changing local conditions (Brooker and Joppe, 2014; Séraphin and Butcher, 2018; Séraphin and Yallop, 2019).

In short, we believe these new cross-cutting groups (such as critical tourism studies) and models (such as ambidextrous tourism management) offer new possibilities for the future of tourism education. But we also need to move beyond the academic and managerial domains and work with local communities and governments that are dealing with the most pernicious form of unsustainable tourism – overtourism.

Overtourism education 'In the Field'

When identifying venues for overtourism and sustainability education, most of us tend to immediately think of universities and tourism schools. However, education can happen in multiple arenas. This section briefly highlights additional beyond-the-classroom venues for effecting change. First we discuss overtourism education in destinations where tourism transpires, highlighting a case study where scholarly research on the life-threatening challenges posed by tourism overdevelopment was shared with local citizens and leaders, with the aim of effecting change. Next we turn to civil society where frustrations with overtourism have led to the development of degrowth social movements. These grassroots mobilisations serve to educate both local officials and broader publics. Finally we look briefly at efforts to deal with overtourism in locations other than major cities and point out that we must learn from these cases as well.

Sharing overtourism research findings locally: pressing for policy revision via educational seminars

One often-overlooked form of education regarding the more subtle ramifications of overtourism takes place in the field, in our scholarly research settings. While overtourism's erosion of the quality of life in places where tourists and locals are crowded elbow-to-elbow is clear to all, in some places its ramifications are more subtle and local stakeholders are less likely to connect the dots between tourism and emerging hardships. In other places, residents are fully aware of the costs of overtourism, but they lack the avenues or agency to push back. In still other locales both these factors are at play.

One example of in-the-field overtourism education comes from the island of Bali, where annual tourist arrivals have outnumbered the population for years. In 2020, prior to the Covid-19's travel disruptions, Bali was poised to host 18.2 million visitors, more than four times its population.[8] On Bali, water is central to local religious practices and wet rice agriculture. It is also prevalent in touristic representations of the island as an exotic paradise, and figures prominently in resort landscape designs. Activist tourism anthropologist-geographer and former tour operator Stroma Cole's political ecology study of water distribution on the island revealed that villagers' ever-increasing difficulties accessing water was tied to the unchecked development of tourism on the island (Cole, 2012; Cole and Browne, 2015). By some estimates, tourists and resorts consume 65% more water than the Balinese, prompting shortages that disproportionately impacted socioeconomically disenfranchised residents. Even middle-class Balinese face low water pressure and irregular waterflow. Cole (2012, p. 1223) notes that scholars such as Charara et al. (2010) have found promise in educational outreach to tourism sector managers and political leaders since many of them lack understanding of water conservation issues. But as Cole and Browne conclude for Bali, 'Whilst there are obvious indications that ... [the island's] water resources are over stretched, there is no feedback loop to the institutional structures that would help enable appropriate responses from the user groups or governance system' (Cole and Browne, 2015, p. 439).

Cole also observes that broader Indonesian cultural orientations further inhibited Balinese from decrying the situation. Indonesia is a highly stratified society and villagers are schooled to enact 'blind obedience' to the national government, as well as to defer to those with economic, political, or cultural power (Erb, 2000; Cole, 2012). Moreover, at the national level, Indonesian ethnic groups are inculcated to put their needs behind those of the nation (Cole, 2008). According to Cole's calculus, locals have limited ability to pressure tourism developers and the state to address the island's growing water crisis by rethinking Bali's current mass tourism model. Thus, in 2015, Cole agreed to play the role of outsider scholar-educator provocateur, and offered a highly publicised public seminar on Bali entitled 'Is Tourism Killing Babies?'[9] As her talk detailed, the (over)tourism-induced water crisis has disproportionately brutal consequences for poorer Balinese women, as their dry wells and unaffordable bottled water prices oblige them to purchase cheaper water from dubious sources, ultimately sickening their infants. Present at Cole's seminar were Bali's Head of the Water Department, the

Chairperson of the Hotel and Restaurant Association and fleets of reporters. The ensuing headlines in local and international newspapers prompted two NGOs to begin promoting public education on the issue, and one charity to install rain catchment water pipes in Bali's driest region.

Cole's post-field research onsite public education efforts are very much in keeping with the principles of public interest anthropology, which advocates not only sharing research results with local stakeholders but actively contributing to the quality of life, social justice, and equality in the locations where we conduct our research (Adams, 2005). Cole's pioneering work illustrates how researchers (especially when they are outsiders) can serve as megaphones to educate tourism decision-makers and government officials about controversial dimensions of overtourism that relatively disempowered locals may not be positioned to comfortably or effectively protest. Moreover, Cole's work shows how public seminars in tourism destinations offer avenues for educating tourists and broader publics about the normally invisible (to non-locals) ramifications of their holidays. On a small scale, such destination-based public education can spur tourists to alter their behaviour and can prompt innovative efforts by NGOs, governments and other enterprises to address the problems posed by overtourism.

Overtourism education of broader publics (and tourists) via social movements

Numerous tourist locations and cities have made important strides in developing strategies for addressing overtourism, showing that local governments and civil society can also help to educate us, and each other, on the need to tackle tourism related problems. Unlike in hierarchical environments like Bali, these European movement participants can fearlessly embrace their rights to set their own local agendas and are more than willing to challenge the tourist industry and local governments. Perhaps the most prominent example are the numerous efforts that neighbourhood groups have pursued in the city of Barcelona, where local struggles with overtourism have been documented for some time (i.e. Fava and Rubio, 2017; Martins, 2018). By 2008, Catalan anthropologist Manuel Delgado had coined the term *turismofobia* to describe the situation, in an article published in the Spanish newspaper *El País* (2008). The term captures the many frustrations that residents of Barcelona felt about the excessive tourism taking place in their city. Since then sentiments against tourists have grown in many other European cities, climaxing in protests in several Spanish cities in summer 2017. The result of these grassroots demonstrations has been the development of social movements focusing on tourism degrowth (Milano, Novelli and Cheer, 2019). These movements towards tourism degrowth have emerged in several other cities, most notably Venice (Bertocchi and Visentin, 2019). These grassroots efforts help to educate their members not only about how to work towards addressing overtourism problems but also on how to pressure local and national governments. In part due to these grassroots pressures, the idea of Smart Tourist Cities is starting to take root, and city governments are beginning to add tourism planning to their sustainable practices (Ivars-Baidal, Garcia-Hernandez and Mendoza de Miguel, 2019). One of the most important outcomes of these grassroots efforts has been the creation of a network of cities – Network of Southern European Cities against Touristification (*Red de ciudades del sur de Europa ante la turistización*) – that are working together to mitigate the negative effects of overtourism. The anti-tourism movements therefore are diffusing in Europe and may diffuse beyond Europe in the future. With these types of social movements education of citizens as well as local and national governments will inevitably occur.

We must learn from the efforts of social movements and local governments. This knowledge would then need to be incorporated into the curriculum of tourism and hospitality programmes and disseminated to local and national governments, as well as to citizen groups (social movements) focused on tourism. The rapid diffusion of information on the ills of tourism and strategies for treating these ills is crucial if we are to achieve even a modest level of sustainable tourism.

Where to from here? Expanding research on overtourism for more comprehensive sustainability education

Having reviewed various venues in which overtourism and sustainability education can transpire, we now shift to briefly discuss the need for expanded studies of those locations taking steps to defend themselves against overtourism. With some notable exceptions, up until the present, the majority of overtourism research has focused on European cities or destinations in the global North (e.g. Ivars-Baidal, García-Hernández and Mendoza de Miguel, 2019; Bertocci and Visentin, 2019; and Milano, Novelli and Cheer, 2019). More research, however, is needed on the experiences and overtourism policies developed in Asian, African, Latin American, and Middle Eastern destinations. Multiple locations in the Non-Western world as well as in the developing world have experienced overtourism and tourism monoculture for decades. Jamieson and Jamieson argue that while overtourism is affecting Asian urban heritage areas, '... many of those responsible for managing urban heritage areas lack the skills and competencies to prevent it or mitigate its effects' (2019, 581). What other factors might be at play in these non-European destinations? As suggested earlier, in some cases the inability to take action against overtourism may not be due to a lack of skills, rather authoritarian states and cultural norms hindering or repressing the emergence of degrowth social movements may pose obstacles (as illustrated by the Bali example). If we are to develop educational strategies for mitigating the negative effects of overtourism in different parts of the world, we need more ethnographically grounded studies of overtourism in different, non-Western locales. Many of these locations have already taken steps towards reducing the ills of unsustainable tourism and we can learn from those efforts.

Some Latin American destinations have attempted to deal with overtourism: their experiences can offer educational and practical insights into sustainable tourism. One case of extreme tourism limitation is that of the Guna (formerly Kuna) indigenous people in Panama. The Guna achieved local autonomy from Panama in 1938, and since that time they have resisted tourism development in their territory, Guna Yala, although this emphasis on curtailing growth has led to some conflict among the Guna (Bennett, 1999). In the 1960s, US investors owned some small hotels in the territory. By the 1970s, the Panamanian Institute of Tourism (IPAT) developed plans to build a large hotel complex, but the Guna resisted these efforts at tourism development on their land (Chapin, 1990). In 1999, the authors visited the autonomous territory of Guna Yala, which spans almost 911 square miles, including over 300 islands (many of them very small) and a wooded fringe of coastal land in the north western coast of Panama. What struck us on our visit was the pristine beauty of the beaches and islands, and the absence of cars, large buildings, and mega-resorts. The hotel in which we stayed, a relatively short canoe ride from the tiny airport on the nearby island of *Porvernir*, was small and relatively spartan. In the years since our 1999 visit, some tourism development has occurred: by 2013, 51 small hotels operated in Guna Yala, with a total occupancy of 854 guests (Savener, 2013, p. 71). Given the size of the territory and its proximity to both the Panama Canal and Panama City (which has fully embraced tourism), however, Guna Yala appears to have achieved a sustainable degree of tourism development. The case of the Guna might help us to understand, and teach other tourist locations, about the potential benefits (but also the potential losses) of severely limiting tourism. Clearly, one advantage of the Guna is their near absolute autonomy. Perhaps, further study of this case might suggest that a potential path towards tourism sustainability for ethnic minorities in nation states lies in establishing some form of regional autonomy, much as Navaho pueblos have done in the American Southwest.

In short, research on overtourism must continue to be expanded beyond the current predominant focus on European cities. We need more case studies from the developing world, as the calculus surrounding debates about overtourism in less wealthy nations is different. These countries have a more pressing need for hard currency and employment opportunities for their citizens. Most of the European cities experiencing overtourism – Barcelona, Venice, Amsterdam – are much better positioned to deal with the loss of tourism revenues than are places like Old Havana, San Cristobal de las Casas, Angkor, and Bali. In short, if we are to effectively teach about shifting away from overtourism towards more sustainable practices, we need additional nuanced case studies from a broader range of nations and destinations.

Necessary steps to promote sustainable tourism holistically: conclusions

While positive steps have taken place at the local, regional and national levels and in the academic world to promote education concerning the negative ramifications of overtourism, as outlined above, global action is needed to address the problem systematically and holistically. Overtourism has all the characteristics of a global problem: global problems are difficult to solve because we live in what international relations theorists describe as an anarchic world, where no central authority exists (Waltz, 2001[1959]). The anarchy in the system makes it exceedingly difficult to solve a collective problem, since there are no agreed on rules and enforcement mechanisms leading most actors to evade the costs of solving the problem. Why would a cruise ship company, a hotel chain, an international restaurant, or a city dependent on tourism dollars unilaterally curtail its revenues if other are not doing the same? The only way to solve a global problem is to find ways to minimise the negative effects of international anarchy.

According to international relations theorists, only three ways exist to solve a global collective action problem in a state of international anarchy (Goldstein and Pevehouse, 2008). One is through force. This solution is clearly not desirable, since it would entail one country or group of countries imposing rules and enforcement mechanisms. A second solution is through ideational change, which would involve convincing all stakeholders that change is necessary, requires immediate action, and is beneficial for everyone in the long term. This is where education can play an essential role, by fostering strong sustainable tourism attitudes in all stakeholders and by educating all stakeholders in strategies for cultivating sustainable tourism (here case studies are especially useful). As we have suggested, however, while sustainable tourism can be (and has already been) introduced in the curriculum of tourism programmes, there is a long way to go before we can claim success in reaching a strong and pervasive sustainable tourism attitude amongst all stakeholders. This strategy should not be abandoned, but rather our educational efforts in and beyond the classroom need to be redoubled before we can hope to address overtourism and foster more environmentally, culturally, and socially sustainable tourism.

Ideational change alone (via education), while an essential start, will not suffice. The third avenue for solving a collective action problem is to develop global rules and norms that promote sustainable tourism. Without global oversight, some destinations will be hesitant to curtail tourism if their efforts simply result in another location gaining tourist dollars at their expense.[10] Moreover, transnational corporations in the tourism industry can pressure cash-strapped nations into accepting unsustainable amounts of tourists and into granting excessive economic concessions, in the classic 'race to the bottom'. The pressures for continued tourism growth are still with us, even though in some affluent countries, cities have started taking measures to reduce tourist visits.

In conclusion, to curtail overtourism and foster sustainable tourism, in tandem with tourism education around the world, a truly global strategy is required. All stakeholders must become convinced that sustainable tourism will be mutually beneficial. In addition, skills must be developed to enable stakeholders to implement strategies that will not only turn tourism into a source of revenue but will also protect the environment and preserve the cultural integrity and lifestyles of local communities. To create this ideational change, educational programmes must retool their curricula in ways that makes sustainable tourism a key goal of all tourist endeavours, drawing on lessons learned in various types of destinations around the world. Tourism locations suffering from overtourism must build bonds with other competing destinations, working together and learning from each other. In addition to education and cooperation, the UNWTO must develop into a more influential international organisation with the ability to establish enforceable rules of conduct that will promote sustainable tourism. Tourism in destinations like Rome, Old Havana, Barcelona, San Cristóbal de las Casas, Dubrovnik, and Bali should not undermine the quality of life of residents of those locations for the sake of tourism income. The answer lies in educating all stakeholders, embracing and promoting policy diffusion, and setting global, enforceable rules that will help us all become savvy travellers, bringing some prosperity directly to communities, while also allowing future generations to travel. Maybe then will tourism's two faces gaze in the same direction.

Notes

1 As *Let's Go Europe, 2008* asserts, 'You can't get more Roman than Trastevere' (Let's Go Inc., 2008, p. 586).
2 See https://www.ehl.edu/en/about-ehl/our-history. Accessed 20 April 2020.
3 See https://sha.cornell.eR.du/about/history/. Accessed 20 April 2020.
4 Nevertheless, we suggest the economic growth value has eclipsed tourism's negative, consequences documented by critical tourism studies. The term 'sustainable tourism' is a good example, since this concept envisions resolving the tensions and contradictions between tourism growth and preserving environments and local lifestyles. The sustainability concept 'has a pervasive obscuring effect' (Mostafanezhad and Norum, 2019, p. 428). Mostafanezhad and Norum further observe that

> a policy of sustainability is constructed around a single Nature, insofar as there are a multitude of natures and a multitude of existing or possible socionatural relations, perpetuates … a condition that forecloses the possibility of a real politics of the environment
>
> (Mostafanezhad and Norum, 2019, p. 428)

These authors underscore the point we make here: pursuing sustainability is desirable, but it is also, paradoxically, often in conflict with the values of economic growth emphasised in our current neoliberal capitalist era.

5 However, Valene Smith, who became a pioneer in tourism anthropology, introduced a 'travel geography' class at Los Angeles City College in 1952, as a Geography Department offering (Smith, 1953).
6 Though Finney and Watson's (1975) Pacific-focused volume of case studies appeared earlier, Smith's *Hosts and Guests* was more widely adopted in tourism anthropology classes.
7 In the intervening years, Adams classes incorporated critiques of these classic theories, as have other tourism studies scholars. For instance, she includes Prideaux's (2000) critique of Butler's TALC model, modules on social justice, ethics, sustainability, and community-based tourism, drawing from Scheyvens (2010), Stronza (2008), Ateljevic, Morgan and Pritchard (2012), Cole (2012, 2014), Cheer and Lew (2017), Adams (2018), and others.
8 This estimate derives from HospitalityNet. See https://www.hospitalitynet.org/news/4089844.html.
9 Personal communication, Stroma Cole, March 2017. Also see: http://equalityintourism.org/stroma-coles-bali-presentation-on-tourism-related-water-shortages-in-bali/.
10 Caribbean islands for example have been hesitant to impose head taxes on cruise ship passengers fearing ships will port elsewhere (Pattullo, 2005).

References

Adams, K. (2005), "Public interest anthropology in heritage sites: Writing culture and righting wrongs," *International Journal of Heritage Studies*, Vol. 11 No. 5, pp. 433–439.

Adams, K. (2018), "Local strategies for economic survival in touristically volatile times: An Indonesian case study of micro-vendors, gendered cultural practices and resilience," *Journal of Tourism Culture & Communication*, Vol. 18 No. 4, pp. 287–301.

Aramberri, J. (2010), *Modern Mass Tourism*, Emerald, London.

Ateljevic, I., Morgan, N. and Pritchard. A. (2012), *The Critical Turn in Tourism Studies: Creating an Academy of Hope*, Routledge, London.

Ateljevic, I., Pritchard, A. and Morgan, N. (2007), *The Critical Turn in Tourism Studies: Innovative Research Methodologies*, Routledge, London.

Bennett, J. (1999), "The dream and the reality: Tourism in Kuna Yala," *Cultural Survival Quarterly*, Vol. 23, pp. 33–35.

Bertocchi, D. and Visentin, F. (2019), "The overwhelmed city: Physical and social over-capacities of global tourism in Venice," *Sustainability*, Vol. 11, pp. 1–19.

Bianchi, R. (2012), "Towards a new political economy of global tourism revisited," in Sharpley, R. and Telfer, D. (Eds.), *Tourism & Development: Concepts and Issues* (2nd Edition), Channel View Publications, Clevedon, pp. 287–331.

Boyle, A., Wilson, E. and Dimmock, K. (2015), "Transformative education and sustainable tourism: The influence of a lecturer's world view," *Journal of Teaching in Travel & Tourism*, Vol. 15 No. 3, pp. 252–263.

Brooker, E. and Joppe, M. (2014), "Developing a tourism innovation typology: Leveraging liminal insight," *Journal of Travel Research*, Vol. 53, pp. 500–508.

Butler, R. (1980), "The concept of a tourism areas cycle of evaluation: Implications for management of resources," *Canadian Geographer*, Vol. 24 No. 1, pp. 5–12.

Butler, R. (2015), "The evolution of tourism and tourism research," *Tourism Recreation Research*, Vol. 40 No. 1, pp. 16–27.

Chapin, M. (1990), "The silent jungle: Ecotourism among the Kuna Indians of Panama," *Cultural Survival Quarterly*, Vol. 14, pp. 42–45.

Charara, N., Cashman, A., Bonnell, R. and Gehr, R. (2010), "Water use efficiency in the hotel sector of Barbados," *Journal of Sustainable Tourism*, Vol. 19 No. 2, pp. 231–245.

Cheer, J. and Lew, A. (Eds.) (2017), *Tourism, Resilience and Sustainability: Adapting to Social, Political and Economic Change*, Routledge, London.

Cohen, E. (1974), "Who is a tourist? A conceptual classification," *Sociological Review*, Vol. 22, pp. 527–555.

Cohen, E. (1984), "The sociology of tourism: Approaches, issues, and findings," *Annual Review of Sociology*, Vol. 10, pp. 373–392.

Cole, S. (2008), "Living in hope: Tourism and poverty alleviation in Flores," in Burns, P. and Novelli, M. (Eds.), *Tourism Development: Hopes, Myths and Inequalities*, CABI International, Wallingford, pp. 272–289.

Cole, S. (2012), "A political ecology of water equity and tourism: A case study from Bali," *Annals of Tourism Research*, Vol. 39 No. 2, pp. 1221–1241.

Cole, S. (2014), "Tourism and water: From stakeholders to rights holders, and what tourism businesses need to do," *Journal of Sustainable Tourism*, Vol. 22 No.1, pp. 89–106.

Cole, S. and Browne, M. (2015), "Tourism and water inequity in Bali: A social-ecological systems analysis," *Human Ecology*, Vol. 43 No. 3, pp. 439–450.

Coles, T., Hall, C. and Duval, D. (2006), "Tourism and post-disciplinary enquiry," *Current Issues in Tourism*, Vol. 9 No. 4/5, pp. 293–319.

Cotterell, D., Hales, R., Arcodia, C. and Ferreira, J. (2019), "Overcommitted to tourism and under committed to sustainability: The urgency of teaching "strong sustainability" in tourism courses," *Journal of Sustainable Tourism*, Vol. 27 No. 7, pp. 882–902.

Crick, M. (1989), "Representations of international tourism in the social sciences: Sun, sex, sights, savings and servility," *Annual Review of Anthropology,* Vol. 18, pp. 307–344.

de Kadt, E. (Ed.) (1979), *Tourism: Passport to Development? Perspectives on the Social and Cultural Effects of Tourism in Developing Countries*, Oxford University Press, New York, NY.

Delgado, M. (2008), "Turistofobia." *El País*, 11 July, available at https://elpais.com/diario/2008/07/12/catalunya/1215824840_850215.html (accessed 27 April 2020).

Dolezal, C., Trupp, A. and Bui, H. (Eds.) (2020), *Tourism and Development in Southeast Asia,* Routledge, Abingdon.

Erb, M. (2000), "Understanding tourists: Interpretations from Indonesia," *Annals of Tourism Research*, Vol. 27 No. 3, pp. 709–736.

Fava, N. and Rubio, S.P. (2017), "From Barcelona: The Pearl of the Mediterranean to Bye Bye Barcelona," in Bellini, N. and Pasquinelli, C. (Eds.), *Tourism in the City*, Springer, Cham, Switzerland, pp. 285–295.

Finney, B. and Watson, K. (Eds.) (1975), *A New Kind of Sugar: Tourism in the Pacific*, East-West Center, Honolulu.

Goldstein, J.S. and Pevehouse, J.C. (2008), *Principles of International Relations*, Pearson/Longman, New York, NY.

Graburn, N. (1980), "Teaching the anthropology of tourism," *International Social Science Journal*, Vol. 32 No. 1, pp. 56–68.

Graburn, N. and Jafari, J. (1991), "Introduction: Tourism social science," *Annals of Tourism Research*, Vol. 18 No. 1, pp. 1–11.

Hall, M., Prayag, G. and Amore, A. (2018), *Tourism and Resilience: Individual, Organizational and Destination Perspectives*, Channel View Publications, Bristol.

Hills, T. and Lundgren, J. (1977), "The impact of tourism in the Caribbean: A methodological study," *Annals of Tourism Research*, Vol. 4 No. 5, pp. 248–267.

Holden, A. and Novelli, M. (2011), "Guest editorial: The changing paradigms of tourism in international development: Placing the poor first – Trojan horse or real hope?" *Tourism Planning and Development*, Vol. 8 No. 3, pp. 233–235.

Hollinshead, K. (2016), "Postdisciplinarity and the rise of intellectual openness: The necessity for "plural knowability" in tourism studies," *Tourism Analysis*, Vol. 21, pp. 349–361.

Inui, Y., Wheeler, D. and Lankford, S. (2006), "Rethinking tourism education: What should schools teach?" *Journal of Hospitality, Leisure, Sport and Tourism Education*, Vol. 5 No. 2, pp. 25–35.

Ivars-Baidal, J., Garcia-Hernandez, M. and Mendoza de Miguel, S. (2019), "Integrating overtourism in the smart cities agenda," *Review of Tourism Research*, Vol. 17 No. 2, pp. 122–139.

Jamieson, W. and Jamieson, M. (2019), "Overtourism management competencies in Asian urban heritage areas," *International Journal of Tourism Cities*, Vol. 5 No. 4, pp. 581–587.

Leite, N. and Graburn, N. (2012), "Anthropological interventions in tourism studies," in Jamal, T. and Robinson, M. (Eds.), *The SAGE Handbook of Tourism Studies*, SAGE, Thousand Oaks, CA, pp. 35–36.

Let's Go Inc. (2008), *Lets Go Europe, 2008,* St. Martin's Press, New York, NY.

MacCannell, D. (1976), *The Tourist: A New Theory of the Leisure Class*, Schocken, New York, NY.

Martins, M. (2018), "Tourism planning and tourismphobia: An analysis of the strategic tourism plan of Barcelona 2010–2015," *Journal of Tourism, Heritage & Services Marketing*, Vol. 4 No. 1, pp. 3–7.

Mihalache, M. and Mihalache, O. (2016), "Organisational ambidexterity and sustained performance in the tourism industry," *Annals of Tourism Research*, Vol. 56, pp. 128–163.

Milano, C., Novelli, M. and Cheer, J. (2019), "Overtourism and degrowth: A social movement perspective," *Journal of Sustainable Tourism,* Vol. 27 No.12, pp. 1857–1879.

Mostafanezhad, M. and Norum, R. (2019), "The anthropocenic imaginary: Political ecologies of tourism in a geological epoch," *Journal of Sustainable Tourism*, Vol. 27, pp. 421–435.

Pattullo, P. (2005), *Last Resorts: The Cost of Cruise Tourism in the Caribbean* (2nd edition), Latin American Bureau, New York, NY.

Prideaux, B. (2000), "The resort development spectrum: A new approach to modeling resort development," *Tourism Management*, Vol. 21 No. 3, pp. 225–240.

Rostow, W. W. (1960), *The Stages of Economic Growth: A Non-Communist Manifesto*, Cambridge University Press, Cambridge.

Sanchez, P.M. and Adams, K. M. (2008), "The Janus-faced character of tourism in Cuba," *Annals of Tourism Research*, Vol. 35 No. 1, pp. 27–46.

Savener, A. (2013), "A host gaze composed of mediated resistance in Panama: Power inversion in Kuna Yala," in Moufakkir, O. and Reisinger, Y. (Eds.), *The Host Gaze in Global Tourism*, CAB International, Oxfordshire, pp. 67–80.

Scheyvens, R. (Ed.) (2010), *Tourism and Poverty*, Taylor and Francis, Abingdon.

Séraphin, H. and Butcher, J. (2018), "Tourism management in the Caribbean," *Caribbean Quarterly*, Vol. 64 No. 2, pp. 254–283.

Séraphin, H. and Yallop, A. (2019), "Proposed framework for the management of resorts Mini Clubs: An ambidextrous approach," *Leisure Studies*, Vol. 38 No. 4, pp. 535–547.

Singh, T. (1978), "Tourism and the environment: Towards better reconciliation," *Tourism Recreation Research*, Vol. 3 No. 2, pp. 5–10.

Smith, V. (1953), "Travel geography courses for a new field," *The Journal of Geography*, Vol. 52 No. 2, pp. 68–72.

Smith, V. (Ed.) (1977), *Hosts and Guests: The Anthropology of Tourism*, University of Pennsylvania Press, Philadelphia, PA.

Stankey, G. and Lime, D. (1973), *Recreational Carrying Capacity: An Annotated Bibliography*, US Department of Agriculture (Forest Service, General Technical Report), Ogden, UT.

Stronza, A. (2005), "Hosts and hosts: The anthropology of community-based ecotourism in the Peruvian amazon," *National Association for Practice of Anthropology Bulletin*, Vol. 23, pp. 170–190.

Stronza, A. (2008), "Partnership for tourism development," in Moscardo, G. (Ed.), *Building Community Capacity for Tourism Development*, CABI, Oxfordshire, pp. 101–115.

Stronza, A. (2010), "Commons management and ecotourism: Ethnographic evidence from the Amazon," *International Journal of the Commons*, Vol. 4 No. 1, pp. 56–77.

Swain, M. (2009), "The cosmopolitan hope of tourism: Critical action and world-making vistas," *Tourism Geographies*, Vol. 11 No. 4, pp. 505–525.

Wall, G. and Wright, C. (1977), *The Environmental Impact of Outdoor Recreation*, Department of Geography Publication Series No. 11, University of Waterloo, Waterloo.

Waltz, K. N. (2001 [1959]), *Man, the State, and War: A Theoretical Analysis*. Columbia University Press, New York, NY.

Wijesinghe, S. and Mura P. (2018), "Situating Asian tourism ontologies, epistemologies and methodologies: From colonialism to neo-colonialism," in Mura, P. and Khoo-Lattimore, C. (Eds.), *Asian Qualitative Research in Tourism: Ontologies, Epistemologies, Methodologies and Methods*, Springer, Berlin, pp. 95–115.

Wilson, E. and von der Heidt, T. (2013), "Business as usual? Barriers to education for sustainability in the tourism curriculum," *Journal of Teaching in Travel & Tourism*, Vol. 13 No. 2, pp. 130–147.

Part II

Practical strategies and impacts

4 Empowering tourism education as a destination management tool

Pinaz Tiwari, Snigdha Kainthola and Nimit R Chowdhary

Introduction

Presently, the parameters of growth in tourism and hospitality industry such as the number of tourist footfalls or contribution in GDP or percentage share in the total employment of a country demonstrates the progressiveness of the sector (UNWTO, 2011, 2018, p. 2). A study reports that the introduction of low-cost carriers increased social media marketing, the convenience of booking online, and increased disposable incomes have contributed to the growth in demand for tourist destinations (Council and JLL, 2019, p. 6). The Skift magazine coined the term overtourism to describe this phenomenon of 'excessive tourism activities' wherein famous destinations face unsustainable consumption practices that majorly impact the local community. Often considered the opposite of responsible tourism (Goodwin, 2017, p. 1), over-tourism requires creative solutions which are strategic enough to create a balance between the economic benefits of tourism and happiness of residents of residents (Perkumienė and Pranskūnienė, 2019, p. 2138).

The idea of lifelong learning has been significant in the tourism industry (Séraphin, Butcher and Korstanje, 2017, p. 176) due to the complexity and dynamic characteristic of the elements involved. Within the same framework, several studies have recommended 'education' as a tool to create awareness and deal with the issue (Weber et al., 2017, p. 2; Seraphin, Sheeran and Pilato, 2018, p. 374; Xi, Sawagvudcharee and Walsh, 2019, p. 23). Education plays a vital role in developing society. It aims to serve a different purpose and holds different connotations for the government, students, managers, and educators (Shahaida et al., 2007, p. 47). Tourism education is multi-disciplinary. It is often considered as a catalyst in sustaining a destination and creating awareness among the people who are part of the tourism system. The contemporary problems in the paradigm of unsustainable management of tourism activities and destination as a whole has led to prominent discourses on tourism education in the last few years (Stergiou and Airey, 2017, p. 3; Femenia-Serra, 2018; Pearce, 2009, p. 145; Dredge, 2015, p. 78; Batra, 2016, p. 89; Godemann, Herzig and Moon, 2013, p. 3; Walmsley, 2017, p. 5; Koens, Postma and Papp, 2018, p. 4384; Capocchi et al., 2019, p. 1). Based on earlier studies which mentioned that knowledge is a vital element for empowerment (Cole, 2006, p. 89; Weng and Peng, 2014, p. 772), the authors found that there is a shortage of literature in highlighting the role of tourism education in managing a destination. This study addressed the question of 'how' to empower this tool for better management of destinations. The chapter aims to give an insight into the four domains wherein tourism education can be empowered, namely, professional education in high schools, capacity building education for stakeholders, tourists' education, and local community awareness about tourism. Also, the study highlights the empowerment of tourism education in the three stages of travel, i.e. pre-visit, during the visit, and post-visit. The authors believe that tourism education, along with large-scale awareness about the multi-fold issues on sustainable development and responsible tourism can help in finding out effective strategies for tourists' destination management. Moreover, the present study will help the overtourism affected destination to add crucial elements of tourism education into their destination management strategies.

The chapter is organised into five sections. After the introduction, the next section mentions an analysis of the current situation of tourism education. This section is followed by two main segments of the study, i.e. empowering tourism education among stakeholders and empowering tourism education at travel stages. The fourth section highlights the contribution of tourism education towards responsible destination management. The last section looks to draw up the conclusion of the study.

Current scenario of tourism education

The concept of tourism education initially originated in Europe with the introduction of tourism training schools (Kunwar, 2018, p. 101) and gradually evolved over a while. Malihah and Setiyorini (2014, p. 3) categorised the evolution of tourism education into four stages. This includes the industrial age (1960–1970s), wherein it was a vocational discipline. Then came the fragmented stage (1980–1990s) wherein uncertainty on the curriculum was predominant due to the multi-disciplinary nature of the domain. This stage was followed by the benchmark stage (2000–2010s) wherein the academic discourses emerged on tourists' behaviour, ethical tourism practices, sustainable tourism, and corporate social responsibility. And, the last stage is the mature stage (2010–till now) which is about knowledge production and innovation. Owing to the multifariousness of the tourism body of knowledge, Kunwar (2018, p. 102) described tourism education as a component of a complex tourism phenomenon whose manifestation is likely to have a direct or an indirect impact on the tourism industry. The study also mentions that vocational tourism training along with education is also vital for obtaining the benefits of tourism at destinations.

The growth of tourism studies increased rapidly after the development of travel-related public and private organisations and increased demand for the professional workforce. This development led to the establishment of tourism and travel-specialised institutes and departments within various universities and colleges to provide higher education (Butler, 1999, p. 99). Dale, Robinson and Gorway (2001, p. 32) suggested that there should be three domains of tourism education. The first degree should be generic that provides for a broad understanding of tourism and interdisciplinary skills. This component should be followed by a functional degree to give specialised knowledge on tourism marketing, information systems, and planning. Finally, there should be a market/product-based degree that focusses on the development of a particular product or market, requiring expertise in the area. These three programs claimed to provide students with the body of knowledge and skills that empower them to work successfully in the industry. However, later studies criticised that tourism education programs merely focus on the formal qualifications in the forms of degrees but fail to comprehend the requirements of the industry (Cooper, 2006, p. 48; Batra, 2016, p. 79). Another critical aspect of the educational programs is designing the curriculum. Inui, Wheeler, and Lankford (2006, p. 32) stated that tourism schools should design their curriculum that aims to develop secure connections with the industry professionals as students are required to take up internships during their course. This exercise would ensure the learning of management techniques and results in skill enhancement of students.

According to earlier studies (Sims and Brinkmann, 2003, p. 72; Bennis and O'Toole, 2005; Felton and Sims, 2005, p. 377; Boyce, 2008, p. 255; Batra, 2016, p. 78; Camargo and Gretzel, 2017, p. 102; Kunwar, 2018, p. 83; Kemper, Ballantine and Hall, 2019, p. 1751), following are the crucial challenges faced by tourism and hospitality education programs in fostering practical knowledge required in the industry to resolve business-related problems:

1   Application of theoretical knowledge into real-time tourism business complexities
2   Curriculum designed and requirements of the industry are unmatched
3   Students lack the application of subjects taught, specifically business ethics, corporate social responsibility or sustainable management
4   Technical competence on subjects of sustainable tourism, corporate social responsibility
5   Limitations of educators and relative expertise on subjects of tourism

To deal with these challenges, PRME was introduced by UNWTO in 2006. It is an initiative with an underlying desire to have a substantial transformation in the education system and also represents the 'wave of change' for management education (Forray and Leigh, 2012, p. 295). For instance, the University of Queensland, Australia reported in their SIP report about its Business Sustainability Initiative in which their research works focus on evaluating the impact of tourism development on climate, resilience, and adaptation by the local community, and trade-off analysis (University of

Queensland, Australia, 2018). Similarly, a transformative tourism education model titled 'Education for Sustainability' was also introduced during the Earth Summit in 1992 (Moscardo, 2015, p. 128).

Therefore, the current situation doesn't completely guarantee responsible and sustainable tourism approaches due to the lack of practical application of the concepts at global scales. It is also to be noted that tourism education is mostly looked as a discipline to be taught in higher educational institutes, but it is not sufficient to attain sustainability in the tourism system. Tourism industry is interconnected and involves multiple stakeholders; thus, education should start from the bottom level (residents, local street vendors, tourists) and go up to top levels (MNCs, officials in national tourism organisations)

Empowering tourism education among stakeholders

This section of the chapter is an extension of the triple-helix model proposed by Leydesdorff and Deakin (2011, p. 53). The model explored the relationship between university, industry, and government in a knowledge-based economy. The model primarily looked into three domains, i.e. reflexive control, organised production of knowledge, and economic wealth creation. With a specific focus on regional development through knowledge, a quadruple helix model was introduced, which added 'wider community' into the triple-helix model (Kolehmainen et al., 2016, p. 28).

The tourism industry is fragmented as it involves various sectors and thus numerous stakeholders who become part of the tourism system. Each stakeholder should assume the responsibility towards the management of a tourist destination. However, over a few years, occurrences of irresponsible behaviour from both tourists and suppliers have resulted in the adverse outcomes of tourism at destinations, for example water pollution created by cruises in the Mediterranean Sea, Airbnb accommodations in the residential area creating havoc for the residents, and tourists' creating litter at famous destinations or invading the privacy of the locals. These kinds of incidents have caused locals to complain about the negative impacts that tourism holds and resulted in phenomena of antitourism movements, overtourism, and touristification at famous destinations (Hughes, 2018, p. 471; Renau, 2018, p. 104; Alonso-Almeida, Borrajo-Millán and Yi, 2019, p. 3356; Cheer, Milano and Novelli, 2019, p. 554). However, education as a tool could be used to effectively manage a destination as it helps in defying deceptive narratives of a destination or perceived impacts attached (Seraphin, Gowreensunkar and Ambaye, 2016, p. 5).

Formal tourism education aids students in taking up important managerial positions wherein they can strategise to market a destination. For instance, Business Enterprises for Sustainable Travel (BEST) is a think tank that primarily consists of academicians and industry professionals developing industry-specific curriculum relevant to the principles of sustainability

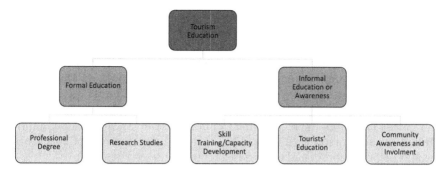

Figure 4.1 The broad domains of tourism education empowerment among stakeholders.

and responsible tourism. This curriculum development is carried out to teach students about different practical aspects of the discipline to ensure a better application of knowledge (Hay, 2016, p. na).

It is criticised that tourism education is majorly limited to a subject which is taught in higher education programmes to assist students in getting higher-paid jobs (Ghoshal, 2005, p. 75; Antunes and Thomas, 2007, p. 384; Kunwar, 2018, p. 85). Conversely, this section highlights the alternative aspects within the realm of tourism education to be empowered towards achieving destination management goals effectively. The following parameters have also been discussed in the quadruple helix model by Kolehmainen et al. (2016, p. 24).

Professional Courses and Research Studies

Education in tourism developed as a vocational discipline in Europe. In 2002, Riley et al., suggested that the tourism professional courses must keep up equilibrium in three aspects namely the upgradation of knowledge, personality development and skill advancement, and practical relevance to the industry. Later, Mazilu and Sitnikov (2010) also said that it is imperative to integrate the educational institutions with the tourism and hospitality industry for professional training of students. However, the tourism professional courses are criticised on the grounds of students' inability in applying their skills to resolve societal problems (Hjalager, 2003, p. 27), or their failure to understand the socio-psychological issues faced by the industry (Inui, Wheeler and Lankford, 2006, p. 27). Education in sustainability is considered crucial to achieve the sustainable tourism goals, but a study conducted on Latin American students (Camargo and Gretzel, 2017, p. 101) reported that students lack technical competence in sustainability-related subjects. The study suggested that content enrichment in tourism courses is a prerequisite to enhance the technical aptitude of students. Thus, knowledge related to sustainability certifications, carbon emission calculations, and tools such as GIS, GPS, and destination management systems to be guided by the educators. Kemper, Ballantine, and Hall (2019, p. 1751) highlighted the role of educators in providing education for sustainability and broadly categorised them into three groups, namely, sustainability transformer, the actioner, and thinker. The authors mentioned that the 'transformer' educator works on transforming students, the 'thinker' encourages students to think critically and develop questioning attitude, and 'actioner' gets the students to work on sustainable projects and get involved in a community that will incite change in them. With the technological advancements, Séraphin, Butcher, and Korstanje (2017, p. 175) suggested that the role of educators would be played by Visual Online Learning Materials (VOLMs).

Higher educational institutes must collaborate with industry professionals and design the curriculum which challenges students to analyse the business problems critically. Empowering tourism education, specifically for professional degree courses, requires close integration with initiatives like PRME so that future leaders can be developed. Camargo and Gretzel (2017, p. 101) and Jamal, Taillon, and Dredge (2011, p. 144) suggested that efforts to interconnect sustainable tourism education with other essential dimensions of the society should be made. Thus, a reflective multi-dimensional education approach is the need of the hour, and educational institutes should rediscover their pedagogy and academic curriculum.

Skill Development of Stakeholders

Multiple stakeholders in the tourism industry are interlinked and interdependent. Since every stakeholder has its role and significance in creating tourists' experience, tourism education should focus on enhancing their skills to cater to the demands of the industry. In literature, substantial recognition has been given to tour guides in designing and delivering the tourism experience (Weiler and Walker, 2014, p. 90; Weiler and Black, 2015, p. 364; Griffin, 2018) as they are often considered as frontline service providers at any destination. As per a study conducted by Hill and Hill (2011, p. 75) in the Amazonia region in Peru, the role of tour guides was magnified in the knowledge exchange process between the service provider to the tourists. Similarly, in India, the Ministry of Tourism, the Government of India conducted various guide training programmes. The purpose is to ensure that guides can assist the tourists in a better way and help in creating enjoyable experiences (Ministry of Tourism, Govt of India, 2017). Tourism education requires common knowledge upgradation and events happening around the world. This knowledge upgradation helps the travel agencies and tour operators to guide their consumers effectively. For instance, an article published in the year 2017 mentioned TUI Group urging tourists to avoid going to destinations affected by overtourism mainly Spain (Petkar, 2017).

Skill-building education or capacity development is considered as 'deep education' which is necessary to connect humans with insightful issues that prevail in society (Caton, 2014, p. 24). In context of the negative impact of tourism on biodiversity, Hall (2011, p. 437) also suggested that education and training programmes for tour operators be provided. Various countries are also introducing such programmes for the stakeholders but timely implementation and reporting progress of these programmes are the challenges posed by the organising authority.

Tourists' Education

Tourist ignorance or lack of awareness is one of the common phenomena at destinations (Zhang, Fyall and Zheng, 2015, p. 110; Trancoso González, 2018, p. 35). In the context of irresponsible behaviour at overtourism affected destinations, a few examples have been quoted by Koens and Postma (2018, p. 4384) such as tourists peeping into the windows of Dutch houses wherein the windows are large or clicking pictures of a 'real European woman' without her permission or drunk driving by tourists are a typical sight in urban cities. These actions often lead to dissonance among locals and tourists. Though not empirically proved, it has been reported that the type of destination can also induce tourists' behaviour. For instance, it is reported specifically at post-conflict or post-disaster destinations that the tourists are motivated to learn and educate themselves owing to a higher degree of rationality and their involvement (Séraphin, Butcher and Korstanje, 2017, p. 171). Also, sometimes tourists conduct irresponsible behaviour unintentionally because of lack of awareness and feeling of disempowerment (Miller et al., 2010, p. 627).

Jacek Borzyszkowski (2015, p. 56) reported that tourist education should be one of the primary objectives of the destination management organisations, along with their core functions of marketing and managing a destination. Similarly, Capocchi et al. (2019, p. 15) also suggested that tourists' education is equally important as managing a destination receiving excessive tourists. According to Kemper, Ballantine, and Hall (2019, p. 1771) providing education at ecological destinations leads to ecological awareness among tourists and develops environmental attitudes in stakeholders. Interpretive tourist programmes (Wearing and Larsen, 1996, p. 117; Hill and Hill, 2011, p. 79) are also central to eco-tourism destinations, wherein tour guides and tour operators ensure that they can inform the tourists about every single detail at a destination in the most effective manner. It aims to educate tourists to appreciate the protected regions being visited by them. For urban destinations, tour companies can provide a list of acceptable socio-cultural norms of a destination to tourists before their visit.

Local Community Awareness

The local community of a destination is the direct receiver of benefits as well as victims of the negative impacts caused by tourism. In the case of Barcelona, the community came up with slogans and raised their voice against the overtourism activities in the city (Russo and Scarnato, 2018, p. 455). The situation of 'too many' tourists disrupted the daily routines of locals as the city became overcrowded due to tourists and subsequently, locals began to displace outside the city. However, Sarantakou and Terkenli (2019, p. 5) noted that deteriorating levels of education in the population also make locals dependent on tourism. Conversely, residents with both higher and lower educational qualifications have a better perception of tourism impacts than those who have none (Muler Gonzalez, Coromina and Galí, 2018, p. 290). The integrated efforts of residents and local organisations are imperative to maintain a balance between conservation of resources and the socio-economic well-being of residents. The Inkaterra Ecological Reserve in Peru outlaws the local people to extract or convert natural resources, and in return, they are paid in cash or kind. Through this practice, the eco-tourism destination is conserved efficiently (Hill and Hill, 2011, p. 75).

Thus, education and creating awareness among the local community concerned with tourism activities allows communities to participate in the tourism planning process (Pearce, 2009, p. 144). It also plays an essential variable in influencing the locals' perception of the tourism impacts (Muler Gonzalez, Coromina and Galí, 2018, p. 277). Redclift and Friedmann (1994, p. n.a) highlighted the need to restore disempowered sectors and communities, by emphasising social learning, community-driven decision-making, and self-reliance. The involvement of the local community is an essential component in the destination management process and behavioural empowerment (Speer and Peterson, 2000, p. 109), which has been a significant ingredient in achieving sustainable tourism development at a destination (Stronza and Gordillo, 2008, p. 449; Nunkoo and Ramkissoon, 2011, p. 964; Strzelecka, Boley and Strzelecka, 2017, p. 554).

Empowering the stages of travel

The tourism consumption process includes three stages widely- pre-visit, during the visit, and post-visit. A destination can be managed effectively by way of improvising tourism activities and implementing tourism education strategies in all the stages.

Pre-visit

Many overtourism affected destinations, face the consequence of conflicts and anti-tourism movements. Such destinations are often considered as post-conflict destinations that pose a challenge to attract tourists owing to the negative image or lack of tourists' education at the pre-visit stage (Séraphin, Butcher and Korstanje, 2017, p. 173). During the pre-visit stage, especially in case of leisure trips, the tourists spend most of their time in searching about the destination they want to visit. The availability of various resources, especially on social media platforms, acts as a catalyst to motivate tourists to visit a place. With the aid of the internet, tourists extract details about the chosen destination, such as the availability of local transport, local cuisine, and unexplored places within the destination. Travel blogs help the potential tourists to know the finest details of a place and get an insight through the traveller's experience writing the blog. The advancement of technology has even led tourists to experience a destination virtually (Neuhofer and Buhalis, 2012, p. 1690).

Tourism education plays a vital role in shaping the demand for a destination at the pre-visit stage. Way back in 1987, Krippendorf appealed for tourists' education at the pre-visit stage to create a system of ethical tourism at the destinations. He also advocated that it is the moral responsibility of the industry. Similarly, Séraphin, Butcher, and Korstanje, (2017, p. 179) in their study suggested that destination managers should focus on the pre-visitation marketing strategies to improve the image of the tourist destination after negative perceptions about the place were felt by visitors. Similarly, various visual online learning materials (VOLMs), a strategy adopted by Haiti Tourism, can also be used to educate the potential tourists about the local culture, people, and other information about a destination. Moreover, this encourages them to select a *destination*. Thus, providing pre-visit awareness about a destination helps in avoiding negative perceptions as well as minimises the gap between expectations and realities, creating a more authentic experience.

During Visit

Tourists consume tourism products or services when they are at the destination. Their satisfaction or dissatisfaction from a destination gets determined during this stage when they will have good or bad encounters. Tourism education at this stage could be useful because stakeholders can practice what they learn at a destination. When people get involved in the learning process, they attain and retain more (Garrison and Cleveland-Innes, 2005, p. 133). The concept of internal destination development (IDD) can be useful for empowering tourism education at this stage (Kaurav et al., 2015, p. 127). This approach includes giving training to the local guides, local transport drivers nearby airports and railway stations on how to help a tourist visiting their destination. An initiative by the Ministry of Tourism, Government of India was carried out in 2015 wherein the boat riders at Varanasi, Uttar Pradesh were trained regarding sensitising them towards tourism and tourists (Uttar Pradesh Tourism, 2018). Similarly, the Indian Government's Cleanliness Drive initiative aims to create awareness among the tour agents and travel operators about ensuring clean surroundings while making their customers' visits to different places within the country. These initiatives indirectly help in managing a destination and directly enhances the tourists' quality of experience (Séraphin, Butcher and Korstanje, 2017, p. 178) reported the benefits of gamification such as experience enhancement, tourist

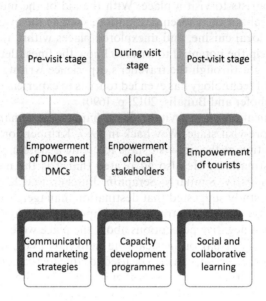

Figure 4.2 The stage-wise and stakeholder-wise tourism education empowerment for destination management.

engagement, loyalty improvement, and change in consumer behaviour as he/she involves themselves in the process.

Séraphin, Butcher, and Korstanje (2017, p. 175) and Séraphin, Zaman, and Fotiadis (2019, p. 110) suggested that appropriate communication strategy should be adopted during this stage as it provides an experience to a tourist when he/she is physically travelling at the destination.

Post-visit

The role of social media has been significant in creating tourism awareness during the post-visit stage. According to Hajli and Lin (2014, p. 38), social media platforms create value towards the development of tourism education by way of informational and emotional assistance. Through it means that social media acts as an open platform wherein people share information about various elements of a destination. And, similarly, emotional assistance is when the set of various information pieces explicitly shows the personal experience of tourists at a specific destination.

Tourism education: a step towards responsible tourism

The phenomenon of overtourism is observed in popular tourist cities like Rome, London, Berlin, Barcelona, Amsterdam, and Venice, among others (Martins and Martins, 2018, p. 3; Milano, Novelli and Cheer, 2019, p. 2;

Perkumienė and Pranskūnienė, 2019, p. 2138). The authorities and the government of the mentioned cities have taken up strategies to prevent the negative impacts by adopting short-term policies like increasing the prices during peak seasons (Dichter and Guevera Manzo, 2017, p. 64), diversifying tourists to other destinations or diversifying their activities (UHERO: The Economic Research Organisation, University of Hawaii, 2017, p. 3), placing a limit on tourist numbers (Peeters et al., 2018, p. 107), and even closing down specific sites for a temporary period such as Maya Beach in Thailand. However, hardly any of the cities have taken up tourism education as an alternative approach to prevent the problem of overtourism, even though the issue can be dealt with education (Koens and Postma, 2018, p. 9).

Capocchi et al., (2019, p. 4) concluded in their study that implementing different approaches is a pre-requisite to sensitised tourists about the locals' customs, traditions, and create awareness among them so that they do not indulge in irresponsible conduct which might deteriorate the destination visited or locals' feelings. The level of awareness could be created at all stages of travel with the help of coordinated efforts by all the stakeholders involved in the tourism industry. Further, the credibility of tourism strategies will depend on the responsible practices undertaken by both suppliers and consumers at a destination. Kunwar (2018, p. 85) mentioned that a well-managed and integrated approach in tourism and hospitality education could increase the value of environmental and cultural resources, bring meaning to places and people, and promote peace. Issues of poverty alleviations, quality of locals' well-being, sociocultural tolerance could be dealt with in a better way. The UNWTO also plays a crucial role in generating knowledge for stakeholders, encourages sustainable tourism policies, and fosters tourism education globally. It collaborates with different institutions and works towards making the tourism industry a useful tool in the development of a destination (Uppink Calderwood and Soshkin, 2019, p. 9).

This study delimits the scope to different stakeholders involved in the tourism system. However, future studies can work on empowering tourism education at different types of destinations affected by overtourism. This study might lead to the planning of strategies tailor-made for destinations and stakeholders involved therein. For instance, at cultural sites, tourist education through interpretive programmes should be provided so that they become culturally aware of the acceptable norms of the destination. A liberal reflective approach needs to be adopted to empower tourism education as this discipline is an amalgamation of multiple disciplines. The management of destinations should also reconsider the humanistic values along with physical attributes to create a responsible and sustainable tourism network. The credibility of tourism strategies will depend on the responsible practices undertaken by both suppliers and consumers at a destination.

Conclusion

Tourism education has been given much importance in the existing literature and suggested as a useful step towards preventing the problem of irresponsible tourism. However, it is crucial to see tourism education from the panorama of both formal education and informal education. Formal education is what has been provided in the educational institutes at higher levels by way of professional courses or research conducted in the tourism domain. On the other hand, informal education is more influential for stakeholders like tourists, locals, tour guides, travel agents, and local administrative staff involved in the tourism industry. The current scenario of formal tourism education requires the implementation of a reflective learning approach to develop future leaders with creative problem-solving skills. Collaboration, internships, and discussions with industry professionals might assist them in understanding the societal challenges faced by the aftermath of harmful tourism activities and other political, economic, and environmental factors. The informal education w.r.t tourists should involve utilisation of effective communication strategies to make them culturally aware of the destinations' attributes, guiding them about the responsible code of conduct, and interpretive programmes during their visit will be some of the useful techniques. Similarly, w.r.t guides and tour operators, training programmes that should primarily include enhancing their linguistic, technological, and soft skills aptitude will assist in creating an experience for tourists. In the same, educating the local community will be the first step towards involving them in the decision-making process specifically in developing nations wherein the top-bottom approach is prominent due to lack of awareness at ground levels.

This study will be useful to policy makers, destination management organisations, and the government to consider tourism education while preparing a policy framework for regulating the negative impacts of tourism. Education is a lifelong learning process, and every destination should explore alternatives to safeguard the interest of locals, service providers, tourists, and destinations as a whole. Within the backdrop of overtourism, definitive steps should be taken to avoid socio-cultural conflicts for better and sustainable management of destinations. The use of technology, artificial intelligence, emotional intelligence techniques will help in dealing with the problem carefully.

References

Alonso-Almeida, M., Borrajo-Millán, F. and and Yi, L. (2019) "Are social media data pushing overtourism? The case of Barcelona and Chinese tourists," *Sustainability*, 11(12), p. 3356. doi: 10.3390/su11123356.

Antunes, D. and Thomas, H. (2007) "The competitive (dis)advantages of European business schools," *Long Range Planning*, 40, pp. 382–404. doi: 10.1016/j.lrp.2007.04.003.

Batra, A. (2016) "Bridging the gap between tourism education, tourism industry and graduate employability: Intricacies and emerging issues in Thailand," *ABAC Journal*, 36(2), pp. 78–89. Available at: http://www.assumptionjournal.au.edu/index.php/abacjournal/article/view/2481.

Bennis, W. and O'Toole, J. (2005) "How business schools lost their way," *Harvard Business Review*, May Issue, pp. 96–104.

Boyce, G. (2008) "The social relevance of ethics education in a global(ising) era: From individual dilemmas to systemic crises," *Critical Perspectives on Accounting*, 19(2), pp. 255–290. doi: 10.1016/j.cpa.2006.09.008.

Butler, R. (1999). "Understanding Tourism," In: E. Jackson and T. Burton, eds. *Leisure Studies: Prospects of the Twenty-first Century*, State College, Venture, pp. 97–116.

Camargo, B.A. and Gretzel, U. (2017) "What do tourism students know about sustainability and sustainable tourism? An exploratory study of Latin American students," *Journal of Teaching in Travel and Tourism*, 17(2), pp. 101–117. doi: 10.1080/15313220.2017.1294038.

Capocchi, A., et al. (2019) "Is 'overtourism' a new issue in tourism development or just a new term for an already known phenomenon?," *Current Issues in Tourism*, 0(0), pp. 1–5. doi: 10.1080/13683500.2019.1638353.

Capocchi, A., et al. (2019) "Overtourism: A literature review to assess implications and future perspectives," *Sustainability (Switzerland)*, 11(12), pp. 1–18. doi: 10.3390/su10023303.

Caton, K. (2014) "Underdisciplinarity: Where are the humanities in tourism education?," *Journal of Hospitality, Leisure, Sport and Tourism Education*, 15(1), pp. 24–33. doi: 10.1016/j.jhlste.2014.03.003.

Cheer, J.M., Milano, C. and Novelli, M. (2019) "Tourism and community resilience in the Anthropocene: Accentuating temporal overtourism," *Journal of Sustainable Tourism*, 27(4), pp. 554–572. doi: 10.1080/09669582.2019.1578363.

Cole, S. (2006) "Cultural Tourism, Community Participation and Empowerment," In: M. Robinson and M. Smith, eds. *Cultural Tourism in a Changing World: Politics, Participation and (Re)Presentation*, Channel View Publications, Clevedon, pp. 89–102. doi: 10.21832/9781845410452-008.

Cooper, C. (2006) "Knowledge management and tourism," *Annals of Tourism Research*, 33(1), pp. 47–64. doi: 10.1016/j.annals.2005.04.005.

Council, W.T. and JLL (2019) *Destination 2030. Global Cities' Readiness for Tourism Growth, WTTC and JLL.*

Dale, C., Robinson, N. and Gorway, R. (2001) "The theming of tourism education: A three-domain approach," *International Journal of Contemporary Hospitality Management*, 13(1), pp. 30–35.

Dichter, A. and Guevera Manzo, G. (2017) "Managing Overcrowding in Tourism Destinations," p. 64. Available at: https://www.wttc.org/-/media/files/reports/policy-research/coping-with-success---managing-overcrowding-in-tourism-destinations-2017.pdf?la=en.

Dredge, D. (2015) "Education for Sustainability in Tourism," In: G. Moscardo and P. Benckendorff, eds. *Education for Sustainability in Tourism: A Handbook of Processes, Resources and Strategies*, Berlin: Springer.

Felton, E. L. and Sims, R. R. (2005) "Teaching business ethics: Targeted outputs," *Journal of Business Ethics*, 60, pp. 377–391. doi: 10.1007/s10551-004-8206-3.

Femenia-Serra, F. (2018). "Smart Tourism Destinations and Higher Tourism Education in Spain. Are We Ready for This New Management Approach?" In B.

Stangl and J. Pesonen, eds. *Information and Communication Technologies in Tourism*, Springer International Publishing, Cham.

Forray, J.M. and Leigh, J.S.A. (2012) "A primer on the principles of responsible management education: Intellectual roots and waves of change," *Journal of Management Education*, 36(3), pp. 295–309. doi: 10.1177/1052562911433031.

Garrison, D. and Cleveland-Innes, M. (2005) "Facilitating cognitive presence in online learning: Interaction is not enough," *American Journal of Distance Education*, 19, pp. 133–148.

Ghoshal, S. (2005) "Bad management theories are destroying good management practices," *Academy of Management Learning and Education*, 4(1), pp. 75–91. doi: 10.5465/AMLE.2005.16132558.

Godemann, J., Herzig, C. and Moon, J. (2013) *Enhancing education for sustainable development in Business and Management, Hospitality, Leisure, Marketing, Tourism, The Higher Education Academy.*

Goodwin, H. (2017) *The Challenge of Overtourism*, available at: http://www.millennium-destinations.com/uploads/4/1/9/7/41979675/rtpwp4overtourism012017.pdf (accessed 15 August 2020)Griffin, K. and Enongene, V. (2018) "The Spirituality of Tour-Guides and their Impact on Visitors' Experience at Sacred Sites" in Pilgrimage and the Evolution of Spiritual Tourism International Conference, Waterford, Ireland, 9th of March, 2018. doi: 10.21427/D7CV07.

Gursoy, D., Chi, C.G. and Dyer, P. (2010) "Locals' attitudes toward mass and alternative tourism: The case of Sunshine Coast, Australia," *Journal of Travel Research*, 49(3), pp. 381–394. doi: 10.1177/0047287509346853.

Hajli, M.N. and Lin, X. (2014) "Social media developing tourism education through social media," *Tourism Planning and Development*, 11(4), pp. 37–41. doi: 10.1080/21568316.2014.883426.

Hall, C. (2011) "A typology of governance and its implications for tourism policy analysis," *Journal of Sustainable Tourism*, 19(4–5), pp. 437–457. doi: 10.1080/09669582.2011.570346.

Hay, R. (2016). *BEST EN Think Tank XVI Corporate Responsibility in Tourism: Standards Practices and Policies.* Townville, Australia, James Cook University.

Hill, J.L. and Hill, R.A. (2011) "Ecotourism in Amazonian Peru: Uniting tourism, conservation and community development," *Geography*, 96(2), pp. 75–85.

Hjalager, A. (2003). "Global tourism careers? Opportunities and dilemmas facing higher education in tourism," *Journal of Hospitality, Leisure, Sport and Tourism Education*, 2(2), pp. 26–37.

Hughes, N. (2018) "'Tourists go home': Anti-tourism industry protest in Barcelona," *Social Movement Studies*, 17(4), pp. 471–477. doi: 10.1080/14742837.2018.1468244.

Inui, Y., Wheeler, D. and Lankford, S. (2006) "Rethinking tourism education: What should schools teach? Educating university level students in tourism," *Journal of Hospitality, Leisure, Sport and Tourism Education*, 5(2), pp. 25–35 doi: 10.3794/johlste.52.122.

Jacek Borzyszkowski (2015) "The Past, Present and Future of Destination Management Organizations (DMO)- The Example of National Tourism Organizations (NTO)," in *Management and Innovation for Competitive Advantage*, Bucharest, pp. 56–66.

Jamal, T., Taillon, J. and Dredge, D. (2011) "Sustainable tourism pedagogy and academic-community collaboration: A progressive service-learning approach," *Tourism and Hospitality Research*, 11(2), pp. 133–147.doi: 10.1057/thr.2011.3.

Kaurav, R.P.S., Baber, R., Chowdhary, N. and Kapadia, S. (2015). "Destination performance: Importance of redefining DMOs," *Asia-Pacific Journal of Innovation in Hospitality and Tourism*, 4(1), pp. 125–142.

Kemper, J.A., Ballantine, P.W. and Hall, C.M. (2019) "Combining the 'why' and 'how' of teaching sustainability: The case of the business school academics," *Environmental Education Research*, 25(12), pp. 1751–1774. doi: 10.1080/13504622.2019. 1667959.

Koens, K. and Postma, A. (2018) "Understanding and Managing Visitor Pressure in Urban Tourism Growth." Available at: https://www.celth.nl/sites/default/files/ 2018-09/Avoiding%20visitor%20pressure%20in%20European%20cities.pdf (accessed 24 October 2019).

Koens, K., Postma, A. and Papp, B. (2018) "Is overtourism overused? Understanding the impact of tourism in a city context," *Sustainability (Switzerland)*, 10(12), p. 4384. doi: 10.3390/su10124384.

Kolehmainen, J. et al. (2016) "Quadruple helix, innovation and the knowledge-based development: Lessons from remote, rural and less-favoured regions," *Journal of the Knowledge Economy*, 7(1), pp. 23–42. doi: 10.1007/s13132-015-0289-9.

Kunwar, R. R. (2018) "Tourism education, curriculum spaces, knowledge production, and disciplinary pluralism," *The Gaze: Journal of Tourism and Hospitality*, 9, pp. 83–155. doi: 10.3126/gaze.v9i0.19724.

Leydesdorff, L. and Deakin, M. (2011) "The triple-helix model of smart cities: A neo-evolutionary perspective," *Journal of Urban Technology*, 18(2), pp. 53–63. doi: 10.1080/10630732.2011.601111.

Malihah, E. and Setiyorini, H.P.D. (2014) "Tourism Education and Edu-tourism Development: Sustainable Tourism Development Perspective in Education," in *The 1st International Seminar on Tourism (ISOT)*, Bandung, pp. 1–7.

Martins, M.M. and Martins, M. (2018) "Tourism planning and tourismphobia: An analysis of the strategic tourism plan of Barcelona 2010–2015," *Journal of Tourism, Heritage and Services Marketing*, 4(1), pp. 3–7. doi: 10.5281/zenodo.1247519.

Mazilu, M. and Sitnikov, C.S. (2010) *Responsibilities in Management of Tourist Destinations, Management and Marketing? Craiova (Management and Marketing-Craiova)*.

Milano, C., Novelli, M. and Cheer, J.M. (2019) "Overtourism and tourismphobia: A journey through four decades of tourism development, planning and local concerns," *Tourism Planning and Development*, 16(4), pp. 1–5. doi: 10.1080/21568316. 2019.1599604.

Miller, G. et al., 2010. "Public understanding of sustainable tourism." *Annals of Tourism Research*, 37(3), pp. 627–645.

Ministry of Tourism, Govt of India. (2017). "Guidelines on the Training Course for Tour Guide and Heritage Tour Guide" [Online], Available at: http://tourism. gov.in/guidelines-training-course-tour-guide-and-heritage-tour-guide [accessed 17 February 2020].

Moscardo, G. (2015). "The Importance of Education for Sustainability in Tourism," In: G. Moscardo, and P. Benckendorff (Eds.) *Education for Sustainability in Tourism*. CSR, Sustainability, Ethics & Governance, Springer, Berlin, Heidelberg.

Muler Gonzalez, V., Coromina, L. and Galí, N. (2018) "Overtourism: Residents' perceptions of tourism impact as an indicator of resident social carrying capacity - Case study of a Spanish heritage town," *Tourism Review*, 73(3), pp. 277–296. doi: 10.1108/TR-08–2017–0138.

Neuhofer, B. and Buhalis, D. (2018) "Understanding and Managing Technology-Enabled Enhanced Torurist Experiences," in *2nd Advances in Hospitality and Tourism Marketing and Management Conference*, pp. 1689–1699. doi: 10.1017/CBO 9781107415324.004.

Nunkoo, R. and Ramkissoon, H. (2011) "Developing a community support model for tourism," *Annals of Tourism Research*, 38(3), pp. 964–988. doi: 10.1016/j.annals. 2011.01.017.

Pearce, P. L. (2009) "From culture shock and culture arrogance to culture exchange: Ideas towards sustainable socio-cultural tourism," *Journal of Sustainable Tourism*, 3(3), pp. 143–154. doi: 10.1080/09669589509510719.

Peeters, P. et al. (2018) *Research for TRAN Committee - Overtourism: Impact and Possible Policy Responses, European Parliament, Policy Department for Structural and Cohesion Policies*. Available at: http://www.europarl.europa.eu/thinktank/en/document.html?reference=IPOL_STU(2018)629184.

Perkumienė, D. and Pranskūnienė, R. (2019) "Overtourism: Between the right to travel and residents' rights," *Sustainability*, 11(7), p. 2138. doi: 10.3390/su11072138.

Petkar, S. (2017). *Spain is quite full' tourists urge to travel elsewhere as protests grip holiday hotspots*, s.l.: Express.co.uk.

Phi, G.T. (2019) "Framing overtourism: A critical news media analysis," *Current Issues in Tourism*, 0(0), pp. 1–5. doi: 10.1080/13683500.2019.1618249.

Redclift, M. and Friedmann, J. (1994) *Empowerment: The Politics of Alternative Development*, Cambridge: Blackwell. doi: 10.2307/3338712.

Renau, R. (2018) "Touristification, sharing economies and the new geography of urban conflicts," *Urban Science*, 2(4), pp. 104. doi: 10.3390/urbansci2040104.

Riley, M., Ladkin, A. and Szivas, E. (2002) *Tourism Employment: Analysis and Planning*. Sydney: Channel View Publications.

Russo, A. P. and Scarnato, A. (2018) "'Barcelona in common': A new urban regime for the 21st-century tourist city?," *Journal of Urban Affairs*, 40(4), pp. 455–474. doi: 10.1080/07352166.2017.1373023.

Saner, T., Bahçelerli, N.M. and Eyupoglu, S.Z. (2016). The importance of practical training in tourism education. *Research Gate,* pp. 916–920.

Sarantakou, E. and Terkenli, T.S. (2019) "Non-institutionalized forms of tourism accommodation and overtourism impacts on the landscape: The case of Santorini, Greece," *Tourism Planning and Development*, 16(4), pp. 1–23. doi: 10.1080/21568316.2019.1569122.

Séraphin, H., Butcher, J. and Korstanje, M. (2017) "Challenging the negative images of Haiti at a pre- visit stage using visual online learning materials," *Journal of Policy Research in Tourism, Leisure and Events*, 9(2), pp. 169–181. doi: 10.1080/19407963.2016.1261146.

Seraphin, H., Gowreensunkar, V. and Ambaye, M. (2016) "The Blakeley Model applied to improving a tourist destination: An exploratory study. The case of Haiti," *Journal of Destination Marketing and Management*, 5(4), pp. 1–8. doi: 10.1016/j.jdmm.2016.07.004.

Seraphin, H., Sheeran, P. and Pilato, M. (2018) "Over-tourism and the fall of Venice as a destination," *Journal of Destination Marketing and Management*, 9, pp. 374–376. doi: 10.1016/j.jdmm.2018.01.011.

Séraphin, H., Zaman, M. and Fotiadis, A. (2019) "Challenging the negative image of postcolonial, post-conflict and post-disaster destinations using events postcolonial, post-conflict and post-disaster destinations using events," *Caribbean Quarterly*, 65(1), pp. 88–112. doi: 10.1080/00086495.2019.1565223.

Shahaida, P., Rajashekar, H. and Nargundkar, R. (2007) "Quality of management education in India: Development of a conceptual framework", *Indore Management Journal*, 2(1), pp. 45–55.

Sims, R. and Brinkmann, J. (2003) "Business ethics curriculum design: Suggestions and illustrations," *Teaching Business Ethics*, 7, pp. 69–86. doi: 10.1023/A:1022602521549.

Speer, P. W. and Peterson, N. A. (2000) "Psychometric properties of an empowerment scale: Testing cognitive, emotional, and behavioral domains," *Social Work Research*, 24(2), pp. 109–118. doi: 10.1093/swr/24.2.109.

Stergiou, D. P. and Airey, D. (2017). "Tourism Education and Industry Expectations in Greece: (re)minding the Gap," In Benckendorff, P. and Zehrer, A. (Eds.), *Handbook on Teaching and Learning in Tourism*, Northampton, MA: Edward Elgar Publishing, pp. 3–4.

Stronza, A. and Gordillo, J. (2008) "Community views of ecotourism," *Annals of Tourism Research*, 35 (2), pp. 448–468. doi: 10.1016/j.annals.2008.01.002.

Strzelecka, M., Boley, B.B. and Strzelecka, C. (2017) "Empowerment and resident support for tourism in rural Central and Eastern Europe (CEE): The case of Pomerania, Poland," *Journal of Sustainable Tourism*, 25(4), pp. 554–572. doi: 10.1080/09669582.2016.1224891.

Trancoso González, A. (2018) "Venice: The problem of overtourism and the impact of cruises," *Investigaciones Regionales-Journal of Regional Research*, 42, pp. 35–52. Available at: https://investigacionesregionales.org/wp-content/uploads/sites/3/2019/01/03-TRANCOSO.pdf.

UHERO: The Economic Research Organisation (University of Hawaii). (2017) *Sustainable Tourism Development and Overtourism*, pp. 1–10. Available at: https://uhero.hawaii.edu/sustainable-tourism-development-and-overtourism/

University of Queensland, Australia. (2018). https://business.uq.edu.au/un-prme. [Online], Available at: https://business.uq.edu.au/files/8398/UN_PRME_Report.pdf, [accessed 12 February 2020].

UNWTO. (2011) *Tourism Towards 2030 Global Overview, UNTWO General Assembly, 19th Session*. Available at: http://www.e-unwto.org.

UNWTO. (2018) "Rebuffing myths," pp. 1–10. doi: 10.18111/9789284419999.

Uppink Calderwood, L. and Soshkin, M. (2019) *The Travel and Tourism Competitiveness Report 2019 Travel and Tourism at a Tipping Point*, pp. 1–129.

Uttar Pradesh Tourism. (2018). *UP Investor Summit,* Lucknow: UP Tourism Government.

Walmsley, A. (2017) "Overtourism and Underemployment: A Modern Labour Market Dilemma Embedding Enterprise and Entrepreneurship in Higher Education View Project Tourism Employment in Nordic Countries View Project Overtourism and Underemployment: A Modern Labour Market Dilemma," in *Responsible Tourism in Destinations 13- Tackling Overtourism-Local Responses*. Available at: https://www.researchgate.net/publication/322489410.

Wearing, S.I. E. N. and Larsen, L. (1996) "Assessing and managing the sociocultural impacts of ecotourism: Revisiting the Santa Elena rainforest project," *The Environmentalist*, 16, pp. 117–133.

Weber, F. et al. (2017) *Tourism Destinations Under Pressure*. Lucerne, Switzerland. Available at: https://static1.squarespace.com/static/56dacbc6d210b821510cf939/t/

5906f31086e6c0c523b565b9/1493627668381/WTFL+study+2017_short+version. pdf (accessed 10th November 2019).

Weiler, B. and Black, R. (2015) "The changing face of the tour guide: One-way communicator to choreographer to co-creator of the tourist experience," *Tourism Recreation Research*, 40(3), pp. 364–378. doi: 10.1080/02508281.2015.1083742.

Weiler, B. and Walker, K. (2014) "Enhancing the visitor experience: Reconceptualising the tour guide's communicative role," *Journal of Hospitality and Tourism Management*, 21, pp. 90–99. doi: 10.1016/j.jhtm.2014.08.001.

Weng, S. and Peng, H. (2014) "Tourism development, rights consciousness and the empowerment of Chinese historical village communities," *Tourism Geographies*, 16(5), pp. 772–784. doi: 10.1080/14616688.2014.955873.

Xi, Q., Sawagvudcharee, O. and Walsh, J. (2019) "Information sources and domestic tourism at Sanyuesan festival, China," *International Business Research*, 12(8), p. 23. doi: 10.5539/ibr.v12n8p23.

Zhang, C., Fyall, A. and Zheng, Y. (2015) "Heritage and tourism conflict within world heritage sites in China: A longitudinal study," *Current Issues in Tourism*, 18(2), pp. 110–136. doi: 10.1080/13683500.2014.912204.

5 Demarketing overtourism

The role of educational interventions

Maximiliano Korstanje and Babu George

Introduction

Overtourism is commonly interpreted as the saturation of visitors and the perceived visual congestion derived from the excess of tourists. This often leads locals to confront with foreign tourists (Bresson and Logossah, 2011; Seraphin, Sheeran and Pilato, 2018). It evinces a tendency widely associated with visiting sites over-crowded or saturated with other visitors. These spaces abound in the world, though the academia gave less attention to it. Overtourism represents a dialectical rupture between hosts and guests which needs mediation (Seraphin, Sheeran and Pilato, 2018). From its outset, the tourism industry has an ecological imprint, which means the need for measuring and controlling the negative effects on non-renewable resources. This academic position leads scholars to the sustainability theory (Britton, 1996; Jamal and Getz, 1995). The idea of sustainability speaks to us of the urgency of planning the activity to find and eradicate those negative consequences which may very well place the destination in jeopardy (Bramwell and Lane, 2011). From its inception, tourism and sustainability were inextricably intertwined. Today, new conceptualisations revolving around degrowth and slow tourism have surfaced captivating the attention of scholarship (Canavan 2014; Hall, 2009). Of course, this would suggest that the term seems to be nothing new, so to speak, unless by the fact that some classic destinations have developed an antitourist sentiment. Echoing H. Goodwin (2017), *overtourism* should be understood as a condition (irreversible or not) where locals and tourists feel an excessive number of visitors on the site. It is important to distinguish overtourism, which connotes the excess of visitors in a place, from antitourism expressions more associated with racism and anti-migration sentiment. Over recent years, some voices have questioned the obsession of authorities and policy makers to adopt tourism as the main economic activity in under-developing countries (Ashley, Goodwin and Boyd, 2000; Tosun, 2006). Poor countries are often obsessed to adopt tourism as their main economic industry creating the conditions towards a vicious circle very hard to break. The tourist-receiving societies gradually experience substantial shifts which oscillate from real estate speculation to inflation. Sooner or later, they ask for financial assistance to construct the necessary infrastructure creating a dependency between tourist-delivering and tourist-receiving economies. Basically, this financial dependency is ultimately aggravated when international segments elect the country as a prime destination (Vanhove, 1997; Richter, 1983; Yong, 2014). Although this has been widely studied in the specialised literature, less attention was paid to the role of degrowth tourism and consumption. As Claudio Milano (2018) puts it, the tourism industry is torn between two contrasting tendencies. Local stakeholders, adjoined to foreign investors, arrive at the community to promote tourism as a genuine form of poverty relief. Since tourism is considered a panacea for economic prosperity, the problem lies in the fact invariably the destination is doomed to be saturated. Second, locals develop hostile attitudes against tourists when they are systematically relegated from profit creation. The quest for profits is directly proportional to local resource exhaustion. Having said this, long-dormant disputes or social discontent arises because of tourism (Comaroff and Comaroff, 2009). For this reason, education plays a crucial role in dismantling the local resistance to visitors as well as the potential conflict host-guest meeting generates (Henthorne, George and Williams, 2010). This chapter brings a reflection on the pros and cons of education in reducing potential situations of conflict created by touristphobia and overtourism. For the Western rationale, the needs of distinguishing the European cultural values as naturally superior or more sophisticated to other forms of organisation, occupy a central position in what anthropologists know as *ethnocentrism*. The archetype of the noble savage was ideologically coined and fabricated to legitimate the European conquest in the overseas colonial territories. Richer nations should protect and help poorer ones not only sharing the economic formulas but also seducing developing nations to trade with them. Just after the Second World War ended, Truman's speech emphasised the importance of assisting developing nations (Burns, 2003). The world was automatically divided into two, developed and undeveloped countries. In tourism and hospitality, this economic-based conception was symbolically framed in the core of scholarship. As de Kadt reminded, tourism – far from being an instrument of wealth production – flourishes successfully in those cultures which were not subject to a past of violence, political stability, or slavery (de Kadt, 1979a, b). For some reason, he does not precise; tourism (like development) fails because of cultural asymmetries (incompatibilities) which are proper of the tourist-receiving society. As the backdrop is given, the debate revolving around overtourism or degrowth tourism are inscribed in the same ideological discourse. Where there is a judgment to be made, it does not question the theory of development as it was originally imagined or designed. Rather, the notion of culture situates here as a tug of war – far from explaining the reasons for the failure – blames natives for the situation.

In this above-noted context, this chapter reflects on the pros and cons of degrowth tourism as well as the role of education in the process. The first section contains a preliminary debate that centres on the use of high digital technology not only saturating the destination but also affecting seriously the small infrastructure. As Milano (2018) observed, tourism rests on a dual contrasting tendency, the need of reaching a standardisation process while avoiding the undesired consequences. Second, we continue the debate left by Jost Krippendorf (1982, 2010) on the cultural values as the founding touchstone of society as well as the alternative solution to the eco-crisis the world faces today. The third and fourth parts are mainly reserved for much deeper exploration about *degrowth tourism* and *undertourism* as catch-all conceptualisations in the years to come. All said and done, in the conclusion section we revisit the question: are educational interventions all that important? If yes, when does it work and when it does not?

Framing the debate

Several scholars have alerted on the problems of overtourism and visual saturation at international destinations (Clark and Chabrel, 2007; Seraphin, Sheeran and Pilato, 2018; Seraphin et al., 2019). In recent years, some voices have pointed out the role of education in overcoming the obstacles of sustainability and, of course, the problems associated with overtourism. For example, an interesting study authored by Kempel, Ballantine, and Hall (2019), alerts on the challenges universities often face to integrate sustainable education with an academic culture which is more prone to profit maximisation and consumption. Based on the administration of semi-structured interviews applied in Australia, Europe, and North America, these researchers develop an interesting model to understand how and why this integration happens. Transformational learning occupies a central position not only in the students' minds but also encouraging critical thought. At the same time, actioners hope to improve the world through practical solutions for big problems.

The expansion of digital technologies such as peer-to-peer accommodation, Airbnb and Couchsurfing are posing a serious challenge for policy makers and experts in tourism management. Destinations which over years were carefully protected from overtourism are now over-crowded by thousands of tourists who look for cheaper options (Shoval and Isaacson, 2007; Hojeghan and Estangareh, 2011; Buhalis and Amaranggana, 2013; Dodds and Butler, 2019). In this respect, in a recently published book entitled *Overtourism: excesses, discontents, and measure in travel and tourism*, Claudio Milano, Joseph Cheer, and Marina Novelli argue convincingly that the industry of tourism rests on two contrasting trends, which oscillates from the quest of profits through the stimulation of mass-consumption and the preservation of local resources. This means that tourism generates benefits we often look for but also negative effects that are overlooked. The discontent of local people or the hostility against tourists seem not to be the same phenomenon. While the former signals a negative reaction to foreign visitors (probably because of racism), the latter refers to much deeper reasons which are enrooted in the saturation of international destinations (Doods and Butler, 2019). The adoption of high digital tech is vital to understand the saturation of classic destinations. In this vein, Daisure Abe (2019) proffers the study case of Kyoto (Japan), which in some extent differs from other cases. Kyoto seems to be an international destination widely marked by the excess of visitors. Since authorities never made the decision of expanding the local infrastructure, such excess was given by the usage of informal digital technologies such as Airbnb or p2p platforms. The digital technologies like Airbnb help in the explosion of informal lodging creating a serious dispute between locals and foreign tourists. In consonance with the other case studies, Kyoto is subject to a gentrification process where local neighbourhoods not only witness gradual inflation but also how the social scaffolding is radically shifted.

As the previous argument is given, in some conditions overtourism is accelerated by the financial mechanism of regulation imposed by the nation state. Francesco Vicentin and Dario Bertocchi (2019) focus on an interesting analysis of Venice city (Italy). Following Milano, Cheer, and Novelli, they hold that tourism stimulates mass consumption which is helpful for local industries. At the same time, tourism brings some undesirable effects as overcrowding, social conflict, and exhaustion of local resources. Recently governments struggled to reverse the overcrowding by the imposition of higher taxes but without any real result. Measures of this calibre created a vicious circle very hard to reverse. Put simply, even if these taxes succeeded in short-run amassing profits for the local budgets, it developed a financial dependency of tourism which aggravated the situation in the long run. As debated, this phenomenon follows a highly complex multi-causality, which is very hard to precise by specialists. Similar findings are obtained by Blazquez-Salom et al. (2019) in their study on the city of Palma de Majorca (Spain). In the same direction of the specialised literature, this research shows how the negative aftermaths caused by overtourism are explained by an interplay of three combined factors: (a) the rise and expansion of the tourist market in small destinations, (b) the real estate speculation which remains unregulated by the state, and (c) the relegation of some lower classes which are pressed to live in the periphery. As a result of this, the touristification process recreates a double effect. On one hand, it prompts the closure of local retail shops affecting the employment of city-dwellers. On the other hand, a gradual process of inflation decreases the purchasing power of middle and lower classes.

To some extent, overtourism reveals two important assumptions. At a first glimpse, the theory of development has some limitations to be applied – at least – in the global South or in some under-developing economies which are characterised by extractive institutions. As Phillip McMichael (2016) puts it, the theory of development starts from the premise that the Global north has the moral mandate to help the South. Quite aside from this panacea, development continues the same ideological root than the theory of noble savage just coined through the European colonialism. McMichael's thesis points out that colonialism arrived to legitimate a process of domination and dispossession where the Non-Western Other occupied a passive and marginal role. While the colonies were governed through the articulation of violence and fear in the European centres, prosperity and democracy certainly prevailed. As a result of this, colonies asked for the same rights and benefits than their White Lords. The growing process of independence in the colonies broke the liaison between the centre and its periphery. The theory of development is ultimately oriented to keep the former colonies under control. Today, the tourism industry echoes many of the old mainstream cultural values imposed by colonialism. By visiting exotic islands and cultures give the European travellers a sign of status, at the time the local resources are devastated. Overtourism, in this context, tells part of the whole story. Second, this complex issue ignites a new stage of conflict where guests are undesired. This was brilliantly evinced by Mathias Pecot and Carla Ricaurte-Quijano. With the basis on research conducted in Las Galapagos (Ecuador), they conclude that unfortunately a whole portion of publications are mainly oriented to show a situation which originated in the global-North. Although interesting their outcomes sometimes do not apply in other cultural contexts. While the tourism industry alludes to the host-guest encounter, which is discursively idealised by the promotion-related campaigns, no less true is that tourism may be very well a source of conflict –if not tension. Overtourism punctuates on a radical rupture between tourists and locals. The Galapagos offers an idealised landscape revolving around the archetype of a lost paradise, in which case, it targets the interests of international demand. Over the years, tourism development situated as a panacea ensuring progress and civilisation for the Island; but today, this destination seems to be saturated because of the ever-increasing demand. Last but not least, in a recently published book, Korstanje (2019) has eloquently explained that overtourism and tourismphobia share at the bottom a similar dynamic. Not only is the *undesired Other* neglected, but it is commoditised as a source of profits. Centred on a critical analysis of capitalist logic, he holds the thesis that 9/11 and terrorism have closed the symbolic borders between the West and the rest of the World. The fear of terrorism had durable effects such as the tightening of controls at borderlines, as well as a recalcitrant climate of hostility against non-Western 'Others'. In this new narrative, the Other is a potential enemy whose intentions remain in the shadows. Foreign tourists, Muslim migrants, and other asylum-seekers are inextricably intertwined. While tourists are commoditised *Others who pay for the hospitality, migrants are suspect of mistrust (undesired Others)*. Tourists are commoditised as vehicles for local profits when they pay for their experiences. In this token, they are rejected when locals are instrumentally excluded from the produced surplus. In parallel, migrants are always considered as potential terrorists because of their incapacity to amass profits. As Korstanje puts it, this evinces the end of hospitality at least as we know it (Korstanje, 2017). As Tzanelli (2018) eloquently noted, the capitalist society has historically divided the coveted gains from the implied costs. This remains encapsulated in the core of Western rationality (instrumentality). Today, locals bid for tourism to captivate foreign investors while embracing economic prosperity, but at the same time, they hate tourists who invade their privacies. Of course, this moot point begs two, more than one pungent question: is overtourism an implicit sign of intolerance to 'the Non-Western Other'? since the Western instrumentality, as well as rational calculation, failed as a mechanism to mitigate the effects of overtourism, to what extent is education a new cure for this social malady?'

Overtourism and education

Beyond the number of publications as well as the interests of scholars to approach over tourism has been increased, no less true seems to be that this phenomenon is multidimensional and was not correctly defined (Koens, Postma and Papp, 2018). Quite aside from this, what is vital to debate is the socio-cultural background which determines overtourism. Koens, Postma and Papp identify five issues already present in the dynamics of saturated destinations such as:

- Overcrowding
- Pervasiveness of visitor impact
- Physical touristification of a destination or city
- Less availability of housing
- Pressure on the local environment

In a landmark paper, Seraphin, Sheeran, and Pilato (2018) suggest notably that the ecological survival of destinations is not associated with the *trexit approach,* which is based on the anti-tourist sentiment. Rather, it should be centred on an *ambidextrous management approach*, alternating the needs of economic exploitation with exploration. Bresson and Logossah (2011) alert on the overtourism as the material asymmetry (inconsistency) between the excessive demand and a low-based infrastructure. Based on an economic analysis of cruise tourism in five Caribbean destinations, they argue that stay-over tourism is a key factor of development in Caribbean nations, but paradoxically their Aquila's kneel. In view of this, overtourism exhibits a much deeper deficiency in the planning process which impedes the strategic long-run vision. Contrariwise, the Spanish anthropologist, Agustin Santana Talavera overtly said that the cultural clash between host and guest is often subject to conflict and disputes. Social pathologies such as racism, negative stereotypes or ethnic prejudices are triggered by the overcrowd of tourists at small destinations (Santana-Talavera, 2006). Under some conditions, staff workers or housekeepers are trained not to show their real sentiments to guests, even stereotypes or bad impressions. The subordination between hotel workers and tourists often leads to a *staged position* where the real sentiments remain hidden. There were interesting works that historically focussed on the host-guest relations. In other studies, i.e. Korstanje (2011), showed that historical disputes between nations remain dormant, placating the in-group conflict. Chilean tourists who arrived in Buenos Aires were well-treated while at the bottom there was dormant prejudice and hostility between Argentinian hotel workers and Chilean Tourists. This conflict dates back to the Beagle dispute as well as the support of Chile to England during the Falkland-Malvinas war. This happens at least until the tourism industry places both groups in different subordinated roles. In the case of Argentina and Chile, a history fraught of geographical disputes and conflict, tourism – far from revitalising the social ties – activated a set of hidden prejudices that fed back a climate of xenophobia and racism. However, since tourism triggers a culture of service where hosts are subordinated to guests, this racism was covert. This position was supported by other studies that focused on the inter-group conflict (Comaroff and Comaroff, 2009; Stephenson, 2004; Causevic and Lynch, 2011). Under some conditions, beyond the sentiment against tourists lies recalcitrant xenophobia, which is culturally hidden. Today's specialists agree that locals often want the positive effects of tourism while avoiding its costs (Tzanelli, 2018). Is education a fertile ground to revert a situation like this?

One of the pioneering voices who alerted on the incongruence between sustainability and tourism was Jost Krippendorf. In Krippendorf's account, education played a crucial role reversing not only the daily behaviour but also the cultural values behind our acts. Although he was not concerned about sustainable issues, he is considered one of the fathers of sustainable tourism theory. It is almost impossible to foster tourism sustainability without inspecting on the cultural values associated with accumulation and consumption which are proper of capitalism. Krippendorf sees tourism as a catalyst developed by society to alleviate psychological frustration. Lay-people are subject to countless situations where their autonomies are systematically undermined. In this respect, tourism helps society to keep united, working like a perfect machine. Tourism is neither good nor bad; rather it reflects the mainstream cultural values of the societal order. Having said this, mass-tourism exhibits the logic of capitalism which standardises production while stimulates consumption. Having said this, education is crucial to change the negative values that lead towards mass-production (Krippendorf, 1982, 1987, 2010; Korstanje, 2015). His legacy and original paradigm was useful and widely cited in tourism fields, but particularly sheds light on the works of a brilliant young anthropologist, Jafar Jafari. Unlike Krippendorf, Jafari is not interested in describing the nature of tourism, but – like him – he was moved by the urgency to create an all-pervading model that helps understanding tourism. Although Jafari coined the term *scientification of tourism* to signal to a state of knowledge production, he laid the foundation for a new conceptual model which was certainly based on four clear platforms: *advocacy, cautionary, adaptancy,* and *knowledge-based*. The advocacy platform concentrates efforts in those studies which note the beneficial effects of tourism such as employment, consumption and economic growth. Over the years, policy makers and professionals acknowledged that the industry has some collateral damages which place the sustainability of the destination in jeopardy. The adaptancy platform combines a mix-based reaction to the good and the bad of tourism. Lastly, Jafari was strongly convinced that tourism would evolve to be a matured science in the passing of years. He believed that the knowledge-based platform was a fertile ground to give rapid and more accurate solutions to the problems created by the industry, even pollution and environmental degradation (Jafari, 2001). In this process, knowledge and education were of paramount importance in transforming the current local practices in good practices (Xiao, 2013). In a seminal book, Stephen McCool and Neil Moisey (2001) revise the concept of sustainability and its intersection with capitalist culture. Per their viewpoint, scholars should start from the premise that sustainability can be successfully achieved only when sustainable institutions are drawn. The question of sustainability raises some interesting points revolving around the figure of political power, or the economic interests of privileged groups. These economic interests prevent tourism to begin with a process of degrowing or embracing some more sustainable forms of exploitation as slow-tourism. One of the challenges of policy makers – no matter the culture or country – associates with the lack of familiarity with the political dimensions of sustainable tourism. As they eloquently put it,

> Tourism has not escaped the discussions concerning sustainability. Indeed, many texts, including this one, have been challenged to frame the question of sustainable tourism, its dimensions and challenges. Clearly, tourism has become a global financial power, achieving a planetary presence unequalled by many other economic sectors … Tourism is no longer the bening economic development tool that the boosterism of the past purported to be yet
>
> (McCool and Moisey, 2001)

Of course, the question of degrowth tourism seems not to be new, but it gained attention in view of the ecological crisis the planet faced, as well as the limitations of sustainable tourism to avoid overtourism. Sabine Panzer-Krause (2017) alerts on the limitations of sustainable theory to achieve more sustainable destinations –at least as we think it today. While in the short term, sustainability networks are going in the correct direction in the co-ordination of shared efforts to slow tourism, no less true is that degrowth strategies should be thought in the long term. Here in this point further investigation is needed.

Undertourism or degrowth tourism

The notion of *degrowth* surfaces in economic theory through the 70s dec-ade, precisely when Nicholas Georgescu-Roegen (1971) introduces in the debate a new interrogation revolving around the limits of the modern econ-omy to expand for-ever. The economic concept of unlimited growth was only possible on a planet with infinite resources. The notion is automatically incorporated into tourism research as a sign of exhaustion which placed the industry between the wall and the deep blue sea. One might speculate the acceleration of green-house effects that triggered climate change was a foundational event for policy makers to interrogate furtherly on the limits of development theory (Borowy, 2013). The question of whether tourism was symbolised as a panacea in the former decades was strictly associated with what Jafari dubbed as an 'advocacy platform'. In consonance with this, a more than interesting point is left by Joo et al. (2020) suggests that collec-tive empowerment is activated in an individual level while the perception (engagement with) the positive outcome of the tourism industry. The polit-ical action, as well as the local reactions against or in favour of tourism de-pends on the collective empowerment the society generates. Empowerment is of vital importance to enable people, organisations and institutions to move resources towards the solution of their daily problems. However, as re-searchers warned, investigations of this nature show some limitations. Some of these types of approaches focus on the non-economic benefits only while the economics of sustainable tourism are not duly considered. Still further, those locals who are familiar with tourism probably would develop a more positive attitude than others. Further research should centre on the material asymmetries of classes as well as individual and collective worldviews.

The turn of the century not only brought uncontemplated risks such as terrorism, climate change or virus outbreaks but also changed the concep-tual paradigm of tourism fields as never before (Somnez and Graefe, 1998; Paraskevas and Arendell, 2007). As K Andriotis puts it, the ideals of tour-ism as a vehicle towards richness and development not only failed to give a coherent explanation to poor countries, but it remains unable to explain why some countries are richer while others are relatively poorer. To some extent, some voices started to revisit the idea tourism should be an ever-growing activity. The term *degrowth tourism* revolves around the needs of down-scaling tourism to alleviate the destination enforcing – if not affirming – a fairer wealth distribution among all the involved stakeholders (Andriotis, 2018). Paradoxically, the tourism industry tends to consolidate an inevitable saturation, because of the fact people want what other people want. When a destination is born, probably as an unconventional place, the campaigns should be put in investing in capital and money. At this stage, the destination is not well-known, but gradually it receives the visits of greater demand. Over the years, the destination will surely reach a point of saturation. The counter-force is equally important, the growth of some destinations implicitly corresponds with the degrowth of other emerging destinations. Michael C. Hall (2009) argues convincingly that the urgency given by climate change to decelerate the current levels of pollution and contamination to the environment leads scholars to think in alternative ways of tourism. This interpretation coincides with the failure of traditional theories to make tourism a sustainable industry. The economic-based paradigm which stipulates that tourism should expand – even when some regulations – fell invariably in discredit. Evoking the Paradox of Common in Hardin's theory, Hall says overtly that individual actors often do not believe their action contributes to environmental degradation. The imposed regulation rarely succeeds in mitigating the negative effects of tourism. Hence, Hall calls the attention on slow consumption as a good alternative path towards degrowth tourism. Here, two assumptions could be made. On one hand, overtourism and degrowth tourism emerge as unquestionable subfields within the constellations of tourism research at least as a reaction to the concrete impacts of the industry in the territory. On the other hand, under some conditions, degrowth tourism helps the destination to prompt a more sustainable change (Canavan, 2014). Put the same in other terms, the tourist system articulates a set of barriers to protect the interests of status quo. As Krippendorf eloquently adheres, a subtle – or radical – change can be applied in the system (or ensured) only if the foundational cultural values are altered. In so doing, the standardised forms of gazing should be gradually reversed towards a new stage of slow-tourism (di Clemente, de Salvo and Mogollon, 2011).

As the previous argument is given, Higgins-Desbiolles et al. (2019) hold that the tourism industry should be contemplated as a key factor of capitalism. In this respect, degrowing tourism is not only conceived as a contradictory concept, but scholars should also pay attention to the global patterns of neoliberal mobility, as it was imagined in the Global North. Tourism should be re-conceptualised in order to give further rights to local communities instead of tourists' rights. In a seminal book, entitled *The Native Tourist*, Krishna Ghimire (2013) contends that the publications in tourism fields are reportedly marked by a great emphasis on profits and businesses. The statistical reports even are issued by governmental agencies that look to foster tourism no matter the consequences. To achieve this goal, further foreign investors should be attracted. In consonance with this, the statistical information is one-sidedly presented or politically manipulated to potentiate the local destination. This has led towards saturation of many emerging destinations geographically located in the developing economies or the Global South. Degrowth tourism, in part, speaks of a new tendency oriented to stimulate a slow consumption in the domestic arena. The native tourist seems to be a neologism used by Ghimire to denote a new locally designed circuit to avoid international tourist fluxes. Although academic supporters of neoliberal capitalism held the thesis that growth can be rationally regulated by private or state actors, no less true is that interesting social studies show precisely the opposite. Here it is important to note overtourism seems to be only the peak of the iceberg. But to what extent is degrowth tourism conducive to the goals of capitalism? or what is worse, in what way, is tourism a good option to rebuild the natives' rights?

Conclusion

Going one step further, we should not shy away from asking whether education is part of the problem or the solution (Higgins-Desbiolles et al. (2019). The answer is not simple. True, numerous researchers have investigated the remedial role of education in correcting unethical behaviour (Armstrong, Ketz, and Owsen, 2003; de Casterlé, Janssen, and Grypdonck, 1996; Luthar and Karri, 2005). Researchers like McKenzie-Mohr et al. (2012) have come to the counter-conclusion that greater education, be it on health, safety, or conservation, does not mean better behaviour. Thus, there is some ambiguity in the literature. To make matters complex, most of these kinds of research are conducted in everyday life situations and not in the context of tourism, which is the 'search for the other'. Individuals invert themselves when they become tourists (George, Henthorne and Williams, 2013). Right conduct in normal situations is expected of well-groomed individuals – if the inversion hypothesis is true, it is uncertain if education would help in redeeming tourists of unethical behaviour. Qualitative research conducted previously by the second author of this chapter indicates this could indeed be the case (Henthorne and George, 2017).

The above research however also highlights the critical role of attraction sequencing: that is, tourists who visit places of eco-cultural importance prior to a beach tend to carry forward the educational and ethical elements they get from their first destination to the second. With a little bit of leap of faith, it could be argued that education that tourists receive *while being tourists*, not from their universities or workplaces, has a significant influence on whether they would conduct appropriately or not. This means that tour operators and destination management organisations should invest in educating and transforming tourists during their very lived experiences of being tourists. When their mindscapes are in routine, work-laden, non-touristic modes, they might grasp the dangers of overtourism; but that knowledge might not translate into appropriate behaviour while they wear their tourist hats.

What then is the missing factor between education and behavioural change? Plausibly, it is motivation (Schultz, 2002). Tourists should be motivated to be a positive influence on places suffering from the ill effects of overtourism. Education does provide directions for the motivated (Schultz, 2011). However, in the absence of motivation, education and the knowledge that it provides has little to no value (Fisher, Fisher, and Shuper, 2009). We believe that the motivation to behave responsibly in the pre-touristic phase of a would-be traveller does not align well with the direction of their touristic motivation. The motivational interventions should be provided even as they liminally transform themselves into tourists.

Now, nothing discussed above speaks of the pivotal role of education in motivating and inducing behavioural intentions in those non-tourist actors such as tourism planners, industry experts, and workers in the tourism destination areas. For these groups of stakeholders, the role of education on behavioural modification could be a much less nuanced pathway (Swain and George, 2007). Say, tourism sector employees who graduated from tourism programmes that stress responsible tourism and sustainable development could be major forces of change in redeeming destinations of the negative impacts of overtourism.

References

Abe, D. (2019). "In Focus 1: Overtourism is invading Kyoto." In Milano, C., Cheer, J., and Novelli, M. (eds.) *Overtourism: Excesses, discontents and measure in travel and tourism.* CABI, Wallingford, pp. 86–90.

Andriotis, K. (2018). *Degrowth in tourism: Conceptual, theoretical and philosophical issues.* CABI, Wallingford.

Armstrong, M. B., Ketz, J. E., and Owsen, D. (2003). Ethics education in accounting: Moving toward ethical motivation and ethical behavior. *Journal of Accounting Education*, Vol. 21, No. 1, pp. 1–16.

Ashley, C., Goodwin, H. I., and Boyd, C. (2000). *Pro-poor tourism: Putting poverty at the heart of the tourism agenda* (Vol. 51). Overseas Development Institute, London.

Blazquez-Salon, M., Blanco-Romero, A., Gual Carbonell, J., and Murray, I. (2019). "Tourist gentrification of retail shops in Palma (Majorca)." In Milano, C., Cheer, J., and Novelli, M. (eds.) *Overtourism: Excesses, discontents and measure in travel and tourism.* CABI, Wallingford, pp. 39–69.

Borowy, I. (2013). Degrowth and public health in Cuba: Lessons from the past?. *Journal of Cleaner Production*, Vol. 38, pp. 17–26.

Bramwell, B., and Lane, B. (2011). Critical research on the governance of tourism and sustainability. *Journal of Sustainable Tourism*, Vol. 19, No. 4–5, pp. 411–421.

Bresson, G., and Logossah, K. (2011a). Crowding-out effects of cruise tourism on stay-over tourism in the Caribbean: Non-parametric panel data evidence. *Tourism Economics*, Vol. 17, No. 1, pp. 127–158.

Bresson, G., and Logossah, K. (2011b). Crowding-out effects of cruise tourism on stay-over tourism in the Caribbean: Non-parametric panel data evidence. *Tourism Economics*, Vol. 17, No. 1, pp. 127–158.

Britton, S. (1996). "Tourism, dependency and development." In Apostolopoulos, Y., Leivadi, S., and Yiannakis, A. (eds.) *The sociology of tourism.* London, Routledge, pp. 155–172.

Buhalis, D., and Amaranggana, A. (2013). Smart tourism destinations. In Xiang Z. and Tussyadiah I. (Eds.), *Information and communication technologies in tourism 2014*. Springer, Cham, pp. 553–564.

Burns, P. (2003). *An introduction to tourism and anthropology*. Routledge, Abingdon.

Canavan, B. (2014). Sustainable tourism: Development, decline and de-growth. Management issues from the Isle of Man. *Journal of Sustainable Tourism*, Vol. 22, No. 1, pp. 127–147.

Causevic, S., and Lynch, P. (2011). Phoenix tourism: Post-conflict tourism role. *Annals of Tourism Research*, Vol. 38, No. 3, pp. 780–800.

Clark, G., and Chabrel, M. (2007). Measuring integrated rural tourism. *Tourism Geographies*, Vol. 9, No. 4, pp. 371–386.

Comaroff, J. L., and Comaroff, J. (2009). *Ethnicity, Inc*. University of Chicago Press, Chicago, IL.

de Casterlé, B. D., Janssen, P. J., and Grypdonck, M. (1996). The relationship between education and ethical behavior of nursing students. *Western Journal of Nursing Research*, Vol. 18, No. 3, pp. 330–350.

De Kadt, E. (1979a). Tourism: Passport to development. *Perspectives on the social and cultural effects of tourism in developing countries*. World Bank Press, New York, NY.

de Kadt, E. (1979b). Social planning for tourism in the developing countries. *Annals of Tourism Research*, Vol. 6, No. 1, pp. 36–48.

Di Clemente, E., De Salvo, P., and Mogollón, J. M. H. (2011). Slow tourism o turismo de la lentitud: Un nuevo enfoque al desarrollo de territorios lentos. *Tourism and Management Studies*, Vol. 1, pp. 883–893.

Dodds, R., and Butler, R. (eds.). (2019). *Overtourism: Issues, realities and solutions* (Vol. 1). De Gruyter Oldenbourg, Berlin.

Fisher, J. D., Fisher, W. A., and Shuper, P. (2009). "The information-motivation-behavioral skills model of HIV preventive behavior." In DeClemente, R., Crosby, R., and Kegler, M. (eds.) *Emerging theories in health promotion practice and research*. Wiley and Sons, San Francisco, CA, pp. 21–65.

George, B. P., Henthorne, T. L., and Williams, A. J. (2013). PAS S. *PAS S*, Vol. 11, No. 3, pp. 47.

Georgescu-Roegen, N. (1971). *The entropy law and the economic process*. Harvard University Press, Cambridge, MA.

Ghimire, K. B. (Ed.). (2013). *The native tourist: Mass tourism within developing countries*. Routledge, Abingdon.

Goodwin, H. (2018) "The challenge of overtourism." In responsible tourism partnership. Working paper 4. Available at: https://haroldgoodwin.info/publications/

Hall, C. M. (2009). Degrowing tourism: Décroissance, sustainable consumption and steady-state tourism. *Anatolia*, Vol. 20, No. 1, pp. 46–61.

Henthorne, T. L., and George, B. P. (2017). The role of eco-cultural attractions in 'perception engineering': A case study conducted in Goa, India. In *The customer is not always right? Marketing orientations in a dynamic business world*. Springer, Cham, pp. 668–671.

Henthorne, T. L., George, B. P., and Williams, A. J. (2010). The evolving service culture of Cuban tourism: A case study. *Tourismos: An International Multidisciplinary Journal of Tourism*, Vol. 5, No. 2, pp. 129–138.

Higgins-Desbiolles, F., Carnicelli, S., Krolikowski, C., Wijesinghe, G., and Boluk, K. (2019). Degrowing tourism: Rethinking tourism. *Journal of Sustainable Tourism*, Vol. 27, No. 12, pp. 1926–1944.

Hojeghan, S. B., and Esfangareh, A. N. (2011). Digital economy and tourism impacts, influences and challenges. *Procedia-Social and Behavioral Sciences*, Vol. 19, pp. 308–316.

Jafari, J. (2001). "The scientification of tourism," In Smith V. L., and Brent M. (eds.) *Host and guest revisted*. Cognizant Communication, Elmsford, pp. 28–41.

Jamal, T. B., and Getz, D. (1995). Collaboration theory and community tourism planning. *Annals of Tourism Research*, Vol. 22, No. 1, pp. 186–204.

Joo, D., Woosnam, K. M., Strzelecka, M., and Boley, B. B. (2020). Knowledge, empowerment, and action: Testing the empowerment theory in a tourism context. *Journal of Sustainable Tourism*, Vol. 28, No. 1, pp. 69–85.

Kemper, J. A., Ballantine, P. W., and Hall, C. M. (2019). Combining the 'why' and 'how'of teaching sustainability: The case of the business school academics. *Environmental Education Research*, Vol. 25, pp. 1–24.

Koens, K., Postma, A., and Papp, B. (2018). Is overtourism overused? Understanding the impact of tourism in a city context. *Sustainability*, Vol. 10, No. 12, pp. 4384.

Korstanje, M. (2015). A portrait of Jost Krippendorf. *Anatolia*, Vol. 26, No. 1, pp. 158–164.

Korstanje, M. (2017) *Terrorism, tourism and the end of hospitality in the west*. Palgrave Macmillan, New York, NY.

Korstanje, M. E. (2011). Influence of history in the encounter of guests and hosts. *Anatolia*, Vol. 22, No. 2, pp. 282–285.

Krippendorf, J. (1982). Towards new tourism policies: The importance of environmental and sociocultural factors. *Tourism Management*, Vol. 3, No. 3, pp. 135–148.

Krippendorf, J. (1987). Ecological approach to tourism marketing. *Tourism Management*, Vol. 8, No. 2, pp. 174–176.

Krippendorf, J. (2010). *Holiday makers*. Routledge, London.

Luthar, H. K., and Karri, R. (2005). Exposure to ethics education and the perception of linkage between organizational ethical behavior and business outcomes. *Journal of Business Ethics*, Vol. 61, No. 4, pp. 353–368.

McCool, S. F., and Moisey, R. N. (eds.). (2001). *Tourism, recreation, and sustainability: Linking culture and the environment*. Cabi, Wallingford.

McKenzie-Mohr, D., Lee, N., Schultz, P. W., and Kotler, P. (2012). *Social marketing to protect the environment: What works*. Sage, Thousand Oaks, CA.

McMichael, P. (2016). *Development and social change: A global perspective*. Sage Publications, London.

Milano, C. (2018). Overtourism, malestar social y turismofobia. Un debate controvertido. Revista Pasos, Vol. 16, No. 3, pp. 551–564.

Milano, C. Cheer, J., and Novelli, M. (2019) *Overtourism: Excesses, discontents and measure in travel and tourism*. CABI, Walingford.

Panzer-Krause, S. (2019). Networking towards sustainable tourism: Innovations between green growth and degrowth strategies. *Regional Studies*, Vol. 53, No. 7, pp. 927–938.

Paraskevas, A., and Arendell, B. (2007). A strategic framework for terrorism prevention and mitigation in tourism destinations. *Tourism Management*, Vol. 28, No. 6, pp. 1560–1573.

Pecot, M., and Ricaurte-Quijano, C. (2019) "Todos a galapagos?: Overtourism in wilderness areas of the global sout." In Milano, C., Cheer, J., and Novelli, M. (eds.) *Overtourism: Excesses, discontents and measure in travel and tourism*. CABI, Wallingford, pp. 70–85.

Richter, L. K. (1983). Tourism politics and political science: A case of not so benign neglect. *Annals of Tourism Research*, Vol. 10, No. 3, pp. 313–335.

Santana-Talavera, A. (2006) *Antropología y Turismo: nuevas hordas Viejas culturas?*. Antropology and tourism: New hordes and old cultures?. Ariel Ed, Barcelona.

Schultz, P. W. (2002). "Knowledge, education, and household recycling: Examining the knowledge-deficit model of behavior change." In Dietz, T., and Stern, P. (eds.) *New tools for environmental protection*. National Academy of Sciences, Washington, DC, pp. 67–82.

Schultz, P. W. (2011). Conservation means behavior. *Conservation Biology*, Vol. 25, No. 6, pp. 1080–1083.

Seraphin, H., Sheeran, P., and Pilato, M. (2018). Overtourism and the fall of Venice as a destination. *Journal of Destination Marketing & Management*, Vol. 9, pp. 374–376.

Séraphin, H., Zaman, M., Olver, S., Bourliataux-Lajoinie, S., and Dosquet, F. (2019). Destination branding and overtourism. *Journal of Hospitality and Tourism Management*, Vol. 38, No. 1, pp. 1–4.

Shoval, N., and Isaacson, M. (2007). Tracking tourists in the digital age. *Annals of Tourism Research*, Vol. 34, No. 1, pp. 141–159.

Sönmez, S. F., and Graefe, A. R. (1998). Influence of terrorism risk on foreign tourism decisions. *Annals of Tourism Research*, Vol. 25, No. 1, pp. 112–144.

Stephenson, M. L. (2004). "Tourism, racism and the UK Afro-Caribbean diaspora." In Coles, T., and Timothy, D. (eds.) *Tourism, diasporas and space*. Routledge, London, pp. 62–77.

Swain, S. K., and George, B. P. (2007). HRD practices in the classified hotels in Orissa: A study of employee perceptions. *Número patrocinado por*, Vol. 5, pp. 81–88.

Tosun, C. (2006). Expected nature of community participation in tourism development. *Tourism Management*, Vol. 27, No. 3, pp. 493–504.

Tzanelli, R. (2018). *Cinematic tourist mobilities and the plight of development: On atmospheres, affects, and environments*. Routledge, Abingdon.

Vanhove, N. (1997). "Mass tourism." In Pilgram, J., and Wahab, S. (eds.) *Tourism, development and growth: The challenge of sustainability*. Routledge, London, pp. 50–77.

Visentin, F., and Bertochi, D. (2019) "Venice: An analysis of tourism excess in an overtourism icon." In Milano, C., Cheer, J., and Novelli, M. (eds.) *Overtourism: Excesses, discontents and measure in travel and tourism*. CABI, Wallingford, pp. 18–83.

Xiao, H. (2013). Jafar Jafari: The platform builder. *Anatolia*, Vol. 24, No. 2, pp. 288–296.

Yong, E. L. (2014). Innovation, tourism demand and inflation: Evidence from 14 European countries. *Journal of Economics, Business and Management*, Vol. 2, No. 3, pp. 191–195.

6 Training of human resources in tourism to mitigate overtourism and promote a sustainable destination

Rita R. Carballo, Carmelo J. León, and María M. Carballo

Introduction

Tourism's potential benefits are clear. However, the mistake is to think that it can only bring good. A mass tourism paradigm continues to dominate as numerous entrepreneurs, planners, students, and faculty perceive that it is beneficial and worthwhile to the economic prosperity of a destination and its culture (Weaver, 2007). Overtourism now appears deadly in light of Covid19 in addition to the mandates to avoid crowded conditions (Benjamin, Dillette and Alderman, 2020). Recent changes in the roles of tourists, the development of sustainable destinations, and the need to implement public-private cooperation in the management and control of local and regional tourism development have become necessary in the current international tourism scenario.

Over the last decade, a more critical attitude has been adopted regarding massive tourism models are increasing, not only in the academic and scientific fields but also in the business and professional tourism sector. Tourism, without any doubt, is one of the most powerful drivers of globalisation and plays an important factor in the evolution of the international economy but, on the other hand, the development of this industry based on massive tourism models is generating negative impacts on the environmental sustainability (Carballo, León and Carballo, 2019). The current model of tourism development is unsustainable since it seeks infinite growth while being based on limited natural resources and a limited capacity to absorb the impacts (Rivera and Rodríguez, 2012).

Notably, the hotel industry has been blamed for the environment-related problems (Singjai, Winata and Kummer, 2018). It has eventually spurred rising criticism about the hotels' policies and actions among the scientific community including interested stakeholders (Seele and Gatti, 2017; Choi et al., 2018). It is necessary to analyse the potential of new forms of tourism 'responsible tourism' and how it contributes to the sustainability of the tourist destination. This concept originated in the early 1990s (Smith, 1990; Cooper and Ozdil, 1992). The First International Conference on Responsible Tourism occurred in 2002, leading to the Cape Town Declaration that defined RT as 'tourism that creates better places for people to live in, and better places to visit' (Cape Town, 2009; Mathew and Thankachan, 2019). We define responsible tourism as the,

> tourism activity that tourists and tourism agents carry out with respect for the host places from an environmental, cultural, social and economic point of view, and which in turn is accepted and respected by the host community and protected and promoted by the public authorities.

Therefore, by definition, it is the opposite of overtourism. Overtourism is sometimes simply a case of numbers: there are too many people in a particular place at a particular time. But in some cases, taking a more responsible approach to tourism can mitigate the negative effects.

The issues of sustainability are not sufficiently integrated in tourist training programmes. This chapter analyses the importance of training in the tourism sector. It examines how training in tourism at the Lanzarote University School of Tourism (EUTL), a centre belonging to the University of Las Palmas de Gran Canaria, and the private industry contribute to fight against overtourism in Lanzarote, one of the main tourist destinations in Spain and in Europe, through training in responsible tourism. The EUTL is located in a sustainable tourism destination, Lanzarote, one of Spain's eight Canary Islands. Lanzarote is a destination that has focused on environmental conservation. Due to its environmental efforts, Lanzarote has been granted various environmental certifications. Since 1993 a Biosphere Reserve was created (UNESCO Biosphere Reserves, 1993) and in 2015, it received the UN declaration of Geopark (UNESCO Global Geoparks, 2015), recognising its environmental management. In addition, in 2015, Lanzarote received the Biosphere Responsible Tourism Certification recognised by the Global Sustainable Tourism Council (GSTC) (Biosphere Responsible Tourism, 2015), a body under the World Tourism Organization. The GSTC acknowledges the trajectory followed by the island in advancing sustainability. The award also recognises social responsibility, economic development, environmental compliance, cultural protection, and the involvement of the tourist at the destination. The current study, in addition to natural and cultural environments, also analyses the extent to which the economic sphere is addressed in tourism training programmes.

This chapter proposes an approach to educational training for professionals in the tourism industry with a focus on sustainable development. It investigates the impact of training in tourism on hotels' sustainability practices and examines how training in tourism by the EUTL influences positively and significantly the sustainability of a tourist destination. Perhaps you can find another way to visit the destinations and make sure to support the local community – from your transportation, to where you stay, what you eat, your touristic activities, and the gifts you purchase (Benjamin, Dillette and Alderman, 2020).

Literature review

Over the decades, tourism has experienced continued growth and deepening diversification. International tourist arrivals (overnight visitors) reached 1.407 million worldwide in 2018, Europe was the most common outbound tourism destination in the world (716 million tourists) following by Asia and the Pacific (348 million), America (216 million), Africa (68 million), and the Middle East (59 million) (UNWTO, 2018).

Tourism has been gaining ground in the world's economy. The contribution of tourism to economic well-being depends on the quality and the revenues of the tourism offer. The continuing growth of this sector has a significant impact on labour markets, since tourism is a significant source of employment, due to its labour-intensive nature. The requirement for tourism destinations to deliver high-quality service and products, coupled with the labour-intensive nature of the industry, results in a need for the tourism sector to recruit and retain well-educated and well-trained professionals. There is also evidence that the reported link between a lack of skills/experience and recruitment difficulties is specific to certain sectors of the industry, in particular to hotels, restaurants and travel agents, and certain operative level occupations, in particular chefs/cooks and waiters/waitresses (Dewhurst, Dewhurst and Livesey, 2007; Thomas et al. 1998; Keep and Mayhew, 1999; Thomas et al., 2000).

Training in tourism in Spain

Despite the importance of the quality of human resources in the tourism sector, the incorporation of Tourism Studies into Spanish universities took place quite late. It was not until 1996 that these studies began to be taught at the university level in a country where tourism is one of the main sources of wealth. Tourism Studies in Spain, a pioneering country in mass tourism, were initiated by the private sector in 1957/58 when the course opened in Madrid, the first Tourism School in Spain. Although the tourism workforce is often associated with low levels of education and limited entrepreneurial and managerial skills, this scenario has been changing. On the one hand, there has been a massive increase in the number of educational programmes offered by schools and higher education institutions in this field. In this case, entrepreneurial skills are of paramount importance (Hernández et al., 2010).

The great development of tourism industry in Spain during the 1960s generated a lot of jobs in companies and establishments dedicated to the sector, which determined the need to organise and officially regulate the training of personnel who would exercise new trades and professions to occupy technical positions in companies and establishments that carried out activities in tourism (Dachary and Arnaiz, 2016).

In addition to this, it should be noted that for years, training in the tourist industry in Spain has been described as 'insufficient' and 'incomplete', despite the attempts to improve the offer of studies (Hernández et al., 2010).

The historical trajectory of the training in tourism, initially corresponded to private schools that were supervised from the public sector by the Official School of Tourism, which took place in a non-university context. Next, the study will focus on the academic level, presenting the scenario reached in the Spanish university with the Diploma for Tourism and the new horizon opened by the undergraduate, master's, and PhD degrees from the new European Higher Education Area (EEES).

At the beginning of the 1990s, Torres (1993) made a diagnosis of training in tourism in Spain. At a time when the country was an important international tourist destination, considers that the training situation was characterised by:

- Insufficient: the number of people trained was small compared to the population employed in the sector and ignored the needs of the tourism market.
- Incomplete: it did not cover the different professional levels and sub-sectors that demanded the evolution of tourist activity.
- Non-integrated: lacking a unitary conception at each level of training and of the interrelations between the different levels.
- Obsolete: training not updated to the changes of the tourist markets.

The creation and implementation of an Observatory of human tourism resources can help to understand human capital needs of sub-sectors. One of the improvements proposed in the study by Bañuls (2009), is the increase in the average education level of the tourism sector due to its significance (Liu and Wall, 2006). Since a sector in which the ability to compete increasingly depends on intangible assets, the empowerment of its human capital in terms of education and training becomes more relevant.

The implications for the recruitment of students to universities and the improvement of the human resource will result in a national gain, and at the micro-level businesses and enterprises will benefit from a better-trained workforce and knowledge transferral (Peacock and Ladkin, 2002). The skills of human resources can significantly improve the tourism experience (Fuentes et al., 2015).

The student placement, once the students have finished their studies, has been a subject of analysis by several authors (Botterill, 1996; Tilley and Johnson, 1999; Simm and Hogarth, 2000; Airey and Johnson, 1999). Industry and education need to work together to ensure that the needs of both of the stakeholders are met (Peacock and Ladkin, 2002).

Tourism and the environment

As suggested earlier, a significant step forward in research on complex systems is that environmental concerns, such as protected areas, often require more than one disciplinary perspective or approach in reaching optimal solutions for discrete points of time (Berkes and Folke, 2000). It should be noted that there is a need to establish different dimensions of tourism training. Tourism development plans have different scales, national, regional, and local (Pearce, 1990). Human capital in tourism should be analysed from this triple consideration to establish the strategies to follow in tourism education that can efficiently serve the training needs of the sector (Bañuls, 2009).

Currently, as a consequence of the pandemic in 2020, tourists are not able to travel and instead are forced to stay home and quarantine. Their absence from sites like Venice brings into focus what can be regained in suspending overtourism; the vacant city's iconic canals are being granted an environmental reprieve and allowed to be cleared of pollution and waste (Benjamin, Dillette and Alderman, 2020).

The environment and tourism are related. This chapter analyses the relationship between university training and the local tourism industry in terms of sustainable tourism and overtourism.

The case study

The empirical study reported here was conducted on the island of Lanzarote, one of Spain's eight Canary Islands. It is a volcanic island with an area of 845,94 km² and 152.289 inhabitants in 2019. The island has focused on environmental conservation. Lanzarote has evolved over the last 50 years as a destination which is recognised by these artistically recreated natural resources with Cesar Manrique as its original creator and contributor. Apart from being an important tourist reference, it was a pioneer territory in the fight against land speculation and overtourism.

In the 1970s, Lanzarote was subjected to a rate of expansion that caused overtourism. Within the period between 1967, a year in which the tourist activity as such began, and 1980 the number of visitors increased from 9.585 to 174.709 which is an increase of 1.722.3% coming mainly from the Nordic countries: Sweden, Holland, Finland, and Norway (Libro Blanco, 1997). In the 1980–1991 the influx of visitors to Lanzarote increased by 493.2%, while the number of tourist beds increased by 152.1%. The population of the island increased by 79.9% from the beginning of the tourist activity until 1990 and a growth of 257.3% until now (Carballo, León and Carballo, 2019).

The fight against overtourism: Lanzarote tourism development plan

The Island Council commissioned the implementation of the sustainable development strategy 'Lanzarote in the Biosphere' (E. L+B) (Lanzarote Biosfera, 1998). An ambitious strategy with two central objectives: to preserve the basic balances of the insular system and to improve the quality of life of the Lanzarote population and its visitors. The strategy proposes a change of direction from the island development model towards sustainability. The alternative that E. L+B proposes to change this situation is the action on transport, energy, heritage, culture, or elimination of waste, among other issues. The Plan is an invitation to stop the development of the tourist construction industry for ten years. It warns of the consequences if Lanzarote did not change the development model adopted in recent years. It cannot afford even one bed more, and better a few thousand less (Gimaral, 1997).

The Plan supports the preservation of the extraordinary natural heritage of the island. Tourism had to be compatible with the environmental and cultural conditions of the island. It proposes a series of actions to solve the situation (Biosfera Lanzarote, 1991):

It drastically reduces the area available for new urban and tourist developments.

It established a ceiling on the number of beds (111,000) that could be allocated to hotels, apartments, and residential housing throughout the island.

It also indicated the restrictions in the construction of new buildings for a period of four years.

It provided for low-density construction, five star hotels, and residential tourism.

In 2000 a reform of the Plan was proposed, limiting urban growth rates and setting a maximum of 10,707 new tourist beds, all of them in hotels. The new hotel beds must be at least four stars, and adapt to the Canary Islands Tourism Law, with a building parameter of 60 m^2 per accommodation. In addition, 17.943 residential spaces can be built in those same tourist areas, for the next ten years (Lanzarote Biosfera, 1998).

Training in tourism in Lanzarote

The EUTL is located in Tahíche, managed by the government and belonging to the University of Las Palmas de Gran Canaria. As reference in tourism studies, the EUTL has invested all its efforts in training highly qualified professionals to cover the needs of the main island sector, in one of the most important destinations at the international level. The mission is to commit itself to the continual improvement of the quality of the destination, promoting sustainability in order to avoid overtourism. Choi et al. (2018) reported that hotels need to arrange environmental training programmes for their employees to inflate their sustainability related knowledge, skills, and capacities.

The EUTL organised a second training programme for future tourism companies interested in joining the 'Club of Tourist Product Biosphere Reserves' of Turespaña. The objective of the programme is to connect the tourism sector with all the sustainable actions that are developed on the island, whether they are private or public, within the framework of the Biosphere Reserve.

The following are the characteristics of the tourist sector in Lanzarote. Table 6.1 shows that the employment in the service sector in Lanzarote is high, exceeding 80% annually.

The study finds a very relevant sector in the country. Undoubtedly the sector has comparative advantages, a sector with a great capacity to generate employment even in unfavourable moments of the economic cycle.

The purpose of collecting this information was to ascertain to what extent the tourism industry had recruited graduate students from the EUTL. An overwhelming 84% of the local tourism companies reported that they had recruited EUTL graduate students permanently over the past six years, while 16% said they had not.

Students graduated in tourism at the EUTL represent the highest rate of labour market insertion compared to the total numbers of students enrolled at the University of Las Palmas de Gran Canaria in the 2015/2016 period (Table 6.2). Even compared to any other degree, the rate is higher only for the degree in relations labour.

Table 6.1 Lanzarote total service sector employment (%) (2009–2019)

Year	Service sector
2009	86.4
2010	87.8
2011	88.8
2012	89.9
2013	90.5
2014	90.1
2015	90.0
2016	89.7
2017	89.4
2018	88.9
2019	89.0

Source: Canary Islands Institute of Statistics (ISTAC).

Table 6.2 Insertion of employment of the graduate students in Tourism (%) (2014–2016)

	2013/2014	2014/2015	2015/2016
EUTL tourism	95.7	83.3	91.7
University of Las Palmas de Gran Canaria (ULPGC) Tourism	78.9	84.4	80.4

Source: Canary Islands Institute of Statistics (ISTAC).

On the other hand, the unemployment rate of graduate students in tourism from the EUTL is only 5% over the last years (Table 6.3).

Concerning the type of contract, employability rate exceeds 90% of graduate students in tourism, with long-term contracts being the most common as they exceed 60% of the total volume (Table 6.4).

Considering these data, the study analyses if training in tourism at both, the EUTL and the tourism companies where the students work once graduate from university, contribute to the sustainability of the tourism destination, through the control of overtourism and other measures. Therefore, the following hypotheses are proposed.

H₁: *Training in tourism at the EUTL influences positively and significantly in the sustainability of the tourist destination*

H₂: Training in tourism at the industry influences positively and significantly in the sustainability of the tourist destination (Figure 6.1)

Table 6.3 Employment and unemployment rate of tourism graduate students by EUTL (%) (2013–2016)

	2013/2014	*2014/2015*	*2015/2016*
Employment rate	94.9	95.9	94.4
Unemployment rate	5.1	4.1	5.6

Source: Canary Islands Institute of Statistics (ISTAC).

Table 6.4 Employment rate according to the modality of the graduates in tourism by EUTL (%) (2013–2016)

Type of contract	*2013/2014*	*2014/2015*	*2015/2016*
Employability rate	91.7	93.4	94.2
Self-employment rate	8.3	6.6	5.8
Long-term contracts	63.9	67.5	66.2
Short-term contracts	24.2	23.9	26.1
No duration of the contract is stated	11.9	8.7	7.7

Source: Canary Islands Institute of Statistics (ISTAC).

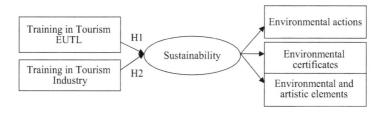

Figure 6.1 Proposed theoretical model.

Data and methodology

An empirical study has been carried out to investigate how training in tourism has contributed to solving the problems of overtourism in Lanzarote. The study, therefore, proposes the hypothesis that training in tourism positively influences the sustainability of the destination and therefore contributes to the control of overtourism.

The survey instrument for this study was developed using a mixed methodology approach. Initially, in-depth interviews were conducted with experts in the hospitality busyness and the Government of Lanzarote, in March 2018. The final questionnaire was developed as the survey instrument including all constructs of the proposed model to investigate training in tourism and the sustainability of the destination.

The questionnaire was designed in Spanish and administered personally to the graduate students who are working in the hospitality business in Lanzarote, and to experts in the sector. All the graduates employed had studied tourism or hospitality programmes at the university. A variety of tourism companies were included in the sample (Table 6.5). Undertaking interviews with tourism businesses may have the added benefit of raising awareness of university activities. A decision was taken at the outset that, where email addresses were available, the questionnaire would be sent electronically. While recognising the difficulties involved in email-based survey research (Witmer, Colman and Katzman, 1999), this was done for ease of access and cost-effectiveness (Peacock and Ladkin, 2002).

The largest types of companies represented in the simple were hotels, resorts and attractions. The hospitality sub-sector, the most representative tourist branch in the sector (Table 6.6)

Most of the companies had been involved with EUTL students through short paid work. One of the reasons for hiring graduates in companies is the size of the company. According to Simm and Hogarth (2000) the relationship between size and involvement in work placements or work experience is significant. The larger companies have an identifiable human resource function to liaise with the university and are more able to provide a more

Table 6.5 Types of tourism companies

Type of company	Percentage of respondents
Hotel	23
Resorts	18
Attraction	17
Air companies	9
Travel agent	8
Ferry operator	8
Hotel booking agency	6
Tourist transport and rent a car	6
Tour operator	5

appropriate learning environment (Peakcook and Ladkin, 2002). This is in line with Cooper and Shepherd (1997) that reflects that the provision of a substantial period of work experience is not an option for many small and medium-sized businesses. The size of an organisation is also likely to play a part in determining an employer's perception of skills shortages and recruitment difficulties. Small tourism and hospitality firms, in particular, are less likely to perceive recruitment difficulties than larger firms (Dewhurst, Dewhurst and Livesey, 2007; Thomas and Long, 2001).

The fieldwork took place during June and August 2018, to ensure an adequate collection of tourism graduate working samples, due to the high occupation of tourists in that period. The population was chosen to represent a range of local tourism businesses, including accommodation, travel agents, tour operators, attractions, entertainment, Tourist Information Office, and transport business (Table 6.5).

A total of 187 usable questionnaires were collected. The selection of individuals was done to meet a set of quotas regarding the following sociodemographic variables: gender, age, occupation. Table 6.7 presents the socioeconomic characteristics of the sample. Nevertheless, the sample size is relatively small, and the data must be treated with caution. However, responses do serve to provide initial findings and to identify areas for further research.

Intending to analyse the interaction between the training in tourism at the university, training in tourism at the industry and the sustainability

Table 6.6 Involvement in work experience and placement

Type of work experience/placement	%
Work placement	13
Short paid work experience	58
Long paid work experience	29

Table 6.7 Demographic data on the sample

Variables	Tourism graduate students	Managers
Country of origin (N)	156	31
Gender (%)	38	59
Male	62	41
Female		
Age (%)	13	0
18–27	29	6
28–37	21	23
38–47	19	31
48–57	13	38
58–67	5	2
More than 67		

of a tourism destination, the first part of the questionnaire focused on the sustainability of tourism destinations and the control of the overtourism on the island. The second part of the questionnaire focused on questions about the sustainability of the destination. There have been various proposals in the literature for the evaluation of sustainability scales (Carballo and León, 2018; Carballo, Carballo and León, 2018; Russell and Pratt, 1980; Russell, Ward and Pratt, 1981). The study utilised a scale based on 10 attributes evaluated with a seven-point Likert-type (1=Very bad; 7=Very good) question format. The last part of the questionnaire collected the personal and socioeconomic characteristics of the tourists.

Modelling

Data were processed utilising SPSS 20 and AMOS 20 statistic packages. The analysis was conducted in two stages. In the first stage, the measurement model is carried out for the underlying dimensions of sustainability. In the second stage, and using the results from the first stage, a Structural Equations Model (SEM) approach was conducted to investigate the above hypotheses of the relationships between the constructs. This technique allows researchers to appraise causal relationships between variables in complex models involving direct and indirect effects, as well as simultaneous relationships between variables. Further, whereas other multivariate techniques can deal only with observable measurements, SEM can work with latent variables, i.e. variables which are not directly measured but are inferred in the model from other variables that are related.

Findings

Measurement model

The Measurement Model analyses the attributes that constitute sustainability at the destination through factorial analysis.

First, an exploratory analysis of scale reliability (EFA) was performed to the multi-attribute dimensions of sustainability at the destination. The purpose of the exploratory factor analysis is to summarise the information of a larger set of variables into fewer constructs that were deemed to represent the underlying dimensions of the variables. Before an evaluation of the structural part of the model, CFA was recommended because it provides further confirmation of the strength of the psychometric properties of the scales (Noar, 2003). Based on the result of EFA and theoretical background, CFA was performed on the measurement model to confirm the structure found in EFA.

The results of EFA applied to the ten environmental attributes of sustainability lead to three factors (Table 6.8). They could be extracted using a principal component analysis with varimax rotation. The KMO measure

Table 6.8 CFA results. List of items and scale reliabilities

Scale and item from sustainability	Factor loadings
Environmental and artistic elements	
Art elements in the destination and design of natural resources	.88
Natural/environmental conservation	.78
Flora and fauna biodiversity	.70
Environmental certificates	
Biosphere Reserve	.89
Biosphere Responsible Tourism	.87
Global Geopark	.80
Environmental actions	
Use of alternative energies	.84
Use of recyclable material	.77
Temperature and humidity	.70

of sampling adequacy of .969 and Bartlett's test of sphericity (X^2=764, df=363; p<.000) confirmed the suitability of the data for factorisation since the relative value of X^2 concerning the degrees of freedom (X^2/df) should not exceed 5 (though below 3 is better) (Chen and Tsai, 2007). One attribute (good recycling system) was deleted due to its low standardised coefficient. Cronbach's alpha values range from .835 for factor 2 to .714 for factor 1. The application of the CFA to the sustainability showed a good fit of the model (GFI=.990; AGFI=.987; CFI=.902; TLI=.921; IFI=.933; RFI=.925; NFI=.911; RMSEA=.048) since the estimated for the model are all above 0.9, and the root mean square error of approximation statistics (RMSEA) is lower than the maximum value of.08, which is considered a good level of fit for the model according to recent studies (Wang, Cole and Chen, 2018; Carballo, León and Carballo, 2017; Mason and Paggiaro, 2012).

Structural model

The SEM approach makes a simultaneous estimation of the relationships between the latent variables and the attributes or observed variables, and the determination of the validity and reliability of the measures (Jorskog and Sorbom, 1989). The study applies the SEM approach to analyse the relationships between the training in tourism and *sustainability of the destination.*

The structural model (Figure 6.2) shows coefficients in a standardised form. The results of the SEM prove that the goodness of fit is satisfactory (X^2/df=2,2; p<.00), the estimated indices are above 0.9 (GFI=.925; AGFI=.914; CFI=.901; TLI=.912; IFI=.985; RFI=.955; NFI=.978; RMSEA=0.6). The statistical significance of parameter estimates was examined through the critical ratio (CR) test statistic. The CRs for paths should be outside the threshold range of ±1.96 to be considered significant (Byrne, 2001) (Table 6.9). All path coefficients were positive and significant at the 5% level with values ranging from a high of 15.28 (Training in tourism at the EUTL → Sustainability of the tourist destination) to a low of 13.25 (Training in tourism at the industry → Sustainability of the tourist destination), which provides evidence of convergent validity (Anderson and Gerbing, 1988).

Among the three factors of sustainability of the destination, 'environmental actions' (β=.83) is the most important explanation, followed by the 'environmental certificates' (β=.74) and the 'environmental and artistic elements' (β=.63).

According to the structural parameters of interest, the estimates are all highly significant; the regression coefficients are significant as they were less than 5% probability. These suggest that the hypotheses are proven with the empirical data thereby accepting the two hypotheses (Table 6.9). Thus, the training in tourism in the EUTL has a positive and significant influence on the sustainability of the destination (β=.68 and p<.000), thereby accepting H_1.

The higher training in tourism in the EUTL the higher sustainability of the destination is. Thus, training of tourism at the Universities contributes to the reduction and control of overtourism and therefore to the sustainability of the tourism destination. In the same way, the training in tourism in the industry, although to a lesser extent than training in university, has a positive and significant influence on the sustainability of the destination (β=.51; p<.000), accepting H_3. Thus, we can say that training in tourism in the industry also contributes to the control of overtourism and the sustainability of the tourist destination.

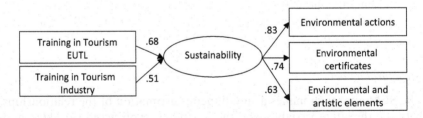

Figure 6.2 The estimated structural model.

Table 6.9 Standardised estimates of structural paths

Direct effect	Estimate	SE	CR	P	Results
H_1: Training in tourism EUTL → Sustainability of the tourist destination	0.68	0.058	15.28	0.00	Accept
H_2: Training in tourism industry → Sustainability of the tourist destination	0.51	0.042	13.25	0.00	Accept

Conclusion

One of the great demands of the tourism business sector has always been closely related to the need to improve employee training (Gestión de Hoteles, 2008). By conceiving of tourism as a social force (rather just a market opportunity) and empowered by studies of humanities and their critical epistemologies, one can see how tourism has the power to change people and societies and, to quote Sheldon, the power to shift from a 'me to we' economy (Benjamin, Dillette and Alderman, 2020). While there are a variety of perspectives on the relative value of different forms of the training intervention, it is widely accepted that training is beneficial to business performance (Thomas and Long, 2001; Kitching and Blackburn, 2002). Despite this, the tourism industry has a reputation as being a poor trainer (Beaver and Lashley, 1998; Jameson, 2000).

Thus, it is a fact that the human resources engaged in tourism are indissolubly linked to the quality of the tourism product, so the competitiveness of companies and/or destinations is closely linked to the professionalism of workers, capable of transmitting a positive image to their customers and providing services that make it possible to meet expectations and to repeat or recommend the destination (Bañuls, 2009). In this sense, the university of the future is already reality, from which we can expect some effects on training in the sector. There is a need to move towards strategies for a greater proportion of workers with medium and higher education. Human resource is a crucial element for the achievement of goals in terms of competitiveness and growth in the tourism sector. There seems to be no doubt that much of the ability to address these challenges will come from improvements in their human resources, which is often identified as part of the service offered (Acosta, Fernández and Mollón, 2002; Lillo, 2007). A less training labour force is at the beginning less likely to generate and/or adopt innovations of all kinds (technological and organisational, among others), has a lower capacity to adapt to changes and is, therefore, less likely to contribute to improving the competitiveness of the sector (Lillo-Bañuls and Casado-Díaz, 2011).

The Department for Culture Media and Sport (DCMS, 2004: 22) warned that

> If the tourism industry is to deliver a truly high-quality product, it must become the career of choice for more of our brightest and most ambitious people. If that is to happen, high-quality training and development strategies are needed, covering the entire range of activities from "hands-on" skills to management, and addressing the needs of both the industry and individuals.

A well-trained and skilful workforce is crucial for tourism to prosper. The sector can provide incentives to invest in education and vocational training and assist labour mobility through cross-border agreements on qualifications, standards, and certifications. In particular youth, women, senior citizens, indigenous peoples, and those with special needs should benefit through educational means, where tourism has the potential to promote inclusiveness, the values of a culture of tolerance, peace and non-violence, and all aspects of global exchange and citizenship. (UNWTO, 2018). On the other hand, this study can state that the tourism promotion of cultural attractions linked to the creative management of natural assets can be managed as useful tools for the regeneration and revitalisation of cultural resources, thereby contributing to the sustainability of tourist destinations (Richards and Marques, 2012). The results show that there is a general acceptance that changes have to occur in the provision of training in the tourism industry in order to improve sustainability. However, these changes are often recommended by academics and not necessarily accepted by the industry.

This study contributes to sustainable tourism research by investigating the usefulness of using creativity and art in sustainable destination management. They are considered important elements that bring opportunities for the differentiation and specialisation of tourist destinations since they are increasingly demanded by tourists and can contribute to the sustainability of the destination. This chapter has addressed the contribution that the creativity factors make to the sustainability of the tourist destinations. From a general point of view, conservation of the cultural heritage has been considered as a dimension of the sustainability of a destination (Carballo and León, 2018; Richards and Wilson, 2006). The perceptions tourists have about the environmental conditions of the destination are found to influence the sustainability of the destination. That is, environmental actions contribute directly to sustainability, followed by the factors of environmental certification and management. Therefore, the results suggest that when there are important artistic environmental attractions at the destination, tourists might perceive the sustainability capability of the destination mostly through the factors of creativity. The implication is that creativity and art creation based on natural resources may be playing an important role in image formation similarly to more conventional approaches to sustainability.

There are two important additional issues to be mentioned here. Sustainable tourism is a holistic approach: it seeks to build the wider aspects of society and the economy as well as tourism, supporting art, culture and conservation (Bramwell and Lane, 1993). Lanzarote brings tourists together with those wider aspects. Furthermore, the growing interest in sustainable tourism marketing 'demonstrates the breadth of approaches that can be utilized to understand how consumers can be influenced to make more sustainable choices that do not compromise their main motivations' (Font and McCabe, 2017). However, when graduate students had been employed all had graduated in tourism and or hospitality rather than in business studies or another discipline. It is difficult to know whether tourism/hospitality graduate students truly have a competitive advantage, or whether this situation simply reacts to graduate students moving from work experience into full-time employment. This needs to be clarified by further research through a comparison with other sectors. It may be the work experience that enables the graduate students to obtain employment, rather than their specific skills or degree titles. Another limitation of this study is that it considers only the environmental aspects of sustainability. More evidence would be welcome regarding the relationships between sustainable tourism and overtourism at a destination.

References

Acosta, A. J., Fernández, N., and Mollón, M. (2002). *Recursos humanos en empresas de turismo y hostelería.* Madrid: Pearson Educación.

Airey, D., and Johnson, S. (1999). "The content of tourism degree courses in the UK." *Tourism Management*, 20(2), 229–235.

Anderson, J. C., and Gerbing, D. W. (1988). "Structural equation modeling in practice: A review and recommended two-step approach." *Psychological Bulletin*, 103(3), 411.

Bañuls, A. L. (2009). "El papel del capital humano en el sector turístico: Algunas reflexiones y propuestas." *Cuadernos de turismo*, 24, 53–64.

Beaver, G., and Lashley, C. (1998). "Barriers to management development in small hospitality firms." *Strategic Change*, 7(4), 223–235.

Becton, S., and Graetz, B. (2001). "Small business—Small minded? Training attitudes and needs of the tourism and hospitality industry." *International Journal of Tourism Research*, 3(2), 105–113.

Benjamin, S., Dillette, A., and Alderman, D. H. (2020). "'We can't return to normal:' Committing to tourism equity in the post-pandemic age." *Tourism Geographies*, 22(3), 476–483.

Berkes, F., and Folke, C. (eds.) (2000). *Linking Social and Ecological Systems: Management Practices and Social Mechanisms for Building Resilience.* Cambridge: Cambridge University Press.

Biosfera Lanzarote. (1991). Available at: http://lanzarotebiosfera.org/ordenacion/instrumentos-deplanificacion/piot.

Biosphere Responsible Tourism. (2015). Available at: https://www.biospheretourism.com/en/entity/lanzarote/136.

Botterill, D. (1996). *Making Connections Between Industry and Higher Education in Tourism*, Guideline No. 5, NLG, The Tourism Society, London.

Bramwell, B. and Lane, B. (1993). "Sustainable tourism: An evolving global approach." *Journal of Sustainable Tourism*, 1(1), 1–5.

Byrne, B. M. (2001). "Structural equation modeling with AMOS, EQS, and LISREL: Comparative approaches to testing for the factorial validity of a measuring instrument." *International Journal of Testing*, 1(1), 55–86.

Cape Town. (2009). *Responsible tourism policy for the city of Cape Town. The City of Cape Town Tourism Department.*

Carballo, R. R., Carballo, M. M., and León, C. J. (2018). The tourist centres' image. In Séraphin, H. and Nolan, E. (Eds.), *Green Events and Green Tourism: An International Guide to Good Practice*, London: Routledge.

Carballo, R., León, C., and Carballo, M. (2019). "Fighting overtourism at Lanzarote (Spain)." *Worldwide Hospitality and Tourism Themes*, 11(5), 506–515. Emerald Publishing Limited 1755–4217. doi: 10.1108/WHATT-06-2019–0043 (In print).

Carballo, R. R., and León, C. J. (2018). "The influence of artistically recreated nature on the image of tourist destinations: Lanzarote's art, cultural and tourism visitor centres and their links to sustainable tourism marketing." *Journal of Sustainable Tourism*, 26(2), 192–204.

Carballo, R. R., León, C. J., and Carballo, M. M. (2017). "The perception of risk by international travelers." *Worldwide Hospitality and Tourism Themes*, 9(5), 534–542.

Chen, C. F., and Tsai, D. 2007. "How destination image and evaluative factors affect behavioral intentions?" *Tourism Management*, 28(4), 1115–1122.

Choi, H. M., Kim, W. G., Kim, Y. J., and Agmapisarn, C. (2018). "Hotel environmental management initiative (HEMI) scale development." *International Journal of Hospitality Management*, Article in press.

Cooper, C., and Ozdil, I. (1992). "From mass to responsible tourism: The Turkish experience." *Tourism Management*, 13(4), 377–386. doi:10.1016/0261-5177(92)90005-r.

Cooper, C., and Shepherd, R. (1997), "The relationship between tourism education and the tourism industry: Implications for tourism education." *Tourism Recreation Research*, 22(1), 34–47.

Dachary, A. C., and Arnaiz, F. C. (2016). "Educación universitaria y turismo." *Revista Latino-Americana de Turismologia*, 2(2), 8–17.

Dewhurst, H., Dewhurst, P., and Livesey, R. (2007). "Tourism and hospitality SME training needs and provision: A sub-regional analysis." *Tourism and Hospitality Research*, 7(2), 131–143.

Font, X., and McCabe, S. (2017). "Sustainability and marketing in tourism: Its contexts, paradoxes, approaches, challenges and potential." *Journal of Sustainable Tourism*, 25(7), 869–883.

Fuentes, R. C., Moreno-Gil, S., González, C. L., and Ritchie, J. B. (2015). "Designing and promoting experiences in a tourist destination. An analysis of research and action needs." *Cuadernos de Turismo*, 35, 435–438.

Gestión de hotels. (2008). *La formación: Objetivo prioritario para las cadenas hoteleras, Gestión de hoteles*, 77, 40–41.

Gimaral, C. (1997). "Lanzarote, reserva de la biosfera, oportunidad o camelo?" Cuadernos del Guincho, 3, 32–41.

Hernández, C. C., Martín, C. A., Jiménez, A. R., Domínguez, C. S., and Bermúdez, I. V. (2010). "La formación en turismo en España: Pasado, presente y futuro en el nuevo Espacio Europeo de Educación Superior." *Cuadernos de turismo*, 25, 45–67.

Jameson, S. M. (2000). "Recruitment and training in small firms." *Journal of European Industrial Training*.

Jorskog, K. G., and Sorbom, D. 1989. *LISREL 7-A Guide to the Program and Applications* (2nd ed.). Chicago: SPSS Publications.

Keep, E., and Mayhew, K. (1999). *Skills Task Force Research Paper 6–The Leisure Sector*. London: DfEE.

Kitching, J., and Blackburn, R. (2002). *The Nature of Training and Motivation to Train in Small Firms*, Research Report RR330, Research Centre Kingston University, available at: https://dera.ioe.ac.uk/4691/1/RR330.pdf

Lanzarote Biosfera. (1998). Available at: http://lanzarotebiosfera.org/biosfera/moratoria/pasa3.htm.

Libro Blanco. (1997). "Atlántida international consultants SL," *Consejería de turismo y Transporte del Gobierno de Canarias. Cabildo de Lanzarote.* Depósito Legal: TF-2.583/97.

Lillo-Bañuls, A., and Casado-Díaz, J. M. (2011). "Capital humano y turismo: Rendimiento educativo, desajuste y satisfacción laboral." *Estudios de economía aplicada*, 29(3), 755–780.

Lillo Bañuls, A., Rodríguez, R., and Sevilla Jjiménez, M. (2007). "El capital Humano como factor estratégico para la competitividad del sector turístico." *Cuadernos de Turismo*, 19, 47–69.

Liu, A., and Wall, G. (2006). "Planning tourism employment: A developing country perspective." *Tourism Management*, 27(1), 159–170.

Mason, M. C., and Paggiaro, A. (2012). "Investigating the role of festivalscape in culinary tourism: The case of food and wine events." *Tourism Management*, 33(6), 1329–1336.

Mathew, P. V., and Thankachan, S. S. (2019). "Responsible and sustainable tourism: A comparison of community perceptions." *Journal of Tourism Management Research*, 6(1), 82–92.

Noar, S. M. (2003). "The role of structural equation modeling in scale development." *Structural Equation Modeling*, 10(4), 622–647.

Peacock, N., and Ladkin, A. (2002). "Exploring relationships between higher education and industry: A case study of a university and the local tourism industry." *Industry and Higher Education*, 16(6), 393–401.

Pearce, D. G. (1990). "Tourism in Ireland: Questions of scale and organization." *Tourism Management*, 11(2), 133–151.

Richards, G., and Marques, L. (2012). *Exploring Creative Tourism*: Editors introduction.

Richards, G., and Wilson, J. (2006). "Developing creativity in tourist experiences: A solution to the serial reproduction of culture?" *Tourism Management*, 27(6), 1209–1223.

Russell, J. A., and Pratt, G. (1980). "A description of the affective quality attributed to environments." *Journal of Personality and Social Psychology*, 38, 311–322.

Russell, J. A., Ward, L. M., and Pratt, G. (1981). "Affective quality attributed to environments a factor analytic study." *Environment and Behavior*, 13(3), 259–288.

Seele, P., and Gatti, L. (2017). "Greenwashing revisited: In search of a typology and accusation-based definition incorporating legitimacy strategies." *Business Strategy and the Environment*, 26(2), 239–252.

Simm, C., and Hogarth, T. (2000). Modern Universities and SMEs: Building Relationships. Available at: http://www.wmin.ac.uk/static/cmushortz.htm.

Singjai, K., Winata, L., and Kummer, T. F. (2018). "Green initiatives and their competitive advantage for the hotel industry in developing countries." *International Journal of Hospitality Management*, 75, 131–143.

Smith, V.L. (1990). "Alternative/responsible tourism seminar." *Annals of Tourism Research*, 17(3), 479–480. doi.org/10.1016/0160-7383(90)90015-j.

Thomas, R., Church, I., Eaglen, A., Jameson, S., Lincoln, G., and Parsons, D. (1998). "The national survey of small tourism and hospitality firms: Annual report 1997–1998." *The national survey of small tourism and hospitality firms: Annual report 1997–1998*.

Thomas, R., Lashley, C., Rowson, B., Xie, Y., Jameson, S., Eaglen, A., and Parsons, D. (2000). *The National Survey of Small Tourism and Hospitality Firms: 2000*,

Skills Demands and Training Practices, Research Report, Nottingham Trent University, available at: http://irep.ntu.ac.uk/id/eprint/6891/Thomas, R., and Long, J. (2001). "Tourism and economic regeneration: The role of skills development." *International Journal of Tourism Research*, 3(3), 229–240.

Tilley, F., and Johnson, D. (1999), "Modernization of universities through greater interaction with small firms." *Industry and Higher Education*, 13(2), 119–126.

Torres Bernier, E. (1993). "Capacitación y formación turística en España." In Marchena, M., Fourneau, F., y Granados, V.(eds) *Crisis del turismo? Las perspectivas en el nuevo escenario internacional*, pp. 93–103.

UNESCO Biosphere Reserves. (1993). Available at: http://www.unesco.org/new/en/natural-sciences/environment/ecological-sciences/biosphere-reserves/europe-north-america/.

UNESCO Global Geoparks. (2015). Available at: http://www.unesco.org/new/en/natural-sciences/environment/earth-sciences/unesco-global-geoparks/list-of-unesco-global-geoparks/spain/lanzarote-and-chinijo-islands/.

UNWTO. (2018). *European Union Tourism Trends. ISBN printed version: 978–92–844–1946-3 ISBN electronic version: 978–92–844–1947-0 | DOI: 10.18111/97892 84419470*

Wang, W., Cole, S. T., and Chen, J. S. (2018). "Tourist innovation in Air travel." *Journal of Travel Research*, 57(2), 164–177.

Weaver, D. (2007). "Towards sustainable mass tourism: Paradigm shift or paradigm nudge?" *Tourism Recreation Research*, 32(3), 65–69.

Witmer, D. F., Colman, R. W., and Katzman, S. L. (1999). *From Paper-and-Pencil to Screen-and-Keyboard*. Thousand Oaks, CA: Sage, pp. 145–162.

7 The impact of tourism education on tourism destination performance and sustainability

Ovidiu I. Moisescu, Oana A. Gică, and Monica M. Coroş

Introduction

Recent years witnessed a change in the tourism competition that shifted from price-centred products (services) towards quality-centred products (services) (Wei, 2015). As this sector is labour-intensive, the quality of the tourist experience depends on employee performance (Andrades and Dimanche, 2019), the qualifications of tourism professionals representing an essential success factor (Chung-Herrera et al., 2003; Marinakou and Giousmpasoglou, 2015; Mbarushimana et al., 2017). Therefore, tourism destinations should strive to improve the level of education within the tourism labour force in order to be competitive.

However, research to date has not examined whether an improvement of education levels brings better tourism destination performance and success. Most previous research regarding the antecedents of tourism destination development have considered traditional determinants such as tourism products' prices and tourists' incomes. Also, little attention has been paid to antecedents that are related to the destinations' level of development such as, for example, the level of education and skills of its workforce. Furthermore, most studies involving the human capital in tourism have been focused on emphasising the industry's potential to create jobs, its low entry barriers to the labour market, or its general image of low salaries, inconsistent working time or few opportunities for career advancement (Duncan et al., 2013; Riley et al., 2002).

The relationship between tourism destination development and its workforce quantity and/or quality is a largely uncharted area within tourism research (Åberg and Müller, 2018). This is not surprising, as specific data regarding public or private investment in tourism education is quasi-absent from mainstream data sources (e.g. OECD, Eurostat). Moreover, data regarding the number of graduates in tourism specific fields of education has been rigorously collected for only a few years, since the introduction of the 2013 International Standard Classification of Education for Fields of Education and Training (UNESCO Institute for Statistics, 2014).

This chapter aims at filling the consistent knowledge gap regarding the relationship between tourism education and tourism destination development, assessing the importance of tourism education for the competitiveness and sustainability of tourism destinations.

Theoretical background

The continuous growth both in the number of tourists and tourism revenue since the Second World War demonstrates that tourism is one of the fastest-growing sectors of the global economy. Tourism is also an important and contemporary area of social life possessing a high capacity for generating new jobs, contributing to the improvement of local life quality and enhancing competitiveness of regions (Maráková et al., 2016). Tourism is a high contact-degree service industry which requires the employees in this industry to have higher competence (Wei, 2015) possessing the skills and knowledge necessary to meet the requirements of employers in the tourism sector (Wang et al., 2010). Tourism as a service industry relies on the quality of its labour to develop and enhance the quality of the tourism product (Ladkin, 2005). A good workforce contributes to the competitive advantage of enterprises by adding value to the product on offer (Cooper and Shepherd, 1997) and being able to rise to the present and future challenges facing the sector (UNWTO, 2009). Education has become increasingly important, as a valuable starting point for the development of human capital, the relationship between jobs and education being central to the development of human capital (Ladkin, 2005).

The fundamental role of training and education in ensuring a professional and productive tourism industry has been recognised by key international bodies such as the World Tourism Organization (WTO), the International Labour Organisation (ILO) and the World Travel and Tourism Council (WTTC) (Cooper and Shepherd, 1997). On the short term, training ensures employees the practical skills and knowledge, while education contributes, on the long term, to improving the quality of both service and personnel within the tourism industry (Cooper and Shepherd, 1997).

While tourism has become a global industry, with more and more international arrivals from year to year, destinations face worldwide competition. Moreover, technology has invaded the tourism sector, implying new challenges for both managers and skilled workforce. In this context, in order to perform well, businesses seek employees who are able to adapt quickly to sectoral changes, meeting novel technological requirements; who are multilingual; who are capable of properly responding to the expectations and desires of the more and more sophisticated contemporary tourists; and who enable businesses to adapt and adopt sustainable policies, which, in their turn, generate significant changes related to the development of existing and new jobs and respective labour skills (OECD, 2011). In order to increase their competitiveness, companies in the tourism sector are implementing a culture of high quality of service provision by improving the educational standards of the workforce (Eurico et al., 2015; Mayaka and King, 2002). As professionalism is a prerequisite of the achievement of quality standards in services there is an agreement that higher education institutions should provide the tourism industry with well-trained graduates (Barron, 2007; Baum, 2007; Choy, 1995, Engberg, 2007).

There is a need for a dynamic and continuous adjustment between the higher education institutions and the tourism industry (Eurico et al., 2015) as the sustainable development of this sector characterised by the intangibility of the services offered depends largely on the skills of its human resources (Ladkin, 2011). The success and sustainability of destinations does not only depend on the quality and attractiveness of their resources and facilities but is strictly linked to the high quality of the provided services. This last aspect is closely dependent on the comprehension, professionalism, commitment, and organising skills of the employees, respectively on the adoption of efficient strategies for the development of human resources (Ţigu et al., 2010). Tourism destinations need to address in a sustainable way the various changes in globalisation, technology, consumption patterns, and an increasing number of global shocks (Cotterell et al., 2019). For this, destinations need professionals able to understand and operationalise diverse problem-solving tools and approaches whilst being cognizant of the complex political and social dynamics shaping the tourism system (Fodness, 2017). Zhang (2017) points out that the greatest sustainable competitive advantage of organisations and, likewise, of destinations, is the ability of the workforce to learn, change, and adapt, while properly facing challenges to cut costs, improve quality, increase productivity, and develop new products and services at a faster pace. Obviously, some destinations manage to cope with increasing demands and expectations, while others struggle or even fail.

All levels of education (vocational training and schooling, secondary schooling, respectively, tertiary or higher education) are considered crucial, being associated with the successful performance of tourist destinations. Strong public-private partnerships are expected to contribute to the market orientation of the educational and training offer, enabling the private sector to contribute directly to the development of the curriculum and course contents, while also generating internship opportunities for practical, on-the-job training and increasing the attractivity of tourism-related careers (OECD, 2011).

Research methodology

In order to assess the relationship between tourism education and tourism destination performance, this study considered four essential indicators as proxies. Thus, the number of graduates in the 'Personal services' field of education (upper secondary vocational, post-secondary non-tertiary vocational, and tertiary education), as defined by the International Standard Classification of Education for Fields of Education and Training – ISCED-F 2013 (UNESCO Institute for Statistics, 2014), was considered as proxy for tourism education. According to this standard, 'Hotel, restaurants and catering' education and 'Travel, tourism and leisure' education represent core components of the 'Personal services' field of education.

Further on, as proxies for tourism destination performance, three important key performance indicators for the accommodation industry were considered: the number of nights spent at tourist accommodation establishments, the turnover in the accommodation industry, and, respectively, the added value (at factor cost) in the industry (the gross income from operating activities after adjusting for operating subsidies and indirect taxes).

All data regarding the indicators presented above were extracted from the Eurostat database in February 2020, for all available years and countries included in the European database. As the number of graduates in the 'Personal services' field of education was only available for five years (between 2013 and 2017), the data were structured considering this specific timeframe. For some European countries (e.g. Croatia, Ireland, Italy, the Netherlands, Switzerland, United Kingdom) data on the target indicators were not available or only partially available for the considered timeframe. Consequently, these countries were excluded from the analysis, the final investigated sample comprising 23 countries (14 developed countries and 9 developing countries). The structured data for the investigated sample of countries are presented in detail in Table 7.1.

Further on, to operationalise the assessment of the relationship between tourism education and tourism destination performance via their proxy indicators, an index has been computed intended to reflect the percentual change of each of the four indicators in the 2013–2017 timeframe:

Change index = Average (2015, 2016, 2017) / Average (2013, 2014, 2015) – 1

As one may notice, the index reflecting the evolution of the indicators was based on moving averages, instead of initial and final values. This was done in order to smooth out short-term fluctuations and emphasise longer-term trends. The change indices for all indicators and countries are presented in detail in Table 7.2.

Results and discussion

The key issue that stands out when scrutinising the data is the fact that developing European countries have generally gone through a decrease in the number of tourism education graduates between 2013 and 2017. The change index values in the case of Estonia and Latvia, for example, are −23.74% and −20.94%, respectively. Czechia and Slovakia have also recorded a significant decrease in the number of tourism education graduates (change index values of −14.37% and −11.99%, respectively). On the other hand, developed European countries have generally benefited from an increase in the

Table 7.1 Proxy indicators for tourism education and tourism destination performance

		Number of graduates in the 'Personal services' field of education[a]					Thousands of nights spent at tourist accommodation establishments				
		2013	2014	2015	2016	2017	2013	2014	2015	2016	2017
Developed countries	Austria	10,523	10,332	10,975	10,366	9,809	110,687	110,441	113,366	117,957	121,127
	Belgium	10,654	10,049	14,361	13,697	17,526	31,448	32,606	38,380	36,855	38,677
	Cyprus	559	617	632	803	696	14,049	13,715	13,375	15,349	16,781
	Denmark	3,222	3,324	2,496	3,874	3,740	28,501	29,647	30,809	31,896	32,158
	Finland	12,055	12,232	13,037	12,459	11,811	20,241	19,786	19,738	20,343	21,914
	France	98,090	108,842	111,802	112,793	113,492	408,126	402,315	410,053	404,763	433,059
	Germany	51,396	50,238	46,695	45,029	44,016	354,871	366,527	378,048	388,852	401,163
	Greece	6,764	5,388	4,681	4,645	7,987	89,105	100,763	106,064	110,020	119,009
	Malta	262	475	396	368	517	8,501	8,781	8,915	8,971	9,580
	Norway	3,539	3,618	3,358	3,319	3,401	29,310	30,614	31,591	32,975	33,297
	Portugal	15,379	19,494	18,707	13,056	12,479	49,888	54,979	59,420	66,014	72,036
	Slovenia	1,836	1,707	2,039	2,755	2,359	9,472	9,470	10,224	11,058	12,460
	Spain	37,642	41,278	42,485	48,595	50,083	389,212	403,963	422,226	454,957	471,200
	Sweden	1,512	5,488	6,125	5,636	5,656	49,710	52,280	55,612	57,234	58,683
Developing countries	Bulgaria	5,802	5,522	5,033	4,800	5,027	21,617	21,698	21,398	25,186	26,054
	Czechia	15,181	13,908	13,200	11,608	11,406	43,308	42,947	47,094	49,697	53,219
	Estonia	1,673	1,443	1,560	1,136	870	5,734	5,809	5,782	6,228	6,509
	Hungary	13,387	11,988	11,133	12,024	11,116	24,426	26,054	27,543	29,291	31,609
	Latvia	2,505	2,821	2,171	1,910	1,846	3,775	4,158	4,110	4,417	4,951
	Lithuania	3,303	3,158	3,296	3,399	3,042	6,089	6,465	6,581	6,993	7,365
	Poland	65,078	62,326	66,706	62,847	64,743	62,959	66,580	71,234	79,394	83,881
	Romania	26,934	22,709	25,621	21,079	23,286	19,302	20,230	23,445	25,275	26,916
	Slovakia	10,692	9,579	8,995	8,866	7,897	11,346	10,781	12,176	13,895	14,668

(Continued)

		Turnover in the accommodation industry (million EUR)					Added value in the accommodation industry (million EUR)				
		2013	2014	2015	2016	2017	2013	2014	2015	2016	2017
Developed countries	**Austria**	8,194.8	8,454.2	8,858.3	9,400.8	9,733.4	4,142.4	4,240.4	4,488.5	4,788.0	4,900.6
	Belgium	2,355.9	2,432.4	2,507.7	2,516.3	2,573.6	1,084.0	1,097.9	1,127.3	1,119.6	1,174.1
	Cyprus	906.9	919.9	932.4	1,077.6	1,192.2	518.2	525.2	541.0	636.2	687.3
	Denmark	1,892.5	2,022.6	2,080.9	2,359.5	2,362.5	789.5	847.0	900.0	1,002.3	968.2
	Finland	1,359.9	1,346.8	1,403.2	1,460.6	1,431.2	420.3	409.4	437.8	512.5	485.5
	France	23,550.1	23,949.0	25,400.1	25,538.0	27,066.5	9,454.3	9,220.3	9,711.4	9,424.8	10,853.5
	Germany	23,880.3	26,391.3	28,574.0	30,095.5	31,331.3	11,548.3	13,026.4	14,210.3	15,559.3	15,870.8
	Greece	3,457.7	4,999.6	5,220.1	5,180.3	6,082.8	1,818.7	2,729.9	2,782.9	2,633.3	3,172.3
	Malta	408.6	442.9	495.5	505.6	603.4	182.4	206.2	223.7	234.1	292.6
	Norway	3,247.7	3,173.5	3,128.7	3,165.2	3,270.0	1,333.3	1,311.4	1,250.5	1,266.0	1,311.4
	Portugal	2,458.2	2,856.1	3,266.7	3,896.3	4,792.7	1,179.7	1,324.0	1,548.5	1,899.8	2,374.0
	Slovenia	565.7	552.7	574.0	623.5	689.4	249.3	242.8	261.8	296.2	329.4
	Spain	17,343.1	18,152.0	20,129.3	22,349.1	24,769.6	8,721.2	9,276.7	10,436.4	11,598.0	13,078.6
	Sweden	4,388.2	4,393.9	4,654.5	5,053.6	5,025.0	1,780.2	1,807.9	2,000.3	2,202.4	2,179.9
Developing countries	**Bulgaria**	757.9	786.7	799.2	934.4	1,013.3	354.2	315.0	348.7	440.7	487.2
	Czechia	1,433.3	1,432.6	1,597.9	1,750.0	2,018.2	516.2	527.6	597.4	651.5	786.2
	Estonia	251.9	265.8	273.0	290.2	323.6	99.8	99.5	113.7	123.4	136.0
	Hungary	822.5	943.3	1,078.1	1,107.6	1,295.2	314.9	375.1	431.5	460.0	564.1
	Latvia	174.5	182.1	186.6	202.4	222.0	72.8	76.1	78.0	83.8	91.1
	Lithuania	178.8	176.1	210.9	237.4	252.4	83.6	67.1	99.7	117.3	133.3
	Poland	2,317.6	2,420.3	2,684.6	2,959.5	3,238.9	877.9	1,025.8	1,140.1	1,234.4	1,418.5
	Romania	929.5	975.1	1,105.2	1,212.0	1,303.7	359.0	457.1	471.6	536.3	631.6
	Slovakia	435.2	364.1	436.1	517.0	544.8	169.7	129.7	157.4	176.5	183.3

Source: https://ec.europa.eu/eurostat/data/database.

a According to the ISCED-F 2013, 'Hotel, restaurants and catering' education and 'Travel, tourism and leisure' education represent core components of the 'Personal services' field of education.

Table 7.2 2013–2017 change indices for the proxy indicators of tourism education and tourism destination performance

		Graduates in the 'Personal services' field of education (%)	Nights spent at tourist accommodation establishments (%)	Turnover in the accommodation industry (%)	Added value in the accommodation industry (%)
Developed countries	Austria	−2.14	5.37	9.74	10.15
	Belgium	30.00	11.21	4.13	3.38
	Cyprus	17.87	10.61	16.06	17.68
	Denmark	11.81	6.64	13.46	13.17
	Finland	−0.05	3.73	4.50	13.28
	France	6.07	2.24	7.00	5.65
	Germany	−8.49	6.24	14.15	17.68
	Greece	2.85	13.23	20.51	17.15
	Malta	13.06	4.85	19.12	22.55
	Norway	−4.16	6.94	0.15	−1.73
	Portugal	−17.43	20.20	39.33	43.68
	Slovenia	28.14	15.69	11.49	17.71
	Spain	16.27	10.94	20.90	23.49
	Sweden	32.70	8.84	9.65	14.21
Developing Countries	Bulgaria	−9.15	12.25	17.20	25.42
	Czechia	−14.37	12.49	20.21	24.00
	Estonia	−23.74	6.89	12.15	19.20
	Hungary	−6.12	13.35	22.40	29.79
	Latvia	−20.94	11.91	12.48	11.46
	Lithuania	−0.20	9.43	23.84	39.90
	Poland	0.10	16.80	19.68	24.61
	Romania	−7.01	20.10	20.30	27.32
	Slovakia	−11.99	18.76	21.25	13.22

number of tourism education graduates between 2013 and 2017, with just a few exceptions such as Austria, Germany, Norway, or Portugal. The change index values in the case of Belgium, Slovenia, and Sweden, for example, are +30%, +28.14 and +32.7%, respectively. Cyprus, Denmark, Malta, and Spain have also recorded a significant increase in the number of tourism education graduates (change index values higher than +10% in all four cases). Nevertheless, even though developed European countries had a much better performance in promoting and fostering tourism education between 2013 and 2017, emerging European economies recorded better evolutions in what concerns tourism destination performance indicators during the same timeframe. At a first glance, these intuitive observations might suggest that a decline in the tourism educational area doesn't generally lead to a worsening of the industry's key performance indicators (at least, not in the case of developing countries), while increasing the number of tourism education graduates does not significantly improve tourism destination performance (at least, not in the case of developed countries).

However, tourism education, by generating an appropriate workforce for the tourism industry, should lead to better service quality in the sector, both via professionalism and via an improved ratio between the number of employees and the number of customers. Further on, as previous research has suggested (e.g. Choi and Chu, 2001; Alexandris et al., 2002; Dortyol et al., 2014), better service quality in the tourism industry leads to higher customer satisfaction, more positive word of mouth and higher price premiums for tourism services. This would consequently lead to more customers for tourism businesses, as well as to higher turnover and added value in the industry. Therefore, theory suggests that increasing the number of tourism education graduates should improve tourism destination performance. Moreover, previous research has pointed out that there are several structural differences between developed and developing countries in what concerns the elasticity of tourism demand in relation to various factors that might influence it (Vanhove, 2017). Also, compared to emerging countries, developed countries are able to export tourism services with a higher added value (Hallak and Schott, 2011), being also able to specialise in more sophisticated tourism products (Gozgor and Can, 2016).

Considering the previously outlined arguments, the relationship between tourism education and tourism destination performance has been further analysed in a comparative manner, splitting our countries' sample into two subsamples, comprising developed and developing countries, respectively. First, the correlation between the change index of the number of graduates in the 'Personal services' field of education and, respectively, the change index of the number of nights spent at tourist accommodation establishments was analysed. As it can be seen in Figure 7.1, a growth in the number of graduates from tourism education programs generally determines an increase in the number of nights spent at tourist accommodation establishments, both in the case of developed and developing European countries. However, the results reveal that this correlation is higher in the case of European emerging countries (Pearson correlation coefficient = 0.68; R^2 = 0.46) as compared to the developed ones (Pearson correlation coefficient = 0.55; R^2 = 0.31).

Second, the correlation between the change index of the number graduates in the 'Personal services' field of education and the change index of turnover in the accommodation industry was assessed. As Figure 7.2 shows, an increase in the number of graduates from tourism education programs is generally associated with a larger turnover in the accommodation industry, both in the case of developed and developing European countries. Nevertheless, the results reveal that the relationship between tourism education and accommodation turnover is higher in developing countries (Pearson correlation coefficient = 0.82; R^2 = 0.67) than in developed countries (Pearson correlation coefficient = 0.56; R^2 = 0.32).

Third, the correlation between the change index of the number of graduates in the 'Personal services' field of education and, respectively, the change index of the added value generated by the accommodation industry was investigated. Figure 7.3 reveals that an increase in the number of graduates

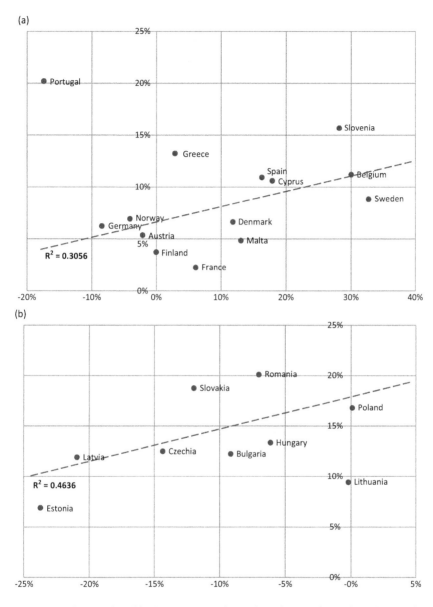

Figure 7.1 The relationship between tourism education and tourism destination performance: tourism education graduates and nights spent in accommodation establishments.

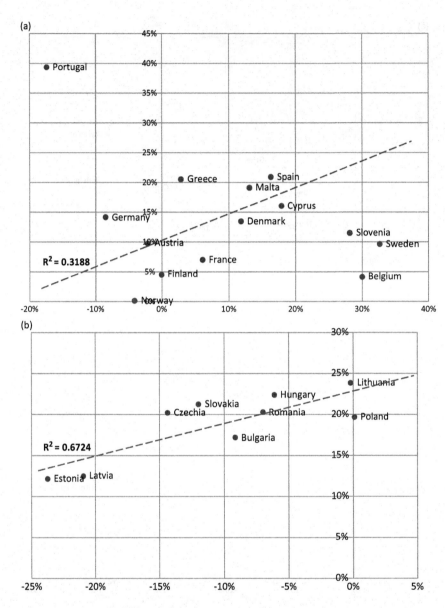

Figure 7.2 The relationship between tourism education and tourism destination performance: tourism education graduates and turnover in the accommodation industry.

Figure 7.3 The relationship between tourism education and tourism destination performance: tourism education graduates and added value in the accommodation industry.

from tourism education programs is generally associated with a growth in the added value of the accommodation industry, both in the case of developed and developing European countries. Similarly to the previously presented analyses, the correlation between tourism education and tourism destination performance, measured in this case via added value in the accommodation industry, is stronger in the case of developing economies (Pearson correlation coefficient = 0.73; R^2 = 0.53) as compared to the developed ones (Pearson correlation coefficient = 0.52; R^2 = 0.27).

The fact that these data suggest a more prominent influence of tourism education on tourism destination performance in the case of developing countries is in line with previous research. Thus, Eugenio-Martin et al. (2008) emphasise the fact that in the case of high-income countries the levels of development in terms of education provision are sufficiently high that further improvements will not make remarkable differences to the number of tourist arrivals. In contrast, in medium- and low-income countries, which generally don't have the threshold levels of education that tourists desire, an increase in the provision of education has a significant positive effect on tourism demand. Overall, the results of this research suggest that tourism education is positively correlated with tourism destination performance in terms of nights spent, turnover and added value. However, the relationship between the two is not unidirectional: tourism education, measured in the number of graduates, is both a cause and an effect of the tourism industry performance. Thus, when tourism demand increases, the need for tourism specialised workforce grows and, consequently, national educational systems respond (at least theoretically) by expanding their tourism related educational offer. Nevertheless, such a response from a national educational system takes years to be implemented, a timeframe in which the market demand may change. On the other hand, when the number of persons with specific skills and competences for the tourism industry increases, the sector should feel the improvement right away. Obviously, tourism education and the quality of the workforce in the sector are not the only factors that determine a tourism destination's performance. There is a vast range of factors that can affect tourism demand such as tourists' income, prices of tourism products, transportation costs, exchange rates, quantity and quality of tourism attractions, use of a common language, shared borders, good weather, and longer coastlines (Eugenio-Martin et al., 2008; Shafiullah et al., 2019).

Tourism education and destinations' sustainability

After showing that tourism education has a positive impact on the quality of the employees and, implicitly, on the performance of tourist destinations, one ought to discuss how education can contribute positively to the sustainability of destinations. There is a wide agreement that regardless of size or scale, the goal of all tourism destinations is sustainability (Clarke, 1997) and that urgent action is needed in this direction. Nevertheless, achieving tourism sustainability has proven to be a difficult task (Higgins-Desbiolles, 2010; Wijesinghe, 2014). Tourism education should communicate sustainability as an important value (Sheldon et al., 2008) and groom professionals able for real-life planning and management of sustainable tourism projects (Jamal et al., 2011). Considering the complexity and interdependence of the tourism system combined with the local realities and power relations at the destination level, Camargo and Gretzel (2017) argue that sustainability-related curricula should not only concentrate on general knowledge of sustainable tourism principles. Practical knowledge, contextualised knowledge of local places and their people (Jamal, 2004), knowledge of ethical precepts (Gretzel et al., 2011; Jamal, 2004), as well as the capacity to consistently make appropriate decisions on a situation at hand (Jamal, 2004) should be developed in a holistic, ethical, and praxis-oriented approach of sustainability education (Jamal, 2004). The goal of education for tourism sustainability should be that of arming graduates with the strongest and most complex conceptualisation of sustainability (Cotterell et al., 2020).

The tourism education futures initiative (TEFI) argues for a value-based approach to teaching sustainable tourism. In the TEFI approach, in order to become leaders and stewards for tourism destinations, the set of values that tourism students should embody on graduation are ethics, stewardship, knowledge, professionalism, and mutuality (Sheldon et al., 2011). Also, sustainable tourism education should develop essential competencies such as creativity, reflective practice, and critical analysis (Camargo and Gretzel, 2017). TEFI leaders identified four key capabilities and knowledge areas that graduates entering the world of the future will need: destination stewardship skills, political and ethical skills, enhanced human resource skills, and dynamic business skills (Padurean and Maggi, 2011). Scholars argue that the multidisciplinary and multidimensional nature of sustainability requires a deep learning educational approach (von Blottnitz, 2006; Jones et al., 2008), aimed at fostering reflection and critical analysis which consequently calls for non-traditional pedagogic practices (Camargo and Gretzel, 2017). Interactive, experiential, transformative, and, most importantly, real-world learning are key strategies to foster sustainability knowledge and competences (Brundiers et al., 2010). Site visits, field trips, group projects and/or internships, as well as working opportunities in sustainable enterprises may contribute to both expanding students' knowledge and providing real-life experiences in sustainability management (Brundiers et al., 2010).

In order to ensure effective changes needed in the 'educational paradigm, purpose, policy and practice' of institutions (Sterling, 2004), required by sustainability, the development of education curriculum should involve all stakeholders (academic managers, teaching staff, students, and administrative staff) (Lozano, 2006).

Conclusions and implications

Overall, our results suggest that tourism education has a positive impact on tourism destination performance in terms of nights spent, turnover, and added value, with a more prominent influence in the case of developing countries. Unfortunately, tourism education, as defined by the International Standard Classification of Education for Fields of Education and Training (UNESCO Institute for Statistics, 2014), has been generally declining between 2013 and 2017 in developing European countries. In other words, the countries which reduced their provision of tourism education were generally the ones which didn't have the necessary threshold levels of such education. Despite the decrease in provisioning adequate education for the tourism industry, the number of nights spent in accommodation establishments, as well as the industry's turnover and added value in developing European countries generally kept growing. However, where the decline in tourism education was less prominent or where the number of tourism graduates was not in decline, tourism destination performance indicators grew at a more rapid pace.

Tourism education is important for all tourism destinations. Especially in developing countries, tourism education and tourism related skills' generation represent a real challenge, particularly in countries experiencing high rates of tourism growth. Developed countries, on the other hand, face the competition from developing and under-developed countries with lower wages, being at the same time pressured to maintain service quality standards. Tourism training and skills' development is therefore essential in developed countries as well, in order to increase productivity and maintain their competitiveness. Researchers expect a doubling or even tripling in the number of travellers over the next four decades (Scott and Gössling, 2015). As long-term prospects for tourism growth are very optimistic, generating an adequate number of tourism education graduates, as well as attracting, training and retaining high quality workforce are essential for the industry's sustainability and long-term growth.

Providing appropriate tourism education and training is extremely important for promoting innovation and achieving productivity improvements in the tourism industry (OECD, 2010). Also, considering the dynamics of the industry, as well as the rapid advancements of information and communications technologies, the tourism industry constantly needs new skills. These can be attained only if appropriate tourism education and training is provided by both national education systems and businesses in the sector. Education is considered to have a major influence on driving societal change towards sustainability. Future tourism managers should be educated in sustainability, as this is critical to achieving improvements in the tourism industry. The concept of education for sustainability calls for transformative ways of teaching and learning which centre on critical reflection, on values, and on the active empowerment of students to make changes. Tourism programs must endow their students with theoretical and practical sustainability knowledge and provide opportunities to work in real-life projects that can increase students' sense of competence and empowerment to work towards a more sustainable world (Camargo and Gretzel, 2017). As OECD specialists suggest (OECD, 2010), tourism strategies should include 'the provision of education and training programs to meet skills shortages and to raise the quality and productivity of the industry's workforce'. Also, considering the pressure on public budgets generated by the need for tourism education and training, governments should take into consideration alternative models of provisioning such education, partially or fully shifting towards the private sector in order to deliver workforce development. In the context of tourism education and destination sustainability, it is also important to take into account the extent to which the hospitality industry is impacted by various pandemics such as SARS, Swine Flu, MERS, and, most recently, COVID-19. Tourism-generated traffic, crowding, and overcrowding are having a significant impact on the spread of various infectious diseases. Consequently, the hospitality industry suffers great losses during such pandemics. Moreover, tourism professionals' knowledge and attitude about the destination- and travel-related diseases will directly or indirectly influence tourists' satisfaction and safety (Hsu et al., 2018). Therefore, tourism education should focus more in the future on knowledge regarding travel health, in order to promote health care for tourists, and be able to minimise the spread of various infectious diseases.

References

Åberg, K. G., and Müller, D. K. (2018), "The development of geographical differences in education levels within the Swedish tourism industry," *Tourism Geographies*, Vol. 20, No. 1, pp. 67–84.

Alexandris, K., Dimitriadis, N., and Markata, D. (2002), "Can perceptions of service quality predict behavioral intentions? An exploratory study in the hotel sector in Greece," *Managing Service Quality: An International Journal*, Vol. 12, No. 4, pp. 224–231.

Andrades, L., and Dimanche, F. (2019), "Destination competitiveness in Russia: Tourism professionals' skills and competences," *International Journal of Contemporary Hospitality Management*, Vol. 31, No. 2, pp. 910–930.

Barron, P. (2007), "Hospitality and tourism students' part-time employment: Patterns, benefits and recognition," *Journal of Hospitality, Leisure, Sport and Tourism Education*, Vol. 6, No. 2, pp. 40–54.

Baum, T. (2007), "Human resources in tourism: Still waiting for change," *Tourism Management*, Vol. 28, No. 6, pp. 1383–1399.

Brundiers, K., Wiek, A., and Redman, C. L. (2010), "Real-world learning opportunities in sustainability: From classroom into the real world," *International Journal of Sustainability in Higher Education*, Vol. 11, No. 4, pp. 308–324.

Camargo, B. A., and Gretzel, U. (2017), "What do tourism students know about sustainability and sustainable tourism? An exploratory study of Latin American students," *Journal of Teaching in Travel & Tourism*, Vol. 17, No. 2, pp. 101–117.

Choi, T. Y., and Chu, R. (2001), "Determinants of hotel guests' satisfaction and repeat patronage in the Hong Kong hotel industry," *International Journal of Hospitality Management*, Vol. 20, No. 3, pp. 277–297.

Choy, D. J. (1995), "The quality of tourism employment," *Tourism Management*, Vol. 16, No. 2, pp. 129–137.

Chung-Herrera, B. G., Enz, C. A., and Lankau, M. J. (2003), "Grooming future hospitality leaders: A competencies model," *Cornell Hotel and Restaurant Administration Quarterly*, Vol. 44, No. 3, pp. 17–25.

Clarke, J. (1997), "A framework of approaches to sustainable tourism," *Journal of Sustainable Tourism*, Vol. 5, No. 3, pp. 224–233.

Cooper, C., and Shepherd, R. (1997), "The relationship between tourism education and the tourism industry: Implications for tourism education," *Tourism Recreation Research*, Vol. 22, No. 1, pp. 34–47.

Cotterell, D., Ferreira, J. A., Hales, R., and Arcodia, C. (2020), "Cultivating conscientious tourism caretakers: A phenomenographic continuum towards stronger sustainability," *Current Issues in Tourism,* Vol. 23, No. 8, pp. 1004–1020.

Dortyol, I. T., Varinli, I., and Kitapci, O. (2014), "How do international tourists perceive hotel quality? An exploratory study of service quality in Antalya tourism region," *International Journal of Contemporary Hospitality Management*, Vol. 26, No.3, pp. 470–495.

Duncan, T., Scott, D. G., and Baum, T. (2013), "The mobilities of hospitality work: An exploration of issues and debates," *Annals of Tourism Research*, Vol. 41, pp. 1–19.

Engberg, M. E. (2007), "Educating the workforce for the 21st century: A cross-disciplinary analysis of the impact of the undergraduate experience on students' development of a pluralistic orientation," *Research in Higher Education*, Vol. 3, No. 48, pp. 283–317.

Eugenio-Martin, J. L., Martín-Morales, N., and Sinclair, M. T. (2008), "The role of economic development in tourism demand," *Tourism Economics*, Vol. 14, No. 4, pp. 673–690.

Eurico, S. T., Da Silva, J. A. M., and Do Valle, P. O. (2015), "A model of graduates' satisfaction and loyalty in tourism higher education: The role of employability," *Journal of Hospitality, Leisure, Sport and Tourism Education*, Vol. 16, pp. 30–42.

European Commission, Eurostat. (2020), *Data: Databases*, https://ec.europa.eu/eurostat/data/database.

Fodness, D. (2017), "The problematic nature of sustainable tourism: Some implications for planners and managers," *Current Issues in Tourism*, Vol. 20, No. 16, pp. 1671–1683.

Gozgor, G., and Can, M. (2016), "Effects of the product diversification of exports on income at different stages of economic development," *Eurasian Business Review*, Vol. 6 No. 2, pp. 215–235.

Gretzel, U., Isacsson, A., Matarrita, D., and Wainio, E. (2011), "Teaching based on TEFI values: A case study," *Journal of Teaching in Travel & Tourism*, Vol. 11, No. 1, pp. 94–106.

Hallak, J. C., and Schott, P. K. (2011), "Estimating cross-country differences in product quality," *The Quarterly Journal of Economics*, Vol. 126, No. 1, pp. 417–474.

Higgins-Desbiolles, F. (2010), "The elusiveness of sustainability in tourism: The culture–ideology of consumerism and its implications," *Tourism & Hospitality Research*, Vol. 10, No. 2, pp. 116–129.

Hsu, S. H., Huang, H. L., Lu, C. W., Cheng, S. Y., Lee, L. T., Chiu, T. Y., and Huang, K. C. (2018), "Tour leaders with detailed knowledge of travel-related diseases play a key role in disease prevention," *Medicine*, Vol. 97, No. 6, pp. 1–5.

Jamal, T. B. (2004), "Virtue ethics and sustainable tourism pedagogy: Phronesis, principles and practice," *Journal of Sustainable Tourism*, Vol. 12, No. 6, pp. 530–545.

Jamal, T., Taillon, J., and Dredge, D. (2011), "Sustainable tourism pedagogy and academic-community collaboration: A progressive service-learning approach," *Tourism and Hospitality Research*, Vol. 11, No. 2, pp. 133–147.

Jones, P., Trier, C. J., and Richards, J. P. (2008), "Embedding education for sustainable development in higher education: A case study examining common challenges and opportunities for undergraduate programmes," *International Journal of Educational Research*, Vol. 47, No. 6, pp. 341–350.

Ladkin, A. (2005), "Careers and employment," In: D. Airey, and J. Tribe (Eds.), *An International Handbook of Tourism Education*, Elsevier, UK, pp. 437–450.

Lozano, R. (2006), "Incorporation and institutionalization of SD into universities: Breaking through barriers to change," *Journal of Cleaner Production*, Vol. 14, No. 9–11, pp. 787–796.

Malmberg, A., and Maskell, P. (2006), "Localized learning revisited," *Growth and Change*, Vol. 37, pp. 1–18.

Maráková, V., Dyr, T., and Wolak-Tuzimek, A. (2016), "Factors of tourism's competitiveness in European union countries," *Economics and Management*, Vol. 19, No. 3, pp. 92–109.

Marinakou, E., and Giousmpasoglou, C. (2015), "Stakeholders' view on the development of a higher education hospitality program in Bahrain: Challenges and opportunities," *Journal of Hospitality and Tourism Education*, Vol. 27, No. 2, pp. 85–92.

Mayaka, M., and King, B. (2002), "A quality assessment of education and for Kenya's tour-operating sector," *Current Issues in Tourism*, Vol. 5, No. 2, pp. 112–133.

Mbarushimana, N., Role, E., and Allida, V. (2017), "Competency-based curriculum in tourism and hospitality: A practical model for Rwanda," *Journal of Research Innovation and Implications in Education*, Vol. 1, No. 3, pp. 96–109.

OECD. (2010), "Tourism 2020: Policies to Promote Competitive and sustainable Tourism." In *OECD Tourism Trends and Policies 2010*, https://www.oecd-ilibrary.org/oecd-tourism-trends-and-policies-2010_5ks8h05nbmbs.pdf.

OECD. (2011), "OECD Studies on Tourism: Italy: Review of Issues and Policies." In *OECD Studies on Tourism*, https://read.oecd-ilibrary.org/industry-and-services/oecd-studies-on-tourism-italy_9789264114258-en#page1.

Padurean, L., and Maggi, R. (2011), "TEFI values in tourism education: A comparative analysis," *Journal of Teaching in Travel & Tourism*, Vol. 11, No. 1, pp. 24–37.

Riley, M., Ladkin, A., and Szivas, E. (2002), *Tourism Employment: Analysis and Planning*, Channel View Publications, Clevedon, UK.

Scott, D., and Gössling, S. (2015), "What could the next 40 years hold for global tourism?" *Tourism Recreation Research*, Vol. 40, No. 3, pp. 269–285.

Shafiullah, M., Okafor, L. E., and Khalid, U. (2019), "Determinants of international tourism demand: Evidence from Australian states and territories," *Tourism Economics*, Vol. 25, No. 2, pp. 274–296.

Sheldon, P., Fesenmaier, D., and Tribe, J. (2011), "The tourism education futures initiative (TEFI): Activating change in tourism education," *Journal of Teaching in Travel and Tourism*, Vol. 11, No. 1, pp. 2–23.

Sheldon, P., Fesenmaier, D., Wöber, K., Cooper, C., and Antonioli, M. (2008), "Tourism education futures, 2010–2030: Building the capacity to lead," *Journal of Teaching in Travel and Tourism*, Vol. 7, No. 3, pp. 61–68.

Sterling, S. (2004), "Higher education, sustainability, and the role of systemic learning," In: P. B. Corcoran, and A. E. J. Wals (Eds.), *Higher Education and the Challenge of Sustainability*, Springer, Dordrecht, pp. 49–70.

Ţigu, G., Andreeva, M., and Nica, A. M. (2010), "Education and training needs in the field of visitors receiving structures and tourism services in the lower Danube region," *Amfiteatru Economic*, No. 12, pp. 735–760.

UNESCO Institute for Statistics. (2014). *ISCED Fields of Education and Training 2013*, http://uis.unesco.org/sites/default/files/documents/international-standard-classification-of-education-fields-of-education-and-training-2013-detailed-field-descriptions-2015-en.pdf.

UNWTO. (2009). "Tourism: Creating opportunities in challenging times," *UNTWO News: Magazine of the World Tourism Organization*, Vol. 13, No. 1, pp. 4–5.

Vanhove, N. (2017). *The Economics of Tourism Destinations: Theory and Practice*. London: Routledge.

von Blottnitz, H. (2006), "Promoting active learning in sustainable development: Experiences from a 4th year chemical engineering course," *Journal of Cleaner Production*, Vol. 14, No. 9–11, pp. 916–923.

Wang, J., Ayres, H., and Huyton, J. (2010), "Is tourism education meeting the needs of the tourism industry? An Australian case study," *Journal of Hospitality and Tourism Education*, Vol. 22, No. 1, pp. 8–14.

Wei, M. (2015), "Construction and evaluation of a performance model of the tourism industry," *Tourism Analysis*, Vol. 20, No. 6, pp. 653–664.

Wijesinghe, G. (2014), "Reimagining the application of sustainability to the hospitality industry through a virtue ethics framework," *Journal of Sustainable Tourism*, Vol. 22, No. 1, pp. 31–49.

Zhang, W. (2017), "Education and tourism in a small open growth economy," *International Journal of Academic Research in Business and Social Sciences*, Vol. 7, No. 11, pp. 643–661.

Part III

Transformative strategies

8 Strategic and transformative tourism education as a valuable approach to educating for sustainable development

Svetla Stoyanova-Bozhkova

Introduction

The core mission of higher education (HE) is to meet the changing societal needs and prepare students for their life after graduation, so they can take their place in society and help tackle the world's grand challenges in the context of a rapidly changing global environment. The debate on strategic and transformative education as a tool for achieving sustainable development (SD) has attracted the attention of scholars and policy makers at international, national, and institutional levels in many counties. Adopted by all United Nations (UN) member states in 2015, the UN Sustainable Development Goals (SDGs) provide a framework at a global level for ending poverty, delivering a better quality of life for all in a way that protects the planet. There is a shared understanding that Higher Education Institutions (HEIs) are key stakeholders in addressing the fundamental societal challenges addressed through the SDGs (Filho et al., 2018; Ali et al., 2017). According to the European Commission report *Modernising Higher Education in Europe* (2013, p. 13),

> higher education institutions are the focal point for imparting what is known, interrogating what is not, producing new knowledge, shaping critical thinkers, problem solvers and doers so that we have the intellectual muscle needed to tackle societal challenges at every level necessary and advance European civilization.

There is a broad consensus that education for sustainable development (ESD) equips graduates for their responsibilities as members of society through incorporating the wider economic, social, and environmental issues in student learning. The need for knowledge and skills for SD is increasingly reflected in the national strategic documents and subject benchmarks. The Quality Assurance Agency (QAA) for HE in the United Kingdom defines ESD as 'the process of equipping students with the knowledge and understanding, skills and attributes needed to work and live in a way that safeguards environmental, social and economic wellbeing, both in the present and for future generations' (Longhurst et al., 2014, p. 7).

The UN initiative, the Decade of Education for Sustainable Development 2005–2014, encouraged HE providers around the world to incorporate sustainability in their policies and action plans. Although slightly inconsistent, progress has been made, evidenced by greening of university campuses, adopting strategic objectives aligned with the SDGs, setting up sustainability networks and conducting research about SD and incorporating the concepts into the curricula.

The initiatives have expanded into the charity and not-for-profit sector. Founded in 2014 as an educational charity, the Students Organising for Sustainability (SOS) has achieved presence on all six continents. Its purpose is to bring student groups globally to lead on learning for sustainability. SOS-UK aims to support the desire of students and young people to respond to the climate emergency and lead society to a better future (SOS-UK, 2020).

Despite the growing body of research on SD and the role of university education in achieving the SDGs, few of these studies look at the context of tourism education. Although SD has implications in all sectors of the economy, it is critical for the tourism and hospitality industries due to their dependence on natural and human resources. Evidence shows tourism development can have a positive impact on destinations and local economies. However, if not planned and managed well, it has the potential to destroy economic, socio-cultural, and natural environments and thus affect the viability of the industry itself. The issue is even more pressing given the forecasts for steady growth of tourism globally and the concerns about what is perceived as a new phenomenon – overtourism (Peeters et al., 2018). Somewhat ironically, the debate on overtourism takes place within the ongoing wider discourse on SD and the recognition of tourism development as a tool to support the SDGs, which questions the effectiveness of the old policies and approaches.

The graduates of HEIs are the next generation of leaders and decision makers who will face the challenges of the growing nature of tourism and its impacts. This calls for joint action of all stakeholders involved in the process, including the industry, academia and the public sector. The HE providers have the responsibility to develop the skills and attributes needed to address the UN SDGs and ensure they are adopted at all levels and in all activities. Nevertheless, it remains unclear how sustainability has been incorporated into the HE curricula and different pedagogies (Slocum et al., 2019).

While notable progress is evident at strategic level, the progress in incorporating sustainability into the classroom has been slow. Evidence shows that the tourism curriculum should be consistently supported by transformational approaches and critical thinking if education for sustainability is to be implemented effectively. A true transformative learning experience is needed to change mindsets and lead to positive outcomes. These include changing the assumptions, beliefs, perspectives, and actions of individuals. As Peter Drucker pointed out, 'learning is a lifelong process of keeping abreast of change. And the most pressing task is to teach people how to learn' (CMI, 2013, p. 128).

This chapter provides a review of previous research carried out on strategic and transformative approaches to education with a particular focus on the area of tourism and hospitality. First, it explores the key concepts of transformative learning and ESD, and how these have evolved into a leading approach to teaching and learning in HE. Next, it looks at the extent to which these have been incorporated or included in HE practices. Finally, it discusses the key challenges facing the HE providers. The review is based on peer-reviewed articles published in English, public policies, and industry reports. It is guided and complemented by the author's experience and prior research in the area.

Achieving ESD is not a matter of changing concepts and policies; it is a matter of changing the way all stakeholders think.

Transformative learning – origins, concepts, and implications

Over the last decade, the terms 'transformative' and 'strategic' have been so often used in relation to HE that they seem to have lost their original meaning. Scholars who have joined HE in the last decade may take for granted that all teaching and learning is transformative, but is it really and how do we know? A few studies explore whether and how transformative learning approaches have been incorporated into the wider HE practices. Even fewer focus on tourism education.

In the area of adult education, the transformative learning theory is associated with the name of Mezirow (Stewart, 2013; Biasin, 2018). Developed between 1970s and 1990s, nowadays its merit is globally acknowledged. It is recognized as a dominant theory in adult education and informs guidance documents developed by international and national organisations. According to Mezirow,

> A defining condition of being human is that we have to understand the meaning of our experience. For some, any uncritically assimilated explanation by an authority figure will suffice. But in contemporary societies we must learn to make our own interpretations rather than act on the purposes, beliefs, judgments, and feelings of others. Facilitating such understanding is the cardinal goal of adult education. Transformative learning develops autonomous thinking
>
> (1997, p. 5)

Inspired by humanistic principles and the constructivist approach, the transformative learning theory is concerned with the role of experiential learning and personal development. It emphasizes the centrality of critical reflection in the process of understanding the real-world issues (Mezirow, 1990). Taking responsibility for one's own learning and development, as well as the ability to use critical judgement and adapt to the changing environment, are acknowledged as key requirements of employers. Schon (1983, in Stewart, 2013) pointed out that teaching methods should enable learners to deal with a wide range of real-world problems and make difficult decisions in complex contexts characterized by economic, political, moral, and ethical issues.

According to the transformative learning theory, the role of the educator is to facilitate and guide learning rather than act as an authority on the subject. The academic is expected to create a 'safe' learning environment to nurture the critically reflective process, enable learners to explore multiple perspectives and different points of view in an empathetic and open way, and make tentative judgements to solve and redefine problems.

By nature, transformative education is learner-centred, participatory, and interactive. It encourages critically reflective thought and involves team work and group problem solving. To achieve this, the learning materials are developed to foster participation in group discussions to assess reasons, examine evidence, and arrive at a reflective judgement. In short, transformative learning takes place through discovery (Mezirow, 1997).

Over the last decades, the transformative learning has evolved from a learning theory into a global diffusion with multiple conceptual orientations, supported by well-developed methodological toolkits (Biasin, 2018). Developing critical thinking is considered a primary objective of HE (Tribe, 2002; European Commission Report, 2013). It is a means to create independent graduates and future professionals who can challenge and reformulate existing worldviews. The role of academia is to prepare students to work in a global, multicultural, complex and interdependent world, facing environmental and cultural dilemmas (Joseph, 2012). These values are seen as fundamental in addressing SD in the HE (Longhurst et al., 2014).

Nowadays, the transformative learning theory has fewer critics than enthusiastic advocates and is in the heart of ESD. However, it has certain pedagogical and ethical limitations. Some are related to the central role of the educator as an active agent of change. Also, the transformation must be voluntary and a result of a conscious rather than a forced decision. Other challenges are related to external factors and the changing nature of academia. Some scholars are warning that the nature of academia is changing to meet changing government priorities, national economic objectives; fill employment gaps; and improve competitiveness (Slocum et al., 2019). Hunt and Chalmers (2013) point out that the corporatisation of academia and the neoconservatism evident in discussions of regulations, quality standards and funding may hinder the effective application of the transformative approaches to education.

The relationship between the transformative theory and education for sustainable development

The 2006 Framework for the UN Decade of Education for Sustainable Development (UNDESD) International Implementation Scheme identified the three pillars of economic, social and environmental sustainability to set out a broad structure for sustainable learning. It helped set out a broad agenda considered essential in order to facilitate ESD, and supported the integration of the key principles and values of SD into education globally, and at all levels of learning. The UNDESD defines ESD as

...a vision of education that seeks to balance human and economic well-being with cultural traditions and respect for the earth's natural resources. ESD applies transdisciplinary educational methods and approaches to develop an ethic for lifelong learning; fosters respect for human needs that are compatible with sustainable use of natural resources and the needs of the planet; and nurtures a sense of global solidarity

(UNDESD, 2005, p. 1)

Current research (Lozano, 2011; Filho et al., 2018; Weiss and Barth, 2019) reveals that SD at universities is a rapidly emerging area. Evidence shows that an increasing number of universities around the world pledge commitment to sustainability in all areas of activities/operations. It has taken decades to reach this point, and the progress should be recognised and celebrated. Although the incentives in HE for research, establishing SD-oriented curricula and other related actions have increased, there have been numerous challenges. As a result, the progress has been rather slow and fragmented.

While the importance of pursuing SD in education has been widely accepted, there have been issues with misconceptions about the concept of sustainability, which hindered its understanding as a process and therefore the actual implementation. Filho (2000) points out that sustainability is often seen as a theoretical and abstract concept that is difficult to operationalise for the benefit of the various national and local stakeholders. The focus on the environmental aspects was stronger and it is not surprising that many universities chose to demonstrate commitment to sustainability through campus greening practices. These include recycling programmes and carbon footprint mapping, dedicated sustainability teams, and solar panel installations, among others (Leihy and Salazar, 2011).

Over the last 40 years, a wide range of strategic documents were published to enforce the process of design of approaches and mechanisms, and encourage universities to incorporate environmental concerns into their policies. The list includes but is not limited to landmark documents, such as: the *Magna Carta of European Universities* (1988), the *Talloires Declaration of University Presidents for a Sustainable Future* (1990), the Halifax document *Creating a common future: an action plan for universities* (1991), the COPERNICUS *Universities Charter for Sustainable Development* (1994), the Lüneburg *Declaration on Higher Education for Sustainable Development* (2001); Ubuntu Declaration on *Education and Science and Technology for Sustainable Development* (2002); Graz Declaration on *Committing Universities to Sustainable Development* (2005); G8 University Summit Sapporo *Sustainability Declaration* (2008), and G8 University Summit: *Statement of*

Action (2010). In reality, very few of these documents were implemented, which shows the disconnect between policy making and taking actions on the ground.

Despite the efforts made throughout the UNDSD, research showed little progress, mostly due to the lack of institutional sustainability policies across academia (Filho, 2015). Organisations have often focused on starting a sustainability initiative; however, they were less successful in implementing and sustaining these initiatives, as well as demonstrating wider impact (Mader et al., 2013). The scepticism might stem partly from the fact that there isn't a consistent and effective way to document and disseminate successful practices of implementing sustainability in HEIs. Thus, the UN SDGs call for more institutional commitment and the use of indicators to measure progress (Hák et al., 2016).

To take the concept to the next level, scholars placed a stronger emphasis on education and capacity-building skills. Transformative education was recognised as critical to achieve education for sustainability due to its focus on deep learning, critical thinking skills, reflection and problem solving, the use of 'real life' experience in developing a greater awareness of social and moral responsibilities in different contexts (Sibbel, 2009; Tilbury and Cooke, 2005). Literature published in recent years shows that progress has been made in different subject areas. The Higher Education Academy (HEA) in the United Kingdom is sharing examples of HEIs best practices of successfully adopting a holistic approach to sustainability across the entire institutional curricula and use of the informal learning environment. The toolkit for university educators created by Bessant et al. (2013) employs problem-based learning (PBL) as a case study for sustainability education. It offers helpful advice, scenarios, and observations about using PBL to teach students about sustainability, with a particular emphasis on how to scale up PBL without it becoming prohibitively expensive.

A few studies have captured the current state of affairs in HE looking at measures and research output. For example, Filho et al. (2018) found that the presence of formal policies is not an effective indicator of institutional commitment when used on its own. Their study examined the extent to which universities that are active in the field of SD have formal policies on SD, and whether such policies are a pre-condition for successful sustainability efforts. This is perhaps one of the largest research efforts of this kind, involving 35 universities in seven countries, including Brazil, Germany, Greece, Portugal, South Africa, the United Kingdom, and the United States. The study found that only 60% of the sampled universities had a policy that specifically addressed SD. However, all of the universities in the sample, regardless of the existence of a formal SD policy, demonstrated engagement with environmental sustainability policies or procedures in some way or another. Weiss and Barth (2019) took a different perspective. Their systematic review of peer-reviewed case studies published over a period of 27 years revealed that while research on sustainability curricula implementation processes in HE produced a growing output in a broad range of journals, most cases were coming from the United States, Europe, and Asia. The cross-country distribution of sustainability curricula implementation processes in HEIs showed that the top countries were the United States (58), United Kingdom (27), Australia (20), Canada (18), and India (10).

Such research brings valuable insights into the different aspects of the ESD, yet more research is needed to advance the understanding of the topic area. The sparsity of academic publications is matched by the limited information about how sustainable education is supported by national policies globally.

In the United Kingdom, the end of the Decade of Education for Sustainable Development was marked by a strong focus on sustainability in national HE documents. The Universities UK Report (2018) acknowledged that the linear model of education-employment-career does not reflect the new realities of the employment landscape and emphasized the need for new modes of delivery and flexible learning approaches, new combinations of skills and experience, and new and innovative partnerships between universities and employers of all sizes. The QAA in collaboration with the HEA produced the Education for Sustainable Development Guidance for UK HE providers (Longhurst et al., 2014), which defined ESD and made a brave attempt to operationalise it through specific pedagogical approaches, teaching and learning methods, and possible assessment strategies. The purpose of this guidance was to complement the UK Quality Code for Higher Education (Quality Code) that sets out the expectations that all providers of UK HE are required to meet and is used in QAA review processes. However, it does not form an explicit part of the Quality Code, which leaves much of it to the priorities and interests of individual universities. Without making explicit reference to the transformation learning theory, the document defines ESD as education which 'encourages students to develop critical thinking and to take a wide-ranging, systemic and self-reflective approach, adapting to novel situations that can arise from complexity' (Longhurst et al., 2014, p. 7).

In general, the strategic educational documents recognise lifelong learning and the strong interdisciplinary, multidisciplinary or transdisciplinary element as a fundamental feature of ESD, reflecting the interconnected nature of many issues in SD. The guidance document recommends transformative learning approaches, seen as well suited to ESD. Nevertheless, the HE educators are encouraged to use the recommended pedagogies creatively, adapt them to fit best the specific subject and discipline, and most importantly, to experiment with innovative teaching and learning methods as appropriate to the discipline (Longhurst et al., 2014).

The significance of ESD is acknowledged by all professional and accreditation bodies, particularly in the area of leadership and management skills. The Association to Advance Collegiate Schools of Business states that good leaders inspire, manage, and cultivate organizations, business systems, and people to enhance the sustainable development of society. The world needs more of them. In the face of complex challenges confronting organizations and communities, leadership is being called on to help create a more just, inclusive, and prosperous global society.

(AACSB, 2020)

Sustainability in tourism higher education

In the field of tourism and hospitality, sustainability has been high on the research agenda for almost four decades, as scholars have increasingly voiced their concern over tourism's social, cultural, and environmental impacts (Dodds and Butler 2019; Wall, 2020). The concept of sustainability has long been present in the tourism curriculum – in fact, the current generation of scholars may draw on their personal experience as students and researchers. Yet, surprisingly, there is scant evidence of sustainability being clearly and consistently embedded throughout tourism, hospitality, and events (TH&E) education (Deale and Barber, 2012; Wilson and von der Heidt, 2013). Researchers have argued that the debate on sustainability in the hospitality industry is academically flawed (Moscardo, 2015), and that has been a barrier to translating the theory of sustainability into practical solutions for businesses (Mihalic et al., 2012; Ali and Frew, 2014). Others have pointed out that a paradigm shift towards sustainability within HE curricula has remained constrained by pedagogical, political, and logistical issues (Leihy and Salazar, 2011; Savelyeva and McKenna, 2011, Slocum et al., 2019).

To understand whether and how Tourism and Hospitality Bachelor's degree courses are using sustainability in their course objectives and descriptions in 2020, this author conducted a systematic review, using the information published by universities on education.com to promote their courses to students globally. The keyword 'sustainable' was intentionally chosen as the terms 'sustainability' and 'sustainable development' brought fewer results. Other HE platforms did not include 'sustainability' in their filters or did not allow a customised search. The results were slightly disappointing and showed that only a small proportion of HE providers showed commitment to sustainability by including 'sustainability' or 'sustainability'-related terms in the description of their courses. The list was led by the United Kingdom, followed by Australia, New Zealand and Switzerland coming third, and Canada and Spain sharing the fourth place. The search found 507 Bachelor's degree tourism and hospitality courses offered by 88 HE providers in the United Kingdom; however, only 10% of them used the term 'sustainable' in the description of their course, including course aims, objectives and units studied. Although the review has its limitations and the data does not provide a complete picture of HE provision, it suggests that HEI's commitment to SD might remain limited to institutional policies and has less (if any) effect on the curriculum. It may also indicate that potential applicants may not make their decisions about where to study based on whether or not SDGs and sustainability are addressed in the course.

In the United Kingdom, the need for skills for SD is reflected in the national strategic documents and subject benchmarks. The UK Subject benchmark statement for Events, Hospitality, Leisure, Sport and Tourism (2019) states that honours degree graduates of courses in this subject grouping should demonstrate a range of behaviours appropriate to their professional context. These include the ability to recognise and respond to moral, ethical, sustainability, and safety issues which directly pertain to the context of study; ability to analyse and reflect on the environmental influences and sustainability issues which impact on hospitality organisations; appreciate the ethical issues associated with the operation and development of tourism; and understand the issues and principles of sustainability and social responsibility in the context of tourism (2019, pp. 15–19). Although the Subject Benchmark is only providing guidance, UK HEI and their campuses abroad are expected to demonstrate how these skills and competencies have been addressed in order to achieve validation (and re-validation) of the relevant degree courses.

Within the wider discourse about what tourism education should represent and incorporate (Dredge et al., 2012; Tribe, 2005), scholars have raised concern about the vocational focus of tourism education and the need for a more balanced, liberal, and vocational style of education (Tribe, 2002), among others. An increasing number of studies aim to critically examine the presence of sustainability and sustainable-related content in the TH&E curriculum. Some researchers point out that there is little evidence of a holistic or integrated approach to sustainable tourism education (Boley, 2011).

The academic perspective

While there is a wide consensus that sustainability is an important principle in tourism education, very few studies (if any) show how sustainability is actually incorporated within their learning and teaching practices, and in the development of the curricula. Some of these studies are briefly presented in Table 8.1.

Studies conducted over the last decade show that despite the significant progress in the area, there is still a long way to go (Deale and Barber, 2012; Boley, 2011). There is common agreement that the concept and principles of SD should be incorporated or included in tourism education. Addressing the SDGs and accomplishment of the Global Code of Ethics in Tourism in the areas of curriculum and pedagogical system, assessment, students, and faculty is a major requirement for achieving the UNTWO TedQual certification in HE (UNWTO, 2020). Nonetheless, the concept of sustainability remains poorly understood, inconsistently applied, left to the discretion of individual academics and driven by personal interests and agendas. It is rarely used as a philosophy underpinning all aspects of teaching and

Table 8.1 Selected studies of the incorporation of sustainability in tourism and hospitality higher education

Author	Description
Airey and Johnson (1999)	**Implementation of sustainability in tourism degree course in the United Kingdom:** The study was based on university prospectuses. The significance and impact of tourism were identified as one of the seven areas of knowledge and covered in the curriculum of 85 out of 99 courses. At the same time, social context/sustainable tourism appeared in the course aims and objectives published in university prospectuses of 19 out of 99 universities and occupied 14th place among the top 20 aims and objectives of tourism degree courses.
Millar et al. (2013)	**Incorporating sustainability into the curriculum at a major US hospitality college:** This research revealed that, in general, academics agree about the importance of incorporating sustainability into hospitality curricula. Nevertheless, they did not feel this was important to them and their classes personally and were less committed to staying on top of such issues. The researchers suggested that limited knowledge and access to appropriate toolkits may be a barrier to addressing sustainability in the classroom. The study recommended providing teaching staff with relevant hospitality sustainability resources as a way to remedy this apparent gap between interest and current teaching methods/approaches.
Wilson and Von Der Heidt (2013)	**Incorporating sustainability in the curriculum of the 1st-year business/tourism curriculum in an Australian university:** The study revealed that despite the institutional commitment to sustainability, action was undertaken in an ad-hoc rather than systematic way; actions were often led by personal interest and personal values of the individual academics. The complexities and priorities of individual departments and the bureaucratic processes that curriculum changes must go through often constrained effective changes such as introducing new units and degrees. The study showed three barriers to incorporating sustainability. These included (i) a pre-determined and crowded curriculum, determined by national benchmark and accreditation standards, requirements of professional qualification, (ii) resistance by staff and students, and (iii) the complexities of the teaching environments (i.e. online courses, international partners, multiple campuses).
Boyle et al. (2014)	**A meta-level website content analysis of 'sustainability' within tourism curriculum at 25 universities across Australia:** The research found that very few TH & E degrees had sustainable/sustainability concepts incorporated throughout the entire degree. Overall, the concept was evident in varying degrees, and there was not always a strong connection between the presence of sustainability or sustainable-related concepts in the subject title and the term actually being included within the subject description.
Ali et al. (2017)	**How hospitality graduate employers perceive sustainable development as a critical graduate skill.** The study found that employers do have knowledge of sustainability and are keen to recruit the best talent for their businesses. However, sustainability is not a priority in the selection of graduates.
Slocum et al. (2019)	**The influence of neoliberalism on the role of HE towards achieving the SDGs:** This exploratory qualitative study examines the perspectives of 14 faculty members in HE institutions across nine countries. The findings suggest that education is becoming increasingly market-driven and neoliberal influences have the potential to change the role of HE in training and development, which may limit their ability to infuse the critical thinking skills needed to sustain the SDGs by future generations. The nature of HE is changing against the background of decreased public support in funding, higher tuition costs, reduced educational quality as colleges attempt to balance budgets by reducing faculty size, limiting course offerings, closing satellite campuses, and increasing focus on student satisfaction, among others. These developments encourage more uniform approaches to learning that aim to meet national, global, and industry economic agendas rather than focus on sustainability issues. The emphasis on neoliberalism appeared most evident in western universities.

learning. On the contrary, practices vary from stand-alone sustainability curriculum module to a broad, 'holistic' approach. As evident from Table 8.1, Ali et al. (2017) add an important perspective to the problem. Public and trade documents often highlight the importance of SD skills for the industry. Nevertheless, academic research shows that SD and graduate employability are considered as divergent, independent considerations. This presents challenges for both hospitality education and the advancement of the industry.

The employer perspective

There is a general consensus that tourism education providers should be aware of the graduate skills and competencies expected by employers and incorporate the development of such skills in the curricula. Nevertheless, there appear to be conflicting views on whether tourism employers consider skills for SD essential or not. This further adds to the complexity of the issue.

Previous research shows that sustainability is an essential skill expected by employers and there is a growing demand for it (Rawlinson and Dewhurst, 2013). As illustrated by Ali et al.'s study (2017) this skill is not a top priority for employers when recruiting graduates. Furthermore, a small proportion of organisational leaders see a SD skill gap (Drayson, 2015). The reasons may vary in the different contexts and industries.

Drawing on evidence from the OECD context, the Next Tourism Generation Alliance report concludes that consumer trends are changing and customers are inclined to show loyalty to companies perceived as socially responsible (NTG, 2019). Industry reports show that employers from the UK's tourism sector place 'green skills' among the top three skills, along with digital and social skills (People 1st, 2019). This is based on a survey which captured the views of 250 UK HR/training and development and operational directors, across a range of tourism businesses of all sizes, in order to identify key current and future skills, skills gaps, and trends in these three areas. The findings suggest that green tourism is growing in popularity with visitors showing preferences for businesses that show commitment to sustainability. To fill in the gap in skills levels, an increasing number of employers are investing in training with most objectives related to the implementation of environmental management systems in tourism. The environmental aspects are dominating and areas where skills are needed include: the promotion of environmentally friendly activities, products and services, energy efficiency, water conservation, and waste management, as well as knowledge on climate change, sustainability, and biodiversity. Sadly, this, again, shows a mismatch between needs, expectations, and educational provision.

Evidence shows that different stakeholders in tourism development have different priorities in achieving SD and these may vary depending on the context and specific settings. In general, sustainability did not fit well in a rapidly changing societal and economic environment. A study of the perceptions of SD of the different stakeholders reveals that the public sector considers as its top priority the development of integrated SD policies, while the industry stakeholders prioritise long-term land-use planning and regulation. Understandably, not-for-profit and pressure groups put 'preserving the environment' at the top of their list of priorities. The lack of collaboration partnership between the stakeholders resulted in some businesses feeling that sustainability is 'a waste of time' and 'lip-service' while declaring commitment to the concept. The 'good sustainability practices' of the stakeholders are often the result of common sense rather than purposive actions to implement the principles of sustainability (Stoyanova-Bozhkova, 2011).

According to the NTG report (2019), a quick scan of job vacancies shows that few (if any) employers expect these skills and they are usually outsourced to other providers. Further studies are needed to understand the industry's needs for green skills (i.e. environmental management skills) within the wider SD skill set when preparing the professionals and leaders of the future.

The student perspective

Students are considered key stakeholders, who have the power to influence the implementation of sustainability in tourism education. Academic research reveals that student resistance to the concept can be a barrier to sustainability agendas (Slocum et al., 2019). In an era when education is seen as a commodity, student satisfaction determines university ranking in league tables and public funding in some geographical contexts, and student participation in the co-creation of the curriculum is seen as a major feature of HE – students are considered customers rather than learners.

A study of Latin American tourism students (Camaro and Gretzel, 2017) revealed that although most of them recognised the importance of sustainability and sustainable tourism, they felt that they had limited knowledge of sustainability principles and technical aspects related to sustainable tourism. In the 2019 NUS Skills Survey, 81% of Bournemouth University students agree or strongly agree that the topic of SD should be incorporated and promoted within courses (BU, 2020). This does not come as a surprise. A longitudinal study of student attitudes towards skills for SD (Drayson et al., 2014, p. 4) consistently showed that students recognised the significance of the SD skill set. Over two thirds of respondents consistently believe that SD should be incorporated into all university courses. Over 60% of UK students and three quarters of international students would like to learn more about SD. Even more importantly, approximately two-thirds of students would be willing to sacrifice £1,000 from an average graduate starting salary to work for a company with a positive social and environmental record, while over two-fifths would sacrifice £3,000 from their starting salary for a specific role that contributes to positive social and environmental change. These findings are very encouraging and convincingly show a shift in value systems.

A notable student-led initiative – The Education for Sustainable Development Community of Practice – has recently been gaining popularity in the western world. The annual *SDG Teach-In* places the SDGs at the heart of education and provides an informal space for academics from all universities to share best practices on embedding sustainability within learning (SOS-UK, 2020).

Unfortunately, tourism-related research appears to be missing and there is insufficient evidence that these results are relevant to the tourism and hospitality courses. Anecdotal evidence shows that many courses offer a separate optional module on environmental sustainability which is chosen by 25%–30% of the students. This suggests that sustainability should be present in all modules and levels of the course as an underlying principle.

Aspirations and current practices

Looking beyond the curriculum and teaching and learning approaches, The *Times Higher Education* (2019) University Impact Ranking is the first global attempt to offer an alternative view of university excellence and assess universities against the UN SDGs. In addition to the hard data on publications and citations, these global performance tables use metrics based on 11 of the 17 UN SDGs to assess the social, environmental, and economic impact of universities on society. The overall ranking includes 462 universities from 76 countries and the results from its first two editions confirm the uneven geographical distribution of commitment to SD evident in previous research (Weiss and Barth, 2019), with Canada, Ireland, and Australia leading the list.

A quick scan of information available in the public domain shows that most UK universities register commitment to delivering the UN SDGs. For example, one of the four main outcomes of the Bournemouth University Strategic Plan 2025 is: 'providing the opportunities for staff and students to develop their sustainability skills and knowledge within a community of learning that align with the SDGs' (BU, 2020). In conversations with the BU Sustainability Team in 2019, 91% of Programme Leaders believed their programmes align to one or more of the goals. To understand how best to integrate the SDGs into the curricula, the university has set up a new Sustainability Academic Network reporting to the Sustainability Committee. The purpose of these new initiatives is to support academics to embed sustainability in the curriculum and align research with the SDGs. Such examples of good practices show the beginning of a positive change towards incorporating the SDGs in all aspects, levels and activities of HE providers. The question remains, whether and how the strategic level aspirations, policies, and initiatives translate into specific actions at the course and unit levels.

Nonetheless, such examples are encouraging in that they show an effective move towards increasing institutional support, without which it will be difficult to see any real results. Many universities claim strong institutional commitment to sustainability through strategic planning documents designed to look comprehensively across divisions and involve all members of the university. The real challenge is often to get all stakeholders of the university (academics, students, and administration) to buy into these policies and adopt the sustainability values in their personal behaviours, attitudes, and teaching and learning practices. In order to be successful, sustainability should be part of the organisational culture and not imposed from the top.

Conclusion

The review of the literature on the implementation of sustainability into HE and that of current practices showed that significant and tangible progress has been made globally and at many levels. Nevertheless, the evidence from the domain of tourism education is limited, fragmented and piecemeal. Tourism is a multi-disciplinary area of study that is deeply embedded in contemporary social and economic life. Tourism education can therefore contribute to understanding and tackling the broader societal challenges within the framework of the SDGs.

Universities operate in a dynamic and rapidly changing environment. Scholars point out that the nature of academia is changing against the neoliberal landscape and under the external pressures of funding cuts, opening HE to competition, improving the efficiencies of course delivery through restructuring of departments and standardisation of curricula and teaching approaches, among others (Dredge et al., 2015). These can be a barrier to a true transformational change and prevent HE providers from effectively addressing the SDGs, thus perpetuating socially and ecologically unsustainable values. As some scholars point out, 'The question at hand is whether tourism academia is focused on sustaining the environment and people, sustaining the tourism industry, or merely sustaining academia' (Slocum et al., 2019, p. 40).

The successful practices reviewed earlier in the chapter convincingly show that commitment to SD declared only through policies is far from enough. Adopting an integrative approach to the commitment to the SDGs and aligning the educational strategy with the institutional strategies on employability, internationalisation, research, and operational sustainability is more likely to bring tangible and rewarding results. It is critical to not only align learning opportunities and research with the SDGs, but also to manage universities' own consumption for the benefit of society at present and into the future. The pillars of sustainability should be embedded throughout the whole course curriculum and teaching and learning strategies, at all levels, with backward and forward linkages between modules. The tourism curriculum should be consciously and purposefully supported by transformational approaches and critical thinking if education for sustainability is to be implemented effectively. Academic leadership and support at all levels is needed to foster capacity building on sustainability, enabling academics to 'teach what they practise and practise what they teach'. Without such actions, tourism curricula will continue to be just 'business as usual' (Wilson and Von Der Heidt, 2013).

Conditions and speed of change vary in different countries, and for this reason SDGs, frameworks and guidelines should be creatively adapted to the specific settings, needs and resources available. While researchers can identify and promote best practices in including SD in tourism education, it is also important to recognise that the one-size-fits-all approach is not effective and decisions should be contextualised.

There is an increasing expectation that universities across the globe can and should lead the way in supporting responsible social and environmental change. Introducing appropriate and innovative measures will allow universities to 'walk the talk' and enable them to raise their profile. Tourism education plays a critical role not only in raising sustainability awareness but also in providing high-impact, quality education. A deeper assessment of the global tourism system requires well-developed decision-making, as well as ethical and critical thinking skills. As scholars point out, it is not about teaching the SDGs specifically, but about educating learners how to apply these concepts for the benefit of future generations, to make informed decisions where social, economic, ecological, and ethical aspects may go hand in hand (Dredge et al., 2013, Slocum et al., 2019).

This chapter shows that further research on the implementation of sustainability in the tourism curricula is needed to better understand the current developments and draw an agenda for the way ahead. More research on student and employer attitudes towards sustainability in the tourism curriculum will help balance the real-world relevance of the HE with the changing nature of student demands and the influence of the industry. The existing business models imply short-term nature and are in contrast with the SGDs and long-term objectives of HE. According to the industry the most important environmental skills in 2030 will relate to habitat management, creation of a common environmental awareness and promotion of environmentally friendly activities and products (NTG, 2019). This, again, is a rather short-sighted forecast that focuses on environmental sustainability while ignoring the other two pillars of SD. Last but not least, more evidence is needed to show that the industry is recognising and rewarding the value of this with the graduates they recruit (Ali et al., 2017).

It is crucial to equip academics with the tools, knowledge, and skills to successfully introduce sustainability into the curriculum (Millar et al., 2013). The importance of train-the-trainer initiatives is even more evident if universities are to motivate and inspire academics' willingness to take action. More research is needed to determine how sustainability is incorporated into curricula and to understand different pedagogies that enhance commitment to achieving the SDGs. This sets the next step in this research agenda, which is to explore the approaches and views of the different academics and courses both in the United Kingdom and internationally.

There is a shared understanding that academia has still a long way ahead to achieve the SDGs. The question remains, is academia tackling 21st century phenomena and challenges with last century approaches? Have we developed new transformative approaches to ESD or simply repackaged and rebranded the transformative learning theory? Without conscious and purposeful actions, it will be *plus ça change, plus c'est la même chose.*

References

AACSB (2020), "Leaders on leadership," available at: https://www.aacsb.edu/publications/researchreports/collective-vision-for-business-education (accessed 10 February 2020).

Airey, D. and Johnson, S. (1999), "The content of tourism degree courses in the UK," *Tourism Management*, Vol. 20 No. 2, pp. 229–235.

Ali, A. and Frew, J.A. (2014), "Technology innovation and applications in sustainable destination development," *Information Technology & Tourism*, Vol. 14 No. 4, pp. 265–290.

Ali, A., Murphy, H.C. and Nadkarni, S. (2017), "Sustainable development and hospitality education: Employers' perspectives on the relevance for graduate employability," *Journal of Teaching in Travel & Tourism*, Vol. 17 No. 3, pp. 159–172.

Bessant, S, Bailey, P., Robinson, Z., Bland Tomkinson, C., Tomkinson R., Ormerod, M. and Boast, R. (2013), *Problem-Based Learning: A Case Study of Sustainability Education A Toolkit for University Educators*, available at: www.keele.ac.uk/hybridpbl/pblandesdresources (accessed 10 January 2020).

Biasin, C. (2018), "Transformative learning: Evolutions of the adult learning theory," *Phronesis*, Vol. 7 No. 3, pp. 5–17.

Boley, B. (2011), "Sustainability in hospitality and tourism education: Towards an integrated curriculum," *Journal of Hospitality and Tourism Education*, Vol. 23, No. 4, pp. 22–31.

Boyle, A., Wilson, E. and Dimmock, K. (2014), "Space for sustainability? Sustainable education in the tourism curriculum space," In Dredge, D., Airey, D. and Gross M. (Eds.), *The Routledge Handbook of Tourism and Hospitality Education*, Routledge, London and New York, pp. 551–564.

BU. (2020), "Update on sustainability in our academia," *Bournemouth University*, available at: https://staffintranet.bournemouth.ac.uk/news/news/thismonth/Updateonsustainabilityinouracademia.php (accessed 12 February 2020).

Camargo, B.A. and Gretzel, U. (2017), "What do tourism students know about sustainability and sustainable tourism? An exploratory study of Latin American students," *Journal of Teaching in Travel & Tourism*, Vol. 17 No. 2, pp. 101–117.

CMI, (2013), "The effective change manager: The change management body of knowledge," *Change Management Institute*, available at: www.change-management-institute.com (accessed on 5 January 2020).

Deale, C. and Barber, N. (2012), "How important is sustainability education to hospitality programs?" *Journal of Teaching in Travel and Tourism*, Vol. 12 No. 2, pp. 165–187.

Deale, C., Nichols, J. and Jacques, P. (2009), "A descriptive study of sustainability education in the hospitality curriculum," *Journal of Hospitality and Tourism Education*, Vol. 21 No. 4, pp. 34–42.

Dodds R. and Butler R. (2019), "The phenomena of overtourism: A review," *International Journal of Tourism Cities*, Vol. 5 No. 4, pp. 519–528.

Drayson, R. (2015), "Employer attitudes towards and skills for sustainable development," QAA-NUS-Change Agents UK, available at: https://www.heacademy.ac.uk/system/files/executive-summary-employers.pdf (accessed 15 December 2019).

Drayson, R., Bone, E., Agombar, J. and Kemp S. (2014), "Student attitudes towards and skills for sustainable development," QAA-NUS-Change Agents UK, available at: https://www.advance-he.ac.uk/knowledge-hub/student-attitudes-towards-and-skills-sustainable-development (accessed 15 December 2019).

Dredge, D., Airey, D. and Gross, M.J. (2015). "Creating the future: Tourism, hospitality and events education in a post-industrial, post-disciplinary world," In Dredge, D., Airey, D. and Gross M. (Eds.), *The Routledge Handbook of Tourism and Hospitality Education*, Routledge, London, pp. 535–550.

Dredge, D., Benckendorff, P., Day, M., Gross, M.J., Walo, M., Weeks, P., and Whitelaw, P.A. (2012), "Building a Stronger Future: Balancing professional and liberal education ideals in undergraduate tourism and hospitality education," *Key Issues in Tourism, Hospitality and Events Curriculum and Design*, Issues paper 1, Canberra: Australian Learning and Teaching Council.

Dredge, D., Benckendorff, P., Day, M., Gross, M.J., Walo, M., Weeks, P. and Whitelaw, P.A. (2013), "Drivers of change in tourism, hospitality, and event management education: An Australian perspective," *Journal of Hospitality & Tourism Education*, Vol. 25 No. 2, pp. 89–102.

European Commission Report. (2013), "Modernising higher education in Europe," available at: https://op.europa.eu/en/publication-detail/-/publication/fbd4c2aa-aeb7-41ac-ab4c-a94feea9eb1f (accessed 2 February 2020).

Filho, W.L. (2000), "Dealing with misconceptions on the concept of sustainability," *International Journal of Sustainability in Higher Education*, Vol. 1 No. 1, pp. 9–19.

Filho, W.L. (2015), "Education for sustainable development in higher education: Reviewing needs," In Filho, W.L. (Ed.), *Transformative Approaches to Sustainable Development at Universities*, Springer, Switzerland, pp. 3–12.

Filho W.L., Brandlin L.L., Becker D., Skanavis C., Kounani A., Sardi C., Papaioannidou D., Paço A., Azeiteiro, U., de Sousa, L.O., Raath, S., Pretorius, R.W., Shiel, C., Vargas V., Trencher G. and Marans R.W. (2018), "Sustainable development policies as indicators and pre-conditions for sustainability efforts at universities: Fact or fiction?" *International Journal of Sustainability in Higher Education*, Vol. 19 No. 1, 2018, pp. 85–113.

Hák, T., Janoušková, S. and Moldan, B. (2016), "Sustainable development goals: A need for relevant indicators," *Ecological Indicators*, Vol. 60, pp. 565–573.

Hunt, L. and Chalmers D. (2013), "Introduction," In Hunt, L. and Chalmers, D. (Eds.), *University Teaching in Focus: A Learning-centred Approach*, Routledge, London and New York, pp. xxi–xxii.

Joseph, C. (2012), "Internationalizing the curriculum: Pedagogy for social justice," *Current Sociology*, Vol. 60 No. 2, pp. 239–257.

Leihy, P. and Salazar, J. (2011), *Education for Sustainability in University Curricula: Policies and Practice in Victoria*. University of Melbourne, Melbourne.

Longhurst, J., Bellingham, L., Cotton, D., Isaac, V., Kemp, S., Martin, S., Peters, C. Robertson, A., Ryan, A., Taylor, C. and Tilbury, D. (2014), "Education for sustainable development: Guidance for UK higher education providers," *Quality Assurance Agency* and *Higher Education Academy*, Technical Report, available at: https://www.qaa.ac.uk/docs/qaa/quality-code/education-sustainable-development-guidance-june-14.pdf?sfvrsn=1c46f981_8 (accessed 15 January 2020).

Lozano, R. (2011), "The state of sustainability reporting in universities," *International Journal of Sustainability in Higher Education*, Vol. 12 No. 1, pp. 67–78.

Mader, C., Scott, G. and Abdul Razak, D. (2013), "Effective change management, governance and policy for sustainability transformation in higher education," *Sustainability Accounting, Management and Policy Journal*, Vol. 4 No. 3, pp. 264–284.

Meyer, J.H.F. and Land, R. (2003) Threshold concepts and troublesome knowledge-linkages to ways of thinking and practicing. u: Rust C. [ur.] Improving student learning - ten years on, Oxford: OCsLD.

Mezirow, J. (1990), *Fostering Critical Reflection in Adulthood*. Jossey-Bass Publishers, San Francisco, pp. 1–20, available at: https://my.liberatedleaders.com.au/wp-content/uploads/2017/02/How-Critical-Reflection-triggers-Transformative-Learning-Mezirow.pdf (accessed 19 January 2020).

Mezirow, J. (1997), "Transformative learning: Theory to practice," *New Directions for Adult and Continuing Education*, Vol. 74, pp. 5–12.

Mihalic, T., Zabkar, V. and Cvelbar, K.L. (2012), "A hotel sustainability business model: Evidence from Slovenia," *Journal of Sustainable Tourism*, Vol. 20 No. 5, pp. 701–719.

Millar, M., Brown, C., Carruthers, C., Jones, T., Kim, Y.S., Raab, C., Teeters, K. and Yang, L.T. (2013). "Implementing environmental sustainability in the global hospitality, tourism, and leisure industries," In Johnson, L. F. (Ed.), *Higher Education for Sustainability: Cases, Challenges, and Opportunities from Across the Curriculum*, Routledge, New York and London, pp. 124–136.

Moscardo, G. (2015), "Tourism and sustainability: Challenges, conflict and core knowledge," In Moscardo, G. and Benckendorff, P. (Eds.), *Education for Sustainability in Tourism*, Springer, Berlin, Heidelberg, pp. 25–43.

NTG (2019), "The next tourism generation alliance report," available at: https://nexttourismgeneration.eu/wp-content/uploads/2019/03/NTG_Desk_Research_Summary_January_2019.pdf (accessed 5 January 2020).

Peeters, P., Gössling, S., Klijs, J., Milano, C., Novelli, M., Dijkmans, C., Eijgelaar, E., Hartman, S., Heslinga, J., Isaac, R., Mitas, O., Moretti, S., Nawijn, J., Papp, B. and Postma, A. (2018), "Research for TRAN Committee - Overtourism: Impact and possible policy responses," European Parliament, Policy Department for Structural and Cohesion Policies, Brussels, available at: https://www.europarl.

europa.eu/thinktank/en/document.html?reference=IPOL_STU(2018)629184 (accessed 20 October 2019).

People 1st. (2019), "The future digital, green & social skill needs in tourism," Insight reports, available at: https://people1st.co.uk/getattachment/Insights/Insight-reports/The-future-digital,-green-social-skill-needs-in/NTG-research-summary-EU.pdf/?lang=en-GB (accessed 10 January 2020).

Rawlinson, S. and Dewhurst, P. (2013), "How can effective university-industry partnerships be developed?", *Worldwide Hospitality and Tourism Themes*, Vol. 5 No. 3, pp. 255–267.

Savelyeva, T. and McKenna, J.R. (2011), "Campus sustainability: Emerging curricula models in higher education," *International Journal of Sustainability in Higher Education*, Vol. 12 No. 1, pp. 55–66.

Sibbel, A. (2009), "Pathways towards sustainability through higher education." *International Journal of Sustainability in Higher Education*, Vol. 10 No. 1, pp. 68–82.

Slocum, S.L., Dimitrov, D.Y. and Webb, K. (2019). "The impact of neoliberalism on higher education tourism programs: Meeting the 2030 sustainable development goals with the next generation," *Tourism Management Perspectives*, Vol. 30, pp. 33–42.

Stewart, M. (2013), "Understanding learning: Theories and critique," In Hunt, L. and Chalmers, D. (Eds.), *University Teaching in Focus: A Learning-centred Approach*, Routledge, London and New York, pp. 3–20.

Stoyanova-Bozhkova, S. (2011), "Tourism Development in Transition Economies: An Evaluation of the Development of Tourism at a Black Sea Coastal Destination During Political and Socio-economic Transition," Unpublished Thesis, Bournemouth University, Bournemouth.

SOS-UK, (2020), "Students organising for sustainability – UK," available at: https://sustainability.nus.org.uk/ (accessed 10 January 2020).

Tilbury, D. and Cooke, K. (2005), *A National Review of Environmental Education and its Contribution to Sustainability in Australia: Volume 1 Frameworks for Sustainability*. Australian Government Department of the Environment and Water Resources and the Australian Research Institute in Education for Sustainability (ARIES).

Times Higher Education. (2019), "The world university rankings," available at: https://www.timeshighereducation.com/news/university-impact-rankings-2019-results-announced (accessed 15 February 2020).

Tribe, J. (2002), "The philosophic practitioner," *Annals of Tourism Research*, Vol. 29 No. 2, pp. 338–357.

Tribe, J. (2005), "New tourism research," *Tourism Recreation Research*, Vol. 30 No. 2, pp. 5–8.

UK Subject benchmark statement for Events, Hospitality, Leisure, Sport and Tourism, QAA. (November 2019), available at: https://www.qaa.ac.uk/docs/qaa/subject-benchmark-statements/subject-benchmark-statement-events-leisure-sport-tourism.pdf?sfvrsn=c339c881_11 (accessed 20 December 2019).

UNDESD. (2005), "Education for sustainable development brief. United Nations Decade of Education for Sustainable Development," *UNDESD*, available at: http://www.unesco.org (accessed 13 January 2020).

Universities UK. (2018), "Solving future skills challenges," available at: https://www.universitiesuk.ac.uk/policy-and-analysis/reports/Documents/2018/solving-future-skills-challenges.pdf (accessed 3 February 2020).

UNWTO (2020), "Quality Assurance for tourism education, training and research programmes," UNWTO.TedQual, available at: https://www.unwto.org/UNWTO-ted-qual (accessed 10 January 2020).

Wall, G. (2020), "From carrying capacity to overtourism: A perspective article," *Tourism Review*, Vol. 75 No. 1, pp. 212–215.

Weiss, M. and Barth, M. (2019), "Global research landscape of sustainability curricula implementation in higher education," *International Journal of Sustainability in Higher Education*, Vol. 20 No. 4, pp. 570–589.

Wilson, E. and von der Heidt, T. (2013), "Business as usual? Barriers to education for sustainability in the tourism curriculum," *Journal of Teaching in Travel & Tourism*, Vol. 13 No. 2, pp. 130–147.

9 Transformative tourism education

An evidence-based framework as best practice in the age of overtourism

Patrick J.N. L'Espoir Decosta, Seleni Matus, Naomi F. Dale and Beverley Wilson-Wünsch

Introduction

This chapter proposes an education practice framework at the nexus of transformative learning theory and evidence-based practice (EBP) to frame the scholarly study of strategic tourism education and overtourism. The practical experience of two of the authors with the framework in a post-graduate immersion consultancy practicum unit in Bali is employed as a case study. We first outline the theoretical rationale to and parameters of the proposed integrated, holistic framework. We then connect tourism and education to highlight the significance of evidence in addressing the challenges of sustainable tourism in light of the phenomenon of overtourism within an evolutionary education framework consistent with the Principles for Responsible Management Education (PRME), supported by the United Nations. We argue that the framework provides not only an inspirational design and practical tourism education strategy but also addresses, within a liberal scholarship of ethical-education-in-action, the broader PRME higher education goals of providing future leaders with the requisite skills and capabilities to address the Sustainable Development Goals (SDGs): a tourism education strategy to deal with overtourism.

The challenge

Since its inclusion as an area of study in higher education nearly half a century ago, tourism has been critically discussed and analysed from a variety of perspectives. In concluding that the emergence of tourism as a discipline 'will not be denied', Jafari and Ritchie (1981: 32) responded to Leiper's (1979) earlier call for the creation of a new discipline of tourism and relied on tourism- and traveller-related problems and the multidisciplinary nature of tourism. Since then, tourism has continuously grown and developed to become well established as both a socio-economic sector and an area of study in tertiary education and research (Airey and Gross, 2015; Airey and

Tribe, 2005). However, progress in curriculum issues has been restrained in the face of the increasing pressures from unabated growth and changes in both the tourism sector and in tertiary education. Despite innovative and forward-looking approaches, such as the Tourism Education Futures Initiative (TEFI) (Sheldon and Fesenmaier, 2015) and the integration of information technology as key advances in curriculum development (Munar and Bodker, 2015), tourism education is not in an 'age of change' (Airey and Gross, 2015) and cannot yet be characterised as a '… means for understanding and responsible action in more widely drawn, complex world of tourism' (Tribe, 2005: 37).

A complex challenge that reflects the recent dramatic evolution of tourism is the phenomenon of overtourism, which since its coinage in the mid-2000s has inflicted dire socio-cultural, natural, and economic consequences, not only on destinations but also on residents, tourists, and tourism as a sustainable and viable sector (Shevachman, 2016; Dodds and Butler 2018). This phenomenon and the perils associated with it have surprisingly attracted almost no academic scrutiny. Indeed, apart from the ambiguity created by overtourism for the broader genus of tourism, it also challenges the provision of tourism education in its depth (research and development of knowledge) and strength (curriculum and teaching development and objectives) (Airey and Tribe, 2015). Tourism education thus needs to update, create, and disseminate knowledge that is stimulating, relevant and transformative to the lives of students, communities and stakeholders (Freire, 1985), with further implications for curriculum, pedagogy, and the student experience (Airey and Tribe, 2015).

This chapter addresses the need for educational change in the face of the uncertainties posed by overtourism by presenting a best practice framework employed by two of the authors in a global immersion programme in Bali, Indonesia as part of a postgraduate sustainable destination course. The framework draws on several concepts of significance to the evolution of higher education in general and tourism education in particular, including knowledge creation and dissemination (Cooper, Ruhanen and Craig-Smith, 2004), critical pedagogy and emancipatory learning (Freire, 1985), problem-based education (Duch, Grow and Allen, 2001), and evidence-based teaching (EBT) (Emerson and Records, 2008). This combined approach is bound by Tribe's underlying principles in 'The Philosophic Practitioner' (2002) that are designed to tease out from a pragmatic liberal education (Roth, 2015) the skills and indispensable capacities of an educated citizen, such as problem solving and thinking critically and analytically to challenge and reconsider the status quo in pedagogy and professional practice. The end goal is to propose a new, different and transformative educational experience for the students, who face crises like overtourism when they enter the workplace. At the core of such a transformative approach is a clear alignment with the goals set for the practicum itself in line with expected graduate attributes as set for the Masters' programme.

From tourism to overtourism

The upsurge in tourism development since the advent of the jet aircraft has led to an ever-increasing number of people and communities around the world being impacted by tourism in one form or another. According to estimates from the United Nations World Tourism Organization (UNWTO), international tourist arrivals have increased from 25 million in the 1950s to nearly 1.4 billion in 2018. While more than two-thirds of tourists arrived in Europe in the 1950s, the distribution had shifted dramatically by 2018, when Europe received just over 50% of total international tourist arrivals, the Americas around 15.5%, the Asia-Pacific region an estimated 24.5%, and the Middle East and Africa sharing the remainder almost equally (Roser, 2020). For less-developed countries (LDCs), tourism is perceived as a potential driver of economic growth and development (UNWTO, 2019) and a force for good in the world (Uniting Travel, April 2018). However, as income levels increase and airfares decrease worldwide while social media draws attention to specific destinations, tourists from both developed and emerging economies are gaining access not only to iconic and popular destinations but also to less-known destinations. Many of these places can no longer cope with the success of their own popularity. During peak periods, cities like Barcelona and Venice, islands like Tasmania and Iceland, and attractions like Angkor Wat in Cambodia and Devil's Tongue in Norway are overrun by tourists, with demand exceeding the carrying capacity of these destinations. The consequences are dire, as local residents experience reduced quality of life due to hordes of tourists, who in turn have a disappointing experience at these destinations.

This pandemonium based on social tensions is the essence of overtourism. The deep economic, environmental and social impacts of the increasing pervasiveness and volume of tourism have been hotly debated for decades 'see Mathieson and Wall (1982)' and have, over the years, placed increasing pressure on resources at destinations (water, waste management, electricity, food, infrastructure). Several studies have focused on environmental and biophysical carrying capacity (Liu and Borthwick, 2011), economic carrying capacity (Snowman, 1987), and social carrying capacity (Navarro et al., 2012). Similarly, Wall (2019) contends that studies on tourism impacts increasingly recognise, for example, 'the importance of the journey' (p. 28), with a focus on the carbon footprint from air travel or on transformations in the very nature and characteristics of an attraction resulting from mass tourism. For instance, Mount Everest and Mount Kilimanjaro are facing 'a conga line of mountaineers [waiting] to approach the summit' (Lowrey, 2019), creating mountains of waste, while wildlife viewing in African safari parks is increasingly influencing wildlife behaviour as these sites gain popularity among adventure tourists. Put simply, overtourism and the dangers associated with it are becoming the bane of tourist destinations, their residents, and attractions worldwide.

Given its severe socio-economic and environmental consequences, as well as interest by academics and researchers in resource management concepts, overtourism has unsurprisingly become a popular topic in university tourism courses, such as tourism planning and policy, tourism economics, destination management, the tourism experience, responsible tourism management, and sustainable destination management. However, as Wall (2019) warns, determining the causal relationships between behaviour and impacts and associated problems is quite complex and requires specialised academic scrutiny for more holistic knowledge, training of tourism researchers in scientific research methods, and education of tourists and of those practicing and involved in tourism. At least two edited books on overtourism were published in 2019, see Milano, Cheer and Novelli (2019); Dodds and Butler (2019), and one in 2020 see Pechlaner, Innerhofer and Erschbamer (2020), addressing the problem from different perspectives, with various theories and methodologies. These three opuses present different perspectives on the origins (Dodds and Butler, 2019), impacts (Qurashi, 2019), and drivers and solutions (Hartmann and Stecker, 2020; Gerritsma, 2019) of overtourism. Case studies include (i) overcrowding in Amsterdam as it strives to strike a balance between trade, tolerance, and tourism (Gerritsma, 2019) and its management strategies (Koens, Postma and Papp, 2020); (ii) the global south, with Thailand becoming too popular for its own good (Hess, 2019); and (iii) the wilderness areas of the Galapagos being overrun by tourists (Pecot and Ricaurte-Quijano, 2019). These edited books also present different disciplinary-grounded theories to critically discuss the complexities (Jóhannesson and Lund, 2019; Visentin and Bertocchi, 2019; Wall, 2019; Butler, 2019), contentions (Canãda, 2019; Clancy, 2020), implications for the tourism experience (Rickly, 2019; Reif, 2020), rhetoric (Nunes Gonçalves, 2019; Canosa, Graham and Wilson, 2019; Volgger, 2020), and approaches (Ioannides, 2019; Kohl, 2019; Reif, 2020) to the study of overtourism. However comprehensive these books are, and notwithstanding the call by Wall (2018) to take a holistic approach to tourism education when dealing with tourism, these works barely consider the strategic role that tourism education can potentially play in the sustainable management and performance of tourism at destinations, in particular the phenomenon of overtourism increasingly faced by such destinations. This chapter addresses this lacuna by proposing a tourism education practice framework based on several approaches to higher education that helps to bridge industry and theory through a practicum under the aegis of a global immersion programme. The following section outlines the foundation to the evidence-based framework applied in the illustrative case study for this chapter by first considering key elements in the evolution of higher education and tourism education (ranging from knowledge to the student experience through the curriculum) to then engage the phenomenon of overtourism with tourism education practice.

Education – the evolution of higher tourism education

Since Jafari and Ritchie's significant foray into tourism education in a special issue of *Annals of Tourism* in 1981, much has been achieved and changed in the higher education of tourism. The definition of tourism as a domain for knowledge building has been thoroughly debated and addressed over the years by academics and various international, national, and regional organisations alike (Yu et al., 2012, United Nations World Tourism Organization [UNWTO], 2019); Frechtling, 2010; Canadian Tourism Commission, 2003; Leiper, 1979; McCabe, 2009; Oppermann, 1992). Jafari and Ritchie's (1981) 'wheel' has been fundamental in forming the foundation for identifying the disciplinary boundaries of tourism and the conceptual elements necessary for tourism education and research. Today, there are approximately 400 journals dedicated to tourism and associated domains (McKercher, 2020) that contribute to the knowledge base and understanding of tourism. This sheer volume of information, data and knowledge has been enabled by advances made by researchers who, throughout the volumes and issues of journals over time, have broadened and shed light on theoretical concepts of interest to the domains. At the same time, their advances have clarified the inter-relationships among tourism, knowledge and tourism curriculum (Tribe, 2002).

As epistemological analysis and advances in tourism increase, Parsons (1991) sees the need for the synergistic development of a core curriculum with input from both education and industry (Koh, 1995), including what is taught (Taylor and Richards, 1985) and the overall educational experiences bundled in a degree programme (Tribe, 2005). The urgency for closer relationships between industry and training needs in tourism (Koh, 1995; Holloway, 1995) was not only geared towards the identification of a body of knowledge on which both academics and the tourism industry could rely and build but also the advocacy of best practices (Goodenough and Page, 1993), including partnerships (Cooper, 1997) and deliberate connections between education and industry (Airey, 2008).

In short, the need for applied research in higher education has been acknowledged. However, applied research has often been criticised for its propensity to consider problems that are too company- or sector-specific and because it deals with concrete and operationally-oriented issues. It is therefore less likely to '… progress the body of knowledge' (Cooper, Shepherd and Westlake, 1994: 126) and is too reminiscent of the vocational origins of tourism education. However, before citing the relationships between tourism education and industry as part of the theoretical rationale for this chapter, it is necessary to consider the broader context and evolution of contemporary higher education to understand, among other things, how industry has impacted the landscape of higher education in general (Lea, 2015) and tourism education in particular (Ayikoru, Tribe and Airey, 2009) through a neoliberal agenda.

From vocational to liberal ideological influences on tourism education

A historical approach to the evolution of tourism education is indispensable because, as tourism education moved from being mere pre-paradigmatic (Kunh, 1971) with a vocational-based and a-theoretical curriculum to taking a more liberal reflective approach to curriculum (Tribe, 2002) based on thinking and reflection (ibid), it developed, in parallel with the tourism world, its own epistemology that was undeniably multi-disciplinary but nonetheless underpinned by scientific method (Tribe, 1997). As a knowledge force field (Tribe, 2006), tourism education relied on a liberal emancipatory approach that prioritised the development of philosophic practitioners equipped with broader knowledge, transferable skills and a strong sense of values, ethics and civic obligation that prepared them to engage and participate in a complex working world (Silver and Brennan, 1988; https://www.aacu.org/). In short, it is more a way of studying (discipline) than a field of study (Tribe, 1997). Tourism was thus intent on developing and consolidating its theoretical base. However, the liberal approach has also meant that the needs of the industry it purportedly supports have been somewhat neglected. This is particularly true of academics who have taken a disciplinary approach to tourism (e.g. the sociology of tourism, the geography of tourism, the economics of tourism), who have overlooked the need for and importance of applied research. See Tribe (1997) and Cooper, Shepherd and Westlake (1994) for a deeper discussion on the differences between a disciplinary approach to tourism studies and applied research, known as a component of 'part 2' production of tourism knowledge in Tribe's 1997 modified 'The creation of tourism knowledge'.)

The added complication of neoliberal influence on tourism education

Major challenges to the liberal academic constructionist approach to tourism education came from the various stakeholders it serves, their different sizes and locations (Sigala and Baum, 2003) and their specific needs (Cooper and Shepherd, 1997). As a major stakeholder, the government has since the 1980s significantly influenced higher education by calling for modifications that reflect and respond to changes in society and the economy (Barnett, 2000) demanded by neoliberalism, ushered in by Thatcher of the UK and Reagan of the United States (Davies, 2015). As an ideology, neoliberalism emphasises progress, international competitiveness, profit, discipline (Apple, 2001), performativity measures, individuality, and free market rationale operationalised through the adoption of managerialism in government, policy and institutions at large (Ayikoru, Tribe and Airey, 2009). The manifestation of the authority of neoliberalism lies in measuring, rating and comparing with the goal of measuring happiness (Davies, 2015) and achieving outcomes (Di Leo, 2017). Universities must therefore compete for students in international markets, and their ability to secure government funding is directly related to their performance, which is itself linked to the universities' academic, research, and societal impact performances (Di Leo, 2017). To Donohue (2008), metrics relating to higher education have led to the advent of the corporate university, which is now required to be accountable and transparent while measuring performance (Page, 2003) and achieve accreditation.

Critics of neoliberalism lament the fact that schools and departments need to defend the public value of their education to the state (Butler, 2014). According to Butler, neoliberalists perceive universities primarily as engines of economic growth to the detriment of the traditional liberal view of the acquisition of knowledge as a public good (Collini, 2012). In their analysis of policy texts on higher education and university course programmes in the United Kingdom, Ayikoru, Tribe and Airey (2009) found that skills and career prospects (part of vocationalism) are neoliberalist ideals that articulate tourism education as a business with industry and employers as its key players. The economic imperatives of higher education are thus legitimised by the government's policy deployment of its education strategy. According to Laclau and Mouffe (1985), these imperatives become hegemonic, as their meanings dominate the educational landscape. Higher education requires conformity on the part of its institutions and individuals. The corporate university is the new measure of higher education run well (Di Leo, 2017), which is the only measure of academic progress in neoliberalism.

Ayikoru et al.'s (2009) confirmation of the influences of neoliberal discourse on tourism higher education institutions, as well as Nussbaum's (2011) connection of the imperatives of such influences to development theories, effectively define tourism by means of business management frameworks (Stuart-Hoyle, 2003), thereby setting the tone for an accelerated process of internationalisation and globalisation (Go, 1998). Globalisation and its link to tourism education is, according to Tribe (2002), dual-faceted. On the one hand, tourism education strives to serve and adapt to the development opportunities of globalisation; e.g., how to deal with mass tourism and overtourism. On the other hand, tourism problematises the threat that globalisation presents to the autonomy of local communities, their culture and lifestyles (Sachs, 1992); e.g., how tourism development can minimise cultural disruption while securing livelihoods. From those needs arose sustainable tourism development and a concomitant 'liberating' and 'transformative' tourism education. The latter requires the integration of stakeholder approaches in its curriculum (Koh, 1995; Tribe, 2002) to address the needs of the various players in tourism, as well as Wall's (2018) call for a deliberate policy of high-quality tourism education that would ramp up training and education in research methods and environmental studies. This is only possible, however, if tourism (education) transcends its business focus to embrace a more flexible pedagogy of transformation akin to the potential for more sustainable and responsible higher education as reflected in the PRME.

From sustainable tourism development to ethical tourism education

The term 'sustainable tourism' can be traced to Butler's (1992) comparison of 'alternative tourism', defined as tourism that respects natural, social, and community values and allows for authentic and shared experiences between hosts and guests (Eadington and Smith, 1992), to sustainable development, referring to a broad, integrated approach to conservation during development, with a focus on the well-being of people and best interests of communities (derived from IUCN's definition of 1980: Section 1.2). Though definitions of sustainable tourism abound, the term generally encompasses inter-generational equity when sustainable development is applied to tourism and reflects some or all of the economic, social, cultural, and environmental connotations of sustainable development (Southgate and Sharpley, 2002). Over the years, sustainable tourism imperatives have been embraced by governments, international organisations, and industry alike (Garrod and Fyall, 1998), and codes of practice with a social and environmental conscience have emerged (Goodwin, 2011), reflected in renowned articulations at global summits such as the Rio Earth Summit in 1992, its +10 in 2002 and +20 in 2012, as well as in specific articulations such as the PRME at the 2006 Global Forum 'Business as Agent of World Benefit'.

The fundamental paradox of sustainable development nonetheless remains the issue of how to maintain development without depleting and damaging the environment, which undermines the very notion of sustainable tourism development. The future of (sustainable) tourism, considered by many countries as a key driver of development spanning several sectors and interests (Cater, 1995), is therefore in jeopardy. The intricacies and complexities of sustainable tourism have been subject to academic scrutiny through the sequential lenses of Jafari's (2001) 'adaptancy' and 'knowledge' platforms. To Macbeth (2005), however, changing environments coupled with progress in sustainable tourism discourse necessitate new platforms of tourism thought to include 'ethical' and reflexivity as opposed to a rigid positivistic-scientific paradigm that views knowledge as objective. Only then can we aspire to a liberal education, one that will provide the space for critical thinking, information evaluation, problem solving, and adaptation (Maimon, 2018), not just for a transformative tourism education but also for defence against the tyranny (Berkes, 2009) of the negative impacts of tourism. Furthermore, the education that accompanies such changes requires a radical overhaul (Sheldon et al., 2011) as tourism sustainability becomes a key priority of local communities, residents, and tourists alike in light of the phenomenon of overtourism. Font and McCabe (2017) advocate for mainstream sustainability into the wider tourism business through product design and more persuasive marketing messages. They insist that globally, the industry is now at a pivotal point in its history, with numerous innovative solutions available to address sustainability challenges. In their edited book on overtourism, Dodds and Butler (2018) conclude that providing tourists with information and education is another way of mitigating the impacts of tourism. Following Boley (2011), we argue that (sustainable) tourism education can be supported through a curriculum that integrates sustainable principles. An initial step in that direction is Tribe's (2002) 'Education for ethical tourism action', in which he links ethical and sustainable tourism, as both are allied to the issue of social responsibility (2002: 310).

Indeed, Tribe (2002) calls for more than just a reflective discourse in the tourism education system. Referencing Schön's (1987) model of reflective practicum, Tribe (2002) proposes a knowing-in-action-oriented ethical education that encourages students to act as advocates for a better tourism society and world (Tribe, 1999). Ethical tourism action as part of a transformational tourism education is a model that emphasises the role of disciplinary-based thinking, responsible reflections and sustainable value that nevertheless gives the students the flexibility to generate their own reflective thinking based on the situation, context and problem at hand, making it less tied to specific disciplinary routines. For example, although an ethnographic approach may be appropriate to the study of the survival of traditional authentic craftsmanship through tourism-based activities, students' reflections on the problem may involve adding cultural diversity as an element of the subject to address cultural imperialism, globalisation and competition.

The art of action: pedagogy in an evidence-based tourism practicum

At the heart of Tribe's approach is the need for an ethical tourism practicum as part of the curriculum that creates a space for experiential learning and improvisation while also applying relevant contemporary technologies, such as virtual spaces, for tourism-related discussion. Beyond the three methods of case studies, role play and work-integrated learning as possible activities to support an ethical-tourism-in-action tourism practicum, we propose in this chapter a variation that required a group of tourism students from the George Washington University (GWU) in the United States to undertake a consulting project in collaboration with local tourism students in Indonesia as part of their Master of Tourism Administration curriculum. The practicum described in this chapter partially addresses the aforementioned issues related to shortcomings in research skills and a rigid education structure with a framework connecting research methods with tourism through an evidence-based approach for transformative (sustainable and responsible) education practices.

The Evidence-Based Transformational Tourism Education Framework (EBTTEF) incorporates evidence-based educational activities that are part of a current trial evidence-based integrated curriculum (Capezio, L'Espoir

Decosta and Keating, 2016) in selected management courses at the Australian National University (ANU) and are endorsed by the Center of Evidence Based Management (CEBMa). The framework is based on the full collaboration and participation of local tourism stakeholders who can contribute unique knowledge and strengths to the research. This participatory research (Palinkas and Soydan, 2012) approach sits within cutting-edge evidence-driven education and research paradigms that draw on extant knowledge and incorporate the engagement and contributions of the three constituencies explicitly recognised by the PRME: students, business (stakeholders), and faculty (www.unprme.org). This approach provides strategic guidance for the development of capabilities in each of these three groups in furtherance of a responsible, sustainable and inclusive global economy (Parkes, Buono and Howaidy, 2017). The goal is to give students hands-on experience with a tourism problem that requires them to rely on extant theoretical knowledge in the domain, tourism research methods, and reflection and critical action towards responsible tourism stewardship that improves the quality of life for stakeholders in the contexts within which tourism is practised (Tribe, 2002; IITS, 2018).

The context: a practicum with an Evidence-based Transformational Tourism Education Framework

A practicum in the form of a consulting project entitled 'Destination sustainability assessment of the Badung Region of Bali, Indonesia: celebrating cultural heritage and promoting community-based tourism' was organised by the GWU International Institute of Tourism Studies (IITS) as part of the university's 2018 global immersion programme. Twelve graduate students and two faculty members from GWU participated in the programme, along with six graduate students and two faculty members from the Sekolah Tinggi Pariwisata (STP) in Bali. The consulting project was carried out on behalf of the Ministry of Tourism's Tourism Institute of Bali and various tourism stakeholders in the Badung region (referred to in the practicum as 'the client'). The main purpose of the project was to assist the Badung region of Bail and the Ministry of Tourism of Bali in identifying areas of priority for the long-term sustainable and responsible vision for tourism growth in light of their present situation of overtourism, increasing population and environmental degradation. Identifying priorities was the first step towards addressing the four main objectives of the GSTC (2013):

1   Demonstrating sustainable destination management.
2   Maximising social and economic benefits for the host community and minimising negative impacts.
3   Maximising benefits to communities, visitors and cultural heritage and minimising negative impacts.
4   Maximising benefits to the environment and minimising negative impacts.

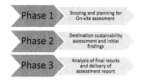

Figure 9.1 Global Sustainable Tourism Council's 3 phases to achieve sustainability.

The work was organised into three broad phases, with phase 1 starting in Washington, DC, merging into phase 2 in Bali, and phase 3 looping back in the United States (Figure 9.1).

The learning outcomes students were expected to achieve in the practicum were developed based on a learning outcomes grid developed by ANU's Research School of Management at the intersection of Bloom's revised taxonomy (Krathwohl, 2002) of cognitive processes and the principles of evidence-based management to reflect the different graduating thresholds expected from basic knowledge acquisition (LO1) to application of skills (LO6). To integrate sustainability education (Stephens et al., 2008) as part of the broader response to overtourism, a link was explicitly established between each evidence-based learning outcome and the respective standard of the UN-supported PRME.[1] In that way, the EB learning outcomes were aligned with the PRME's vision to realise the SDGs as expressed in the four pillars of the GSTC. The table below illustrates the initial part of the EBPF, which connects the evidence-based learning outcomes set for the practicum with the PRME and the four main pillars of the GSTC.

Phase 1 – Pre-departure goal setting, scoping, and planning for on-site assessment

Preparation for this project began in Washington, DC three months prior to departure. Students were paired online with their Indonesian counterparts and were introduced to Indonesia and Bali through a presentation by an Indonesian partner who is also a professional guide in the country. Students received education on tourism sustainability and research methods and were introduced to steps in EBP and research strategies to identify reliable sources of evidence (from academic literature, industry and organisations, and stakeholders such as practitioners), as well as learning strategies, including critical thinking and the use of metacognitive skills in reflection. These elements were embedded in the research methods of the EBTTEF that students would later employ to assess the health of the tourism industry of the Badung region of Bali, Indonesia against the Global Sustainable Tourism Council's (GSTC) destination level criteria, which had recently been adopted by the Indonesian Ministry of Tourism as a national standard for the sustainability of their destinations. Following Barends and Rousseau (2018), these elements (skills and capabilities) were deemed critical in the

Table 9.1 Evidence-based learning outcomes set for the practicum through a link with PRMEs and aligned with the four pillars of the GSTC

Evidence-based learning outcomes	Principles for responsible management education (PRME)	Pillars of the Global Sustainable Tourism Council (GSTC)
Identify the problem faced by the stakeholder and community and translate it into an answerable question	P1 – Purpose P2 – Values	Destination Management • Current approaches and mechanisms for planning and management of tourism
Incorporate extant theoretical knowledge into action relevant to the problem	P2 – Values P4 – Research	• Assessment of destination stewardship
Systematically search for and retrieve the best available evidence to circumscribe the problem under scrutiny	P4 – Research	• Diversification of the tourism product Community Involvement and Economic Impacts
Apply research methods to collect data and information and enhance students' and stakeholders' collaborative and learning experiences	P3 – Method P5 – Partnership	• Assessment of economic benefits resulting from tourism • Assessment of community involvement in visitor economy
Explicate noteworthy phenomena and data for their own sake (Barends and Rousseau, 2018)	P1 – Purpose P3 – Method P4 – Research P5 – Partnership P6 – Dialogue	Cultural and Natural Heritage Management Environmental Conservation
Develop knowledge regarding the current level of tourism sustainability in the Badung region of Bali within a sustainability framework that applies the GSTC criteria for destinations	P1 – Purpose P2 – Values P3 – Method P4 – Research P5 – Partnership P6 – Dialogue	• Assessment of management of water, solid waste, natural resources, and transportation • Responses to changes in climate

Source: The authors.

transformative learning of participants as they apply theoretical knowledge, searching skills, critical and analytical skills and reflections to:

1 Identify the best evidence for practice and decision-making
2 Use different sources of evidence to lead in research, collaboration and policy proposal
3 Acquire evidence and appraise its relevance and usefulness to the problem under study
4 Obtain practical insights into how to turn evidence into action

The second objective of the practicum was to identify key issues and priorities for sustainable destination management related to overtourism in Bali.

Bali's breathtaking tropical landscapes, white sandy beaches, its kind and tolerant people, and rich Hindu culture and temples have drawn millions of tourists (international and domestic) to its shores every year. Bali has been experiencing impacts from a ballooning population, the accumulated effects of mass tourism morphing into overtourism, and uncontrolled consumption of resources. The destination sustainability assessment results will provide tourism leaders, practitioners, educators and stakeholders with a snapshot of the destination's current performance on key sustainability indicators and help it to establish priorities for future development strategies. Pre-departure preparation also included cross-cultural training provided by GWU's global and experiential education department. The objective was to provide students the skills to communicate with and support local tourism stakeholders in making evidence-based decisions related to the problematic processes and issues under scrutiny.

Subjects of interest identified by students prior to departure during desk searches and analyses related to the problem of overtourism, including overcrowding, excess carrying capacity, commodification and erosion of culture, conflicts between residents and tourists, and the destruction of ecosystems (Dodds and Butler, 2018). Connections between (over)tourism as a phenomenon and tourism as an area of study were identified at the level of key tourism dimensions: (i) the tourist, (ii) businesses, (iii) host community, (iv) host environment, (v) host government, and (vi) generating country (Tribe, 1997). This structure was adopted to enable students to identify relevant theories and to be more focused during the problematisation phase. These descriptions are also significant, as they help to understand the assumptions underlying the EBT-TEF and the respective sets of principles for students, faculty, and local stakeholders to follow during the practicum and when applying the framework.

Phase 2 – practicum in situ

In order to efficiently address the issues identified in phase 1, students organised themselves into two teams while in Bali, each with three Indonesian counterparts. Each team focused on two different pillars of the GSTC destination sustainability criteria to,

1 Confirm the list of key stakeholders in the sector based on the exercise carried out in phase 1
2 Identify the key documents necessary to verify the indicators for assessment through reports and information from GSTC
3 Identify missing evidence/documentation about performance in the sector under each of the four pillars
4 Confirm the research methods identified in phase 1 as part of the triangulation (of methods, respondents and researchers) process adopted and implemented during the practicum
5 Appraise the literature collected related to key dimensions of tourism, including tourists' motivations, government policy and planning at both

the tourism and intersectoral levels, host community and socio-cultural impacts, host environment and ecological impacts, and host economy and business and economic impacts

6   Analyse the data and information gathered to assess and evaluate the state of destination sustainability national standards since Indonesia's adoption of the GSTC destination level criteria and indicators

7   Develop a Destination Sustainability Assessment Report for local stakeholders and deliver evidence-based recommendations to the government and community to address areas of priorities in view of the challenges that overtourism and concomitant problems represent to Bali's long-term sustainable and responsible tourism growth

Ultimately, the groups gathered evidence and information through primary data (in-depth interviews with key local stakeholders, local industry experts, community leaders and members, and participant observation), secondary data collection (industry reports, official local and national government reports, previously commissioned consultancy reports, and UNWTO and World Bank reports), and on-site evaluation. In the analysis phase, with the help of accompanying and local faculty members, students made sense of the data collected to answer questions related to the different GSTC criteria of assessment under each pillar. These answers were then critically appraised using extant literature to ascertain the evidence-based recommendations in the Destination Sustainability Assessment Report, which was finalised on the students' return to the United States.

Educational practices explicitly included in the practicum

The different learning outcomes and foci associated with the practicum and the Destination Sustainability Assessment Criteria respectively were operationalised through the following educational practices.

Core theoretical knowledge

The goal is for students to achieve intellectual coherence through theoretical knowledge[2] acquired during phase 1. At this level, disciplinary knowledge and thinking underpin the recommended tourism action. Units of basic tourism knowledge and theories are set to vertically integrate the broader curriculum under which the practicum sits, thereby assuring that graduate objectives are organised around impactful knowledge and research, collaborative and multidisciplinary scholarship, global outlook, technological and innovative education, problem-based and community learning, and field experience.

Research (evidence-based and basic research methods)

In this practicum, students are active participants, responsible for their learning, finding and assessing sources of evidence and information related to the problems they rationalise, the questions they ask, the research design they use, and the recommendations they make to the client based on their research results. To aid in that effort, the faculty members provided them the research skills to encourage inquisitiveness, creativity, and a thirst for knowledge. The practicum thus provided a curriculum employing a combined, aligned, and mutually complementary research-method and evidence-based approach. It required students to be aware of existing research and knowledge in the field to ultimately become reflective practitioners by evaluating both existing and their own research.

It was important for both faculty and students to understand the relationship between EBP and research. At several points during the practicum, students were challenged to integrate practical evidence (from literature, stakeholders, organisations, and practitioners) under each of the four pillars they were studying (for example, site interpretation as part of cultural and natural heritage management and water management and waste water as part of environmental conservation). Helping students incorporate the four sources of evidence into the research design required a deliberate shift in the delivery of education on methods and inquiry (Benner et al., 2019). One assumption is that the questions framing the research allow for critical perspectives and are fully ethical in line with the universal principles of right action, in accordance with the UNWTO Global Code of Ethics for tourism (https://www.unwto.org/global-code-of-ethics-for-tourism).

By embracing EBPs, students effectively undertook the following mix of actions based on Drisko and Grady's (2012) six steps of EPB, typically applied in nursing education:

a   Appreciate the situation of the client: This was achieved in phase 1 from desk research, case study, problem identification related to each of the four pillars, and a literature search for scientific evidence and existing 'similar' and 'dissimilar' cases for comparison and context to evaluate the evidence. The assumption is that the questions framing the research allow for critical perspectives and are fully ethical.

b   Circumscribe the client's goals, values and wishes: Following the above, students must understand the assumptions, motivations, goals, values, and wishes of the client in each of the four pillars. For example, under 'community involvement and economic benefits', the differing views of leaders and younger community members on preventing exploitation by the tourism sector had to be reconciled to incorporate differences in generational approaches to tourism practices and respect for cultural heritage and religious ceremonies.

c   Learn and appreciate solutions that 'work' based on the best available research identified in (a): The quality of and completeness of conceptualisations and the collected data are assumed to be fully adequate to determine what works (Drisko and Grady, 2012). For example, in their presentation to community leaders and local faculty members, students provided examples from published research relating to other countries that were working to reduce wastewater and solid waste in resorts under the 'environmental conservation' pillar.

d   Discuss client views about the recommendation to consider cultural and other differences, and to honour client self-determination and autonomy: Under the pillar 'destination management', for example, an assessment of criterion A3 revealed no evidence of an official or unified inventory of tourism assets and attractions for the Badung region. The recommendation that a list be agreed on and documented by the Bali Tourism Board and linked to the Badung Tourism Authority required holding public meetings to discuss which assets to include, as local communities and their leaders have strong opinions on the need for including local residents in that decision-making process.

e   Clarify with the client what the groups can, and cannot, provide fully and ethically (Gambrill, 2003; Gilgun, 2005): As part of what Tribe (2002) called ethical tourism practicum, this creates a space that encourages interactions and '... where communicative reason ... guide reflection for good action' (p. 320) and helps to assess that action.

Ultimately, actions derived from EBP were useful to both students and the client. The considerable attention paid to the different sources and quality of evidence led to 'many ways of knowing' (Hartman, 1990) the phenomenon of overtourism, making choices about ways to diagnose problems and impacts related to the phenomenon, and selecting interventions or programmes with the least negative impact or harm possible.

Transformational and experiential learning

The integration of EBP in the curriculum of sustainable tourism requires a transformation of the instructional and learning strategies for the practicum. This approach relies on students having an inquisitive mindset (in this example regarding overtourism and its social, economic and environmental impacts in Bali), access to information of what works (episteme), and how to make it work by applying methods and acquiring skills (techne). This allowed for the creation of a space where students were able to ask provocative questions about the use of evidence and their role in the maintenance of dominant ideas, particularly when community values, ideas, or approaches were not readily embraced by tourism policies and forms of practice.

During the practicum in Bali, respect for and protection of cultural authenticity was an expressed and understood value, albeit difficult for authorities to implement because the destination is continuously overrun by tourists. In that sense, the evidence-based framework provided both students and educators opportunities to discover the best answers to all questions relating to industry and educational practice. In fact, the literature provides evidence of the role of early tourism planning in the obstruction and traffic resulting from the 'savage build up' of tourism (Wall, 1998, 2018) along routes that held Balinese public ceremonies, such as the Siwa Ratree[3] or the Tumpek Uduh.[4]

Our knowledge of sustainable tourism – the framework for dealing with the relentless vagaries of mass tourism to ensure our future – tends to emerge from a mix of science, research, opinions, rituals, and traditions. This practicum has given students, community leaders and members, stakeholders, and faculty alike the knowledge and skills to embrace objective management of evidence and respect for the specificity of local knowledge and context (Jamal, 2004). The Tri Hita Karana award, for example, is a local ontological take on sustainability standards and practices. Interactions and interviews with local stakeholders and practitioners enabled the students to clearly understand the local assumptions underpinning the award, beyond its implementation in the tourism sector.

The EBTTEF model employed here also pays attention to the experience and expertise of practitioners, such as environmental and cultural experts. The wisdom (experience and expertise) they bring to the empirical evidence collected through scientific research (by students) is foundational to the rigor of the methods supported by educational aspects (Boswell and Cannon, 2016). The research skills and evidence-based capabilities that students developed, applied and reflected on in the practicum, coupled with their field experience, created a transformative learning experience that was essential for a 'know-in-action' tourism education.

Community- and problem-based learning

An instructional strategy cognisant of students' need to integrate field-based applied learning in tandem with community partners requires community- and problem-based learning. In terms of Tribe's (2002) use of the term 'phronesis' (that which aims at developing a disposition towards good action), students as practitioners must learn to identify, abstract, and apply contextual, situation-specific principles from extant scientific knowledge, combined with practitioners' knowledge, to take advantage of a sustainable tourism curriculum (Jamal, 2004). The practicum required students to confront a real-world problem and thereby prepared them for work and life after their studies. Without critical thinking and structured reflection, however, it would be difficult for them to leverage classroom learning to inform community practices. Understanding the principles of sustainable tourism, together with local knowledge and research skills, is necessary to develop a community-based strategy to address excessive tourism growth, (overtourism in this instance). Students' engagement and interactions with local communities throughout the practicum provided them with direct field experience, while benefiting from the supervision and coaching of experts, which helped to develop their professional skills.

Conclusion

This chapter described the implementation of a framework that seeks to implement best practices for sustainable tourism education. There are core skills that are essential to sustainable tourism education, which in this chapter involved the best approach to educate and train tourism students to face the problems created by overtourism. This chapter incorporated Tribe's intentional steps of EBP (2002) to connect with the PRME in an international field practicum. The EBTTEF demonstrates how a tourism practicum course can employ an evidence-based approach to the education of future tourism practitioners. The EBP-related course learning objectives and outcomes expected from students were clearly articulated at the outset.

While the framework is theoretically sound and contains the necessary elements for successful operationalisation, practical constraints (lack of time and resources) meant that its implementation was imperfect. Post-practicum, the participants stated that they would have benefited from a more substantial combined course on research methods and evidence-based approaches and that two seminar sessions were insufficient to convey the required knowledge. However, application of the framework in a field context proved to be feasible. Since the framework incorporates flexibility at various stages and assumes an iterative approach, teaching and moments of learning transformation occurred throughout the practicum. For example, practitioners, faculty, and students alike received a spontaneous presentation in the field on the significance of EBPs and how their incorporation in the teaching and learning design can help students to practice sustainable tourism management effectively and responsibly.

Notes

1 For details about the six principles of the PRME, please go to: https://www.unprme.org/about-prme/the-six-principles.php
2 Theories and knowledge with which students familiarised themselves include: Social Exchange Theory, Doxey's Irridex, Butler's five conditioning factors of relationships between residents and tourists, Upchurch and Teivane's (2000) use of Butler's (1980) tourism area life cycle (TALC), Ap and Crompton's (1993) attitude scale, Fishbein and Ajzen's theory of reasoned action, social action theory (Andriotis, 2003), and social carrying capacity (Saveriades, 2000).
3 Siwa Ratree is a ceremony in honour of Lord Shiva. Part of the ritual involves fasting, staying awake all night, and walking to the temples for prayers.
4 Tumpek Uduh is a ceremony devoted to Sanghyang Sangkara, Lord of all food and plants, during which a blessing ceremony is held for good crops and products. The ceremony is a long march along every plantation and farm throughout the island.

References

Airey, D. and Gross, M.J. (2015), *The Routledge Handbook of Tourism and Hospitality Education*, Routledge, London and New York.

Airey, D. and Tribe, J. (2005), *An International Handbook of Tourism Education*, Elsevier, London.

Andriotis, K. and Vaughan, R.D. (2003), "Urban residents' attitudes toward tourism development: The case of Crete," *Journal of Travel Research*, Vol. 42, pp. 172–185.

Ap, J. (1992), "Residents' perceptions on tourism impacts," *Annals of Tourism Research*, Vol. 19, pp. 665–690.

Ap, J. and Crompton, J.L. (1993), "Residents' strategies for responding to tourism impacts," *Journal of Travel Research*, Vol. 32, pp. 47–50.

Apple, M.W. (2001), "Comparative Neo-liberal projects and inequality in education," *Comparative Education*, Vol. 37 No. 4, pp. 409–423.

Australian National University, "Evidence-based MBA programme," https://www.cbe.anu.edu.au/study/programs/master-of-business-administration/ (Accessed on 18 April 2020).

Ayikoru, M., Tribe, J. and Airey, D. (2009), "Reading tourism education: Neoliberalism unveiled," *Annals of Tourism Research*, Vol. 36 No. 2, pp. 191–221.

Barends, E. and Rousseau, D.M. (2018), *Evidence-Based Management: How to Use Evidence to Make Better Organizational Decisions,* Kogan Page, New York.

Barnett, R. (2000), "Supercomplexity and the curriculum," *Studies in Higher Education*, Vol. 25 No. 3, pp. 255–265.

Benner, P., Sutphen, M., Leonard, V. and Day, L. (2009), *Book Highlights from Educating Nurses: A Call for Radical Transformation,* Jossey-Bass Publishers, Hoboken, NJ.

Berkes, A. (2009), *A bill for the more general diffusion of knowledge.* https://www.monticello.org/site/research-and-collections/bill-more-general-diffusion-knowledge (Accessed on 18 April 2020).

Boley, B. (2011), "Sustainability in hospitality and tourism education: Towards an integrated curriculum," *Journal of Hospitality and Tourism Education*, Vol. 23 No. 4, pp. 22–31.

Boswell, C. and Cannon, S. (2016), "Connection between evidence-based practice and nursing education," In Cannon, S. and Boswell, C. (Eds.), *Evidence-based Teaching in Nursing: A Foundation for Educators*, 2nd ed., Burlington, MA: Jones & Bartlett Learning, pp. 129–154.

Butler, R. (1992), "Alternative tourism: The thin edge of the wedge", In Smith, V.L. and Eadington, W.R. (Eds.), *Tourism Alternatives: Potentials and Problems in the Development of Tourism,* University of Pennsylvania Press, Philadelphia, PA, pp. 31–46.

Butler, R.W. (1974), "Social implications of tourism development," *Annals of Tourism Research*, Vol. 2, pp. 100–111.

Butler, R.W. (1980), "The concept of a tourist area cycle of evolution: Implications for management and resources," *Canadian Geographer*, Vol. 25, pp. 5–12.

Butler, R.W. (2019), "Overtourism and the tourism area life cycle" (Chapter 6), In Dodds, R. and Butler, R.W. (Eds.), *Overtourism: Issues, realities and solutions*, Berlin: De Gruyter, pp. 76–97.

Cañada, E. (2019), "Responses to overtourism in Guanacaste (Costa Rica): A rural water conflict perspective," In Milano, C., Cheer, J.M. and Novelli, M. (Eds.), *Overtourism: Excesses, Discontents and measures in Travel and Tourism*, CABI, Boston, MA, pp. 107–124.

Canadian Tourism Commission, Instituto de Estudios Turísticos, Turist Delegationen (2003), *Measuring Visitor Expenditure for Inbound Tourism: International*

Experiences, Model Border Survey: WTO Proposal, World Tourism Organization, Madrid.

Capezio, A., L'Espoir Decosta, J.N.P. and Keating, B. (2016), "Evidence-based management competency grid," Unpublished internal report, *Evidence-Based Management Integrated Curriculum*, Research School of Management, Australian National University.

Capocchi, A., Vallone, C., Pierotti, M. and Amaduzzi, A. (2019), "Overtourism: A literature review to assess implications and future perspectives," *Sustainability*, Vol. 11, p. 3303.

Canosa, A., Graham, A. and Wilson, E. (2020), "My overloved town: The challenges of growing up in a small coastal tourist destination (Byron Bay, Australia)," In Milano, C., Cheer, J.M. and Novelli, M. (Eds.), *Overtourism: Excesses, Discontents and measures in Travel and Tourism*, CABI: Boston, MA, pp. 190–204.

Cater, E. (1995), "Environmental contradictions in sustainable tourism," *The Geographical Journal*, Vol. 161 No. 1, pp. 21–28.

CEBMA. https://www.cebma.org/ (accessed on 17 April 2020).

Clancy, M. (2020), "Overtourism and resistance: Today's anti-tourist movement in context," In Pechlaner, H., Innerhofer, E. and Erschbamer, G. (Eds.), *Overtourism: Tourism Management and Solutions*, Routledge, London and New York, pp. 14–24.

Coca-Stefaniak, A., Morrison, A., Edwards, D., Graburn, N., Liu, C., Pearce, P., Ooi, C., Pearce, D., Stepchenkova, S., Richards, G., So, A., Spirou, C., Dinnie, K., Heeley, J., Puczkó, L., Shen, H., Selby, M., Kim, H. and Du, G. (2016), "Editorial," *International Journal of Tourism Cities*, Vol. 2 No. 4, pp. 273–280.

Collini, S. (2012), *What Are Universities For?*, Penguin, London.

Cooper, C. (1997), "A framework for curriculum planning in tourism and hospitality," In Laws, E. and Conroy, B. (Eds.), *The ATTT Tourism Education Handbook*, London: Tourism Society, pp. 24–27.

Cooper, C. and Shepherd, R. (1997), "The relationship between tourism education and the tourism industry: Implications for tourism education," *Tourism Recreation Research*, Vol. 22 No. 1, pp. 34–47.

Cooper, C., Shepherd, R. and Westlake, J. (1994), *Tourism and Hospitality Education*, University of Surrey, Guildford.

Cooper, C. P., Ruhanen, L. M. and Craig-Smith, S. J. (2004), "Developing a knowledge management approach to tourism research," *Proceedings of conference on Tourism: State of the ARt II*, Glasgow England.

Davies, W. (2015), *The Happiness Industry: How Government and Big Business Sold Us Well-being*, London, UK: Verso Books.

Di Leo, J.R. (2017), "Higher Education under late capitalism; identity, conduct, and the neoliberal condition," In Saltman, K. J. (Ed.), *New Frontiers in Education, Culture and Politics*, London: Palgrave Macmillan.

Dodds, R. and Butler, R.W. (2018), *Overtourism: Issues, Realities and Solutions*, De Gruyter, Boston, MA.

Donohue, F. (2008), *The Last Professors: The Corporate University and the Fate of the Humanities*, Fordham University Press, New York.

Doxey, G. (1975), "A causation theory of visitor-resident irritants: Methodology and research inferences." In *Sixth Annual Conference Proceedings of the Travel Research Association, Travel Research Association*, San Diego, CA, pp. 195–198.

Drisko, J. and Grady, M. (2012), *Evidence-based Practice in Clinical Social Work*, Springer-Verlag, New York.

Duch, B.J., Groh, S.E. and Allen, D.E. (2001), (Ed.). *The Power of Problem-based Learning*, Stylus Publishing, Sterling, VA.

Dyer, P., Gursoy, D., Sharma, B. and Carter, J. (2007), "Structural modelling of resident perceptions of tourism and associated development on the Sunshine Coast, Australia," *Tourism Management*, Vol. 28, pp. 409–442.

Eadington, W. and Smith, V. (1992), "Introduction: The emergence of alternative forms of tourism," In Smith, V. and Eadington, W. (Eds.), *Tourism Alternatives: Potentials and Problems in the Development of Tourism,* University of Pennsylvania Press, Philadelphia, PA, pp. 1–13.

Emerson, R.J. and Records, K. (2008), "Today's challenge, tomorrow's excellence: The practice of evidence-based education," *Journal of Nursing Education*, Vol. 47 No. 8, pp. 359–370.

Fishbein, M. and Ajzen, I. (1975), *Belief, Attitude, Intention, and Behavior*, Addison-Wesley, Reading, PA.

Font, X. and McCabe, S. (2017), "Sustainability and marketing in tourism: Its contexts, paradoxes, approaches, challenges and potential," *Journal of Sustainable Tourism*, Vol. 25 No. 7, pp. 869–883.

Frechtling, D. (2010), "The tourism satellite account: A primer," *Annals of Tourism Research*, Vol. 37 No. 1, pp. 136–153.

Freire, P. (1985), *The Politics of Education: Culture, Power, and Liberation,* Bergin and Garvey, South Hadley, MA.

Gambrill, E. (2003), "Evidence-based practice: Implications for knowledge development and use in social work," In Rosen, A. and Proctor, E. (Eds.), *Developing Practice Guidelines for Social Work Intervention*, Columbia University Press, New York, pp. 37–58.

Garrod, B. and Fyall, A. (1998), "Beyond the rhetoric of sustainable tourism?" *Tourism Management*, Vol. 19 No. 3, pp. 199–212.

Gerritsma, R. (2019), "Overcrowded Amsterdam: Striving for a balance between trade, tolerance and tourism," In Milano, C., Cheer, J.M. and Novelli, M. (Eds.), *Overtourism: Excesses, Discontents and Measures in Travel and Tourism*, CABI, Boston, MA, pp. 125–147.

Gilgun, J. (2005), "The four cornerstones of qualitative research," *Qualitative Health Research*, Vol. 16 No.3, pp. 436–443.

Go, F. (1998), "Globalization and emerging tourism education issues", In Theobald, W. (Ed.), *Global Tourism*, London: Routledge.

Goodenough, R.A. and Page, S.J. (1993), "Planning for tourism education and training in the 1990s: Bridging the gap between industry and education," *Journal of Geography in Higher Education*, Vol. 17 No. 1, pp. 57–72.

Goodwin, H. (2011), *Taking Responsibility for Tourism*, Goodfellow Publishers Limited, Oxford.

Gretzel, U. (2019), "The role of social media in creating and addressing overtourism" (Chapter 5), In Dodds, R. and Butler, R.W. (Eds.), *Overtourism: Issues, Realities and Solutions*, Berlin: De Gruyter, pp. 62–75.

GWU https://business.gwu.edu/ (Accessed on 18 April 2020).

Hartman, A. (1990), "Many ways of knowing," *Social Work,* Vol. 35 No. 1, pp. 3–4.

Hartmann, R. and Stecker, B. (2020), "Development of core indicators for the assessment and analysis of sustainable city tourism," In Pechlaner, H., Innerhofer, E. and Erschbamer, G. (Eds.), *Overtourism: Tourism Management and Solutions*, Routledge, London and New York, pp. 81–92.

Hess, J. S. (2019), "Thailand: Too popular for its own good," In Dodds, R. and Butler, R.W. (Eds.), *Overtourism: Issues, Realities and Solutions*, Berlin: De Gruyter, pp. 62–75.

Holloway, J.C. (1995), "Towards a core curriculum for tourism: A discussion paper," The National Liaison Group for Higher Education in Tourism, London.

IITS. (2018), *GW Tourism Consulting Project Scope of Work Bali*, Indonesia.

Ioannides, D. (2019), "Greenland's tourism policy making and the risk of overtourism," In Milano, C., Cheer, J.M. and Novelli, M. (Eds.), *Overtourism: Excesses, Discontents and measures in Travel and Tourism*, CABI, Boston, MA, pp. 209–223.

IUCN https://www.iucn.org/theme/global-policy/our-work/sustainable-development-goals (Accessed on 21 April 2020).

Jafari, J. and Ritchie, B.J.R. (1981), "Toward a framework for tourism education: Problems and prospects," *Annals of Tourism Research*, Vol. 8 No. 1, pp. 13–34.

Jamal, T.B. (2004), "Virtue ethics and sustainable tourism pedagogy: Phronesis, principles and practice," *Journal of Sustainable Tourism*, Vol. 12 No. 6, pp. 530–545.

Jóhannesson, G. T. and Lund, K.A. (2019), "Beyond overtourism: Studying the entanglements of society and tourism in Iceland," In Milano, C., Cheer, J.M. and Novelli, M. (Eds.), *Overtourism: Excesses, Discontents and Measures in Travel and Tourism*, CABI, Boston, MA, pp. 91–106.

Koens, K., Postma, A. and Papp, B. (2020), "Management strategies for overtourism: From adaptation to system change," In Pechlaner, H., Innerhofer, E. and Erschbamer, G. (Eds.), *Overtourism: Tourism Management and Solutions*, Routledge, London and New York, pp. 149–159.

Koh, K. (1995) "Designing the four-year tourism management curriculum: A marketing approach," *Journal of Travel Research*, Vol. 24 No. 1, pp. 68–72.

Kohl, J. (2019), "In focus 4: Managing overtourism through a holistic lens," In Milano, C., Cheer, J.M. and Novelli, M. (Eds.), *Overtourism: Excesses, Discontents and Measures in Travel and Tourism*, CABI, Boston, MA, pp. 224–226.

Krathwohl, D.R. (2002), "A revision of Bloom's taxonomy: An overview," *Theory into Practice*, Vol. 41 No. 4, pp. 212–218.

Kunh, T.S. (1971), "Notes on Lakatos, Boston," *Studies in the Philosophy of Sciences*, Vol. 8, pp. 137–146.

Laclau, E. and Mouffe, C. (1985), *Hegemony and Socialist Strategy: Towards a Radical Democratic Politics*, Verso Books, London.

Lea, J. (2015), *Enhancing Learning and Teaching in Higher Education: Engaging with the Dimensions of Practice*, Open University Press, Maidenhead, Berkshire.

Leiper, N. (1979), "The framework of tourism: Towards a definition of tourism, tourist, and the tourist industry," *Annals of Tourism Research*, Vol. 4, pp. 390–407.

Liu, R.Z. and Borthwick, A.G.L. (2011), "Measurement and assessment of carrying capacity of the environment in Ningbo, China," *Journal of Environmental Management*, Vol. 92 No. 8, pp. 2047–2053.

Lowrey, A. (2019, June 4), "Too many people want to travel," https://www.theatlantic.com/ideas/archive/2019/06/crowds-tourists-are-ruining-popular-destinations/590767/ (Accessed on 18 April 2020).

Macbeth, J. (2005), "Towards an ethics platform for tourism," *Annals of Tourism Research*, Vol. 32 No. 4, pp. 962–984.

Maimon, E.P. (2018), *Leading Academic Change: Vision, Strategy, Transformation*, Stylus, Sterling, VA.

Martín Martín, J.M., Guaita Martínez, J.M. and Salinas Fernández, J.A. (2018), "An analysis of the factors behind the citizen's attitude of rejection towards tourism in a context of overtourism and economic dependence on this activity," *Sustainability*, Vol. 10, pp. 2851.

Mathieson, A.R. and Wall, G. (1982), *Tourism: Economic, Physical and Social Impacts,* Longman, Harlow, Essex.

McCabe, S. (2009), "Who needs a holiday? Evaluating social tourism," *Annals of Tourism Research*, Vol. 36 No. 4, pp. 667–688.

McKercher, B. (2020), List of journals – Trinet communication Jan. 20, 2020 Trinet via lists.Hawaii.edu.

Milano, C., Cheer, J.M. and Novelli, M. (2020), *Overtourism: Excesses, Discontents and measures in Travel and Tourism*, CABI, Boston, MA.

Navarro, E., Tejada, M., Almeida, F., Cabello, J., Cortes, R., Delgado, J. and Solis, F. (2012), "Carrying capacity assessment for tourist destinations: methodology for the creation of synthetic indicators applied in a coastal area", *Tourism Management*, Vol. 33 No. 6, pp. 1337–1346.

Nunes Gonçalves, D. (2019), "In Focus 3: Brazilian media not yet concerned with overtourism," In Milano, C., Cheer, J.M. and Novelli, M. (Eds.), *Overtourism: Excesses, Discontents and Measures in Travel and Tourism*, CABI, Boston, MA, pp. 205–209.

Nussbaum, M. (2011), *Creating Capabilities: The Human Development Approach*, Belknap Press, Cambridge, MA.

Oppermann, M. (1992), "International tourist flows in Malaysia," *Annals of Tourism Research*, Vol. 19, pp. 482–500.

Page, S.J. (2003), "Evaluating research performance in tourism: The UK experience," *Tourism Management*, Vol. 24 No. 6, pp. 607–622.

Palinkas, L.A. and Soydan, H. (2012), *Translation and Implementation of Evidence-Based Practice*, Oxford University Press, New York.

Parkes, C., Buono, A.F., and Howaidy, G. (2017), "The Principles for Responsible management Education (PRME): The first decade – What has been achieved? The next decade – Responsible management education's challenge for the Sustainable Development Goals (SDGs)," *The International Journal of Management Education*, Vol. 15 No. 2, pp. 61–65.

Parsons, D. (1991), "The making of managers: Lessons from an international review of tourism management education programmes," *Tourism Management*, Vol. 12 No. 3, pp. 197–207.

Pechlaner, H., Innerhofer, E. and Erschbamer, G. (2020), *Overtourism: Tourism Management and Solutions*, Routledge, London and New York.

Pecot, M. and Ricaurte-Quijano. (2019), "'Todos a Galápagos?' Overtourism in wilderness areas of the global south," In Milano, C., Cheer, J.M. and Novelli, M. (Eds.), *Overtourism: Excesses, Discontents and Measures in Travel and Tourism*, CABI, Boston, MA, pp. 70–85.

Prayag, G., Hosany, S., Nunkoo, R. and Alders, T. (2013), "London residents' support for the 2012 olympic games: The mediating effect of overall attitude," *Tourism Management*, Vol. 36, pp. 629–640.

Qurashi, J. (2019), "The hajj: Crowding and congestion problems for pilgrims and hosts," In Dodds, R. and Butler, R.W. (Eds.), *Overtourism: Issues, Realities and Solutions*, Berlin: De Gruyter, pp. 185–198.

Reif, U. (2020), "Constantly adapting – Approaches for effective visitor monitoring and adaptive visitor guiding in the Black Forest National Park," In Pechlaner, H., Innerhofer, E. and Erschbamer, G. (Eds.), *Overtourism: Tourism Management and Solutions*, Routledge, London and New York, pp. 93–103.

Rickly, J.M. (2019), "Overtourism and authenticity," In Dodds, R. and Butler, R.W. (Eds.), *Overtourism: Issues, realities and solutions*, Berlin: De Gruyter, pp. 46–61.

Roser, M. (2020), "Tourism." Published online at OurWorldInData.org. https://ourworldindata.org/tourism (Accessed on 18 April 2020).

Roth, M. (2015), *Beyond the University: Why Liberal Education Matters*, Yale University Press, New Haven, CT.

Sachs, W. (1992), *The Development Dictionary: A Guide to Knowledge as Power*, Zed Books, London.

Saveriades, S. (2000), "Establishing the social tourism carrying capacity for the tourist resorts of the east coast of the Republic of Cyprus," *Tourism Management*, Vol. 21, pp. 147–156.

Schon, D.A. (1987), *Educating the Reflective Practitioner*, Jossey-Bass, London.

Seraphin, H.S., Sheeran, P. and Pilato, M. (2018), "Over-tourism and the fall of Venice as a destination," *Journal of Destination Marketing Management*, Vol. 9, pp. 374–376.

Sheldon, P. and Fesenmeir, D. (2015), "Tourism education futures initiative: Current and future curriculum influences" (Chapter 12), In Airey, D. and Gross, M.J. (Eds.), *The Routledge Handbook of Tourism and Hospitality Education*, Routledge, London and New York, pp. 155–170.

Sigala, M. and Baum, T. (2003), "Trends and issues in tourism and hospitality higher education," *Tourism and Recreation Research*, Vol. 4 No. 4, pp. 367–375.

Silver, H. and Brennan, L. (1988), *A Liberal Vocationalism*, Hodder and Stoughton, London.

Southgate, C. and Sharpley, R. (2002), "Tourism, development and the environment," In Sharpley, R. and Telfer, D.J. (Eds.), *Tourism and Development: Concepts and Issues*, Channel View Publications, Clevedon, pp. 231–262.

Stephens, J.C., Hernandez, M.E., Roman, M., Graham, A.C. and Scholz, R.W. (2008), "Higher education as a change agent for sustainability in different cultures and context," *International Journal of Sustainability in Higher Education*, Vol. 9 No.3, pp. 317–338.

Stuart-Hoyle, M. (2003), "The purpose of undergraduate tourism programmes in the United Kingdom," *Journal of Hospitality, Leisure, Sport and Tourism Education*, Vol. 2 No. 1, pp. 49–74.

Taylor, P.H. and Richards, C. (1985), *An Introduction to Curriculum Studies*, NFER-Nelson, Windsor.

Tribe, J. (1997), "The indiscipline of tourism," *Annals of Tourism Research*, Vol. 24 No. 3, pp. 638–657.

Tribe, J. (2002a), "Education for ethical tourism action," *Journal of Sustainable Tourism*, Vol. 10 No. 4, pp. 309–324.

Tribe, J. (2002b), "The philosophic practitioner," *Annals of Tourism Research*, Vol. 29 No. 2, pp. 338–357.

Tribe, J. (2006), "The truth about tourism," *Annals of Tourism Research*, Vol. 33 No. 2, pp. 360–381.

United Nations World Tourism Organization (UNWTO). *World Tourism Barometer* (2019), available at: https://www.unwto.org/world-tourism-barometer-2019-nov (Accessed 27 April 2020).

Upchurch, R.S. and Teivane, U. (2000), "Resident perceptions of tourism development in Riga, Latvia," *Tourism Management*, Vol. 21, pp. 499–507.

Volgger, M. (2020), "The end of tourism through 'localhood' and 'overtourism'?: An exploration of current destination governance challenges," In Pechlaner, H., Innerhofer, E. and Erschbamer, G. (Eds.), *Overtourism: Tourism Management and Solutions*, Routledge, London and New York, pp. 206–220.

Visentin, F. and Bertocchi, D. (2019), "Venice: An analysis of tourism excesses in an overtourism icon," In Milano, C., Cheer, J.M. and Novelli, M. (Eds.), *Overtourism: Excesses, Discontents and Measures in Travel and Tourism*, CABI, Boston, MA, pp. 18–38.

Wall, G. (1998), "Landscape resources, tourism and landscape change in Bali, Indonesia," In Ringer, G. (Ed.), *Destinations: Cultural Landscapes of Tourism*, Routledge, London, pp. 51–62.

Wall, G. (2019), "Perspectives on the environment and overtourism" (Chapter 3), In Dodds, R. and Butler, R.W. (Eds.), *Overtourism: Issues, Realities and Solutions*, Berlin: De Gruyter, pp. 27–45.

Yu, X., Kim, N., Chen, C.C. and Schwartz, Z. (2012), "Are you a tourist? Tourism definition from the tourist perspective," *Tourism Analysis*, Vol. 17, pp. 445–457.

10 Designing strategic and transformative tourism education programmes and education strategies

Tammi J. Sinha

Introduction

This chapter brings together the disciplines of transformative education, strategy development, and performance and role of tourism education to enrich and embed sustainability in our future tourism leaders. ESD (Educating for sustainable development) is a crucial part of the UN Sustainable Development Goals, as SDG4 (Quality Education) and SDG 13 (Climate action) are intrinsically linked. Bringing in the dimensions of transformative tourism education, will ensure that all we leave behind as travellers/tourists 'are foot-prints'. Treading lightly on the earth is a formula for tourism, tourism education AND transformative tourism education. Working the golden thread of this book, that is, the focus on 'overtourism and education', this chapter weaves the following into a rich tapestry: developing strategies with a focus on sustainability, developing transformative curriculum using good practice to enable 'flow', developing the governance themes to enable informed strategy development through portfolios of work (strategies), programmes of work (tertiary education programmes), and individual projects linking the themes of sustainability, flow, and tourism education. The research questions for this chapter are:

How can we design strategic and transformative approaches to tourism education?
What good practice can we draw on?
What does our roadmap and framework look like?
What are the paths through the roadmap?
What are the pitfalls? What are the delights?

The chapter begins with the foundations of the following theoretical constructs and themes: tourism strategy, transformative education in tourism, flow, designing strategic tourism education programmes, and overtourism and education.

Towards a best practice framework of strategic and transformative education

The chapter provides a framework which enables educators to develop strategies with a focus on sustainability, when developing transformative curriculum in tourism using good practice to enable 'flow'. This is informed by developing governance themes to enable informed strategy development through the classical approach of PPP – portfolios, programmes, and projects, that is, providing a framework for *portfolios* of work at a strategic level, *programmes* of work delivered through tertiary education programmes, and individual *projects* linking the themes of sustainability, flow, and tourism education through case studies and stories (Table 10.1).

Setting the scene – tourism strategy

Tourism generates growth, investment, employment, and cross-cultural experiences. The sector benefits local and national communities with this in mind, to develop economically, and lift communities out of poverty. However, the positive aspects of tourism bring a dearth of challenges at different systemic levels. The impact on the environment and social structures of mass consumerism and overtourism, has catastrophic impacts on the environment. There is a risk of depletion of natural resources, exploitation of the local population, lack of oversight, modern slavery, and distrust. The movement of energy between tourists and the communities welcoming

Table 10.1 Portfolio, programme, and project management applied to tourism education development

Portfolio – Strategy		Programmes – Education		Projects – Modules
National Tourism Strategy Choices	Content Process Stakeholders	Tertiary Tourism Education Programmes		Tourism Education Module
Impact				
–VE	+VE	Theory	Planning	Perspectives
Overtourism	Growth	T	Fit	Value
Mass consumerism	Cross-cultural	O	Emergence	Philosophy
Modern slavery	experience	U	Positioning	Balance
Depletion of	Investment	R	Resource-based	
national	Employment	I	Stakeholder	
treasures	Transformational	S		
		M		

Source: The author.

them, needs to be a positive experience for all stakeholders. The benefits of updating infrastructure, public services, transport, and the hospitality industry have the potential to bring positive and negative outcomes to communities (Ramirez and Rangel, 2018). Strategy may be defined as the setting of the direction and portfolio of work for a defined entity (APM Body of Knowledge, 2016). In the context of tourism strategy, as the impact of tourism on the economy and social justice is high, nationals and intra-national organisations must work together to ensure tourism strategy benefits all stakeholders. SSP – strategy- structure-performance – are a useful way to develop approaches which will have an impact on the communities hosting tourism, and the tourists visiting the communities. When exploring strategy and outcomes, it is helpful to link the 'content' they want (what), the 'process' (how), and 'stakeholders' (who) when setting a strategic course. Mishra and Mohanty (2020) provide 6 themes which help craft strategies for tourism, and transformative tourism education programmes to provide the leaders to plan and enact these strategies. These can be used as a checklist: planning, fit, emergence, positioning, resource-based, and stakeholders. Salazar (2019), a social cultural anthropologist, exposes the hypocrisy that tourism is mainly beneficial for development. He asserts that we must use multiple criteria for success. The measures should be developed using different perspectives, values, and philosophies, to ensure the balance of the local communities and tourists who visit. Whatever lenses are used in developing strategies, choices must be made, values embedded, and action plans initiated, as a finely crafted tourism strategy is worth nothing unless it is enacted.

Setting the scene – transformative education

Transformation and transformative are emotional terms. Sometimes transformation can be beneficial, and sometimes not. Kubler-Ross (1969) in her *On death and dying* provides a helpful model to show the stages we go through when some type of transformation is enacted: denial and isolation, anger, bargaining, depression, and acceptance. Transformation and change are sometimes about loss – loss of innocence, loss of rose-coloured glasses, loss of ignorance. Transformative tourism education benefits from this cycle, and educators need to be skilled in holding the space for students; if the education programme is truly transformative, the emotions experienced may follow this pattern. Researchers are starting to pay attention to the delivery and content of sustainable development education and tourism; however, the identification of the skills, knowledge, and attributes held and required by tourism students is at an early stage (Camargo and Gretzel, 2017). The Tourism Education Futures Initiative (TEFI) provides a hub for exploring the current and future needs of Tourism Education; originally set up in the 1990s, the forum has evolved to take a progressive and contemporary approach to tourism education. This means that tourism educationalists are working together to collaborate through pluralism and intercultural communication, in order to embed values of sustainable development education into their discipline.

Mezirow's (1997) Transformative Learning Theory offers four learning types:

1   Developing on existing frameworks and understanding
2   Downloading and learning new frameworks and understanding
3   Transforming routines and habits
4   Transforming points of reference and view

However, Yacek (2019) questions the premise that all transformation is positive in the fact that shifting and providing transformative experiences should not be taken lightly. Emotionally intense and potentially existential risky situations need to be risk assessed, thought through and led by experienced educators, who are also able to hold the space for their students, and able to provide appropriate lessons learned and debriefs. Yacek (2019) further outlines his view of transformative education as initiation through ethical experiences in the classroom. Transformation can be described as causing a marked change in the state of a person or an object. In this chapter we have constructed a good practice framework for strategic and transformative education, weaving sustainability and tourism as the context for the work. Therefore, it is helpful to outline the general qualities of a transformative education experience.

Should transformative tourism education be momentous, irreversible, discontinuous, and rapid? Some key issues that we should face as educators include consent and controversial direction. The other side of the coin is that travel and tourism ARE transformative. The word 'travel' comes from 'travail', to work, to toil, to engage in hard labour, both physically and intellectually. Therefore, we could argue that transformative travel is physically and intellectually momentous, irreversible, discontinuous, and rapid (Walker and Manyamba, 2019).

Transformative tourism education is crucial for our students, as it gives them the opportunity to transform in a 'safe space' to experience it before they may experience it in the 'outside world'.

> Transformative learning is the expansion of consciousness through the transformation of basic worldview and specific capacities of the self; transformative learning is facilitated through consciously directed processes such as appreciatively accessing and receiving the symbolic contents of the unconscious and critically analyzing underlying premises
>
> Elias (1997, p. 3)

Mezirow (1997) included the following phases as part of his transformative learning theory.

Phase 1: a disorienting dilemma. Phase 2: a critical self-examination with feelings of guilt and shame. Phase 3: a critical assessment of epistemic, sociocultural, or psychic assumptions. Phase 4: recognition that one's discontent and the process of transformation are shared and that others have negotiated a similar change. Phase 5: exploration of new options for new roles, relationships, and actions. Phase 6: planning a course of action. Phase 7: acquisition of knowledge and skills for implementing one's plan. Phase 8: provisional trying of new roles. Phase 9: building of competence and self-confidence in new roles and relationships. Phase 10: a reintegration into one's life on the basis of conditions dictated by one's perspective.

Stone and Duffy (2015) provide an insight into this through their Systematic Literature Review (SLR), 53 papers included both transformative learning theory and tourism studies. They support the need to hold the space for our students when they are disorientated especially in experiences that are novel, exposed, different routines, and the need for us as educators to be flexible, and able to teach and hold spaces for our students to encourage transformative learning. Pritchard et al. (2011) add to the debate with their 'hopeful' tourism pedagogy, which 'engage[s] democratic and emancipatory learning agendas, [and] transform[s] the traditional hierarchical character of much pedagogic practice ... and value[s] multiple worlds and knowledge experiences in the classroom ...'.

According to Mezirow (1997), our frames of reference consist of: meaning perspectives (taken-for-granted ways of being in the world), meaning schemes (fixed ways of seeing and being which emerge out of our meaning perspectives), habits of mind (habitual ways of thinking, feeling, acting, and seeing, which emerge from our meaning schemes), and points-of-view (resulting from our habits of mind which lead us to a particular interpretation). To build on these theories, the work of Csikszentmihalyi (2014) is a powerful addition to the mix of transformative tourism education.

Setting the scene – achieving flow

'Flow' according to Csikszentmihalyi (1996) is one of eight states of learning and occurs when we are engaged in a learning activity that is challenging to our skills and fully immersed and concentrating on the task in hand. This experience is a function of skills and challenges in a specific activity. Moneta and Csikszentmihalyi (1996) present four dimensions required for flow.

Concentration, Happiness, Involved, and *Wished* to engage in the activity. When we are engaged in a learning activity, our mental states from anxiety, apathy, boredom, arousal, relaxation, control, worry, and FLOW. Flow can be experienced in any activity, from education, candy crush to music. It has been described as being 'in the zone' where you are fully, joyfully immersed in the activity at hand.

This statement from Csikszentmihalyi's' interview with *Wired* magazine puts it beautifully:

> being completely involved in an activity for its own sake. The ego falls away. Time flies. Every action, movement, and thought follows inevitably from the previous one, like playing jazz. Your whole being is involved, and you're using your skills to the utmost.

And 'the holistic sensation that people feel when they act with total involvement' (Csikszentmihalyi and Csikszentmihalyi, 1988, p. 36). We can develop educational environments to enable the learner and educator to achieve flow through: (a) *Psychological triggers:* intense concentration, clear goals and instant feedback; (b) *Environmental triggers:* rich environments and a deep sense of place; (c) *Social triggers:* serious play and concentration, clear and shared goals, appropriate communication, familiarity, full participation, element of risk; and (d) *Creative triggers*: pattern recognition and risk taking (Csikszentmihalyi, 2014; Moneta and Csikszentmihalyi, 1996).

Designing strategic educational programmes for tourism futures

Developing robust and resilient approaches require clear definitions for foundations. Slack and Brandon-Jones (2019) explain strategy as a pattern of decisions and actions, that position the organisation within its environment, that enable long term goals to be realised.

In this context, strategy concerns the pattern of strategic decisions and actions pertaining to Tourism Futures Education, and sets the role objectives and activities of the educational operation. It can be used to articulate a vision for the contribution to the success of the university strategy.

The **process** is the activities taken to compose and action the strategy. There are four key perspectives to strategy: top down, which links organisational objectives to the sustainable and tourism education strategy; outside in, which links student needs and wishes; and inside out, which embodies the idea of the reflective practitioner, and Bottom up which links practice in the field and cases. It is worth remembering to engage our full range of stakeholders, both within and outside of our institution when developing these strategies and these strategic frameworks.

As previously mentioned, strategy consists of the process element and the content element. Returning to the **Process Element**.

There are four typical stages to developing strategy:

The first is **Formulation**. Such as 'An Educational Tourism Strategy to equip future tourism leaders with the skills, knowledge and attributes required to bring equity to the sector in terms of positive and negative effects. 'What are the steps needed?

The second stage is **Implementation**. How do we implement the above? What processes, technology, and team development are needed to enact the strategy? An example of this is the rapid move to online learning with the lockdown experienced with the COVID-19 pandemic, which requires a rapid enactment of a change in face to face teaching to online platforms with minimal training and many challenges.

Third phase is **Monitoring**. How do we ensure that the actions that we are taking and the decisions that we're making are contributing to our transformative educational strategy? Checking in with stakeholders and being able to respond to the changing environments is important in this phase.

And finally, the fourth stage is **Control**. How do we ensure that we control what we're doing and ensure that we get best outcomes for our students, our educators and our institution? This part embeds governance within the tourism education programme. The internal and external checks to ensure positive aspects are embedded, and negative aspects are engineered out of the delivery.

Another useful cycle, drawn from the Six Sigma body of work, developed by General Electric, and Motorola, in the early 1990s is affectionately known as **DMAIC.**

D stands for **DEFINE**. This is where we define the scope of the framework for developing strategies for transformative education. The second phase is **MEASURE**. This is where we look at the current situation and decide if the current situation fits with our strategy, and whether we actually need to make some adjustments, these adjustments could be incremental in nature, or they could be radical in nature. The third phase in DMAIC is **ANALYSE** where data shows the current state. What is working well, not working well and what could make this even better. Appreciative inquiry developed by Whitney and Cooperrider (2011) is used here. Next comes IMPROVE where the current situation, the analysis enables us to identify feasible changes, whether they're incremental again, or whether they are transformational. Final phase is **CONTROL** where the changes are embedded in business as usual.

Hays and Wheelwrights (1985) model shows how we could contribute to the education and educational experience of our students, developed from analysing 'excellent' organisations. It can be very helpful in looking at good practice in developing these types of frameworks.

STAGE ONE

The Tourism Education Programme is internally neutral. This means that they still need to correct the worst problems and are not addressing the concerns of the sector or students.

STAGE TWO

Externally neutral, when Tourism Education Programmes start to adopt good practice. Educators are starting to implement relevant and robust education strategies.

STAGE THREE

Internally supportive. Higher Education Institutions Tourism Education Programme strategy, is now transformative in nature, linking the strategy with the educational values and operations.

STAGE FOUR

Externally supportive, tourism education programmes that we offer and the work that we do as educators are seen as giving the department/university/school an advantage.

So, stage one, holding the organisation back, stage two, as good as our competitors, stage three, the best in our educational sector, and stage four, redefining expectations. The notion of maturity can be applied to sustainable tourism education. The paradigm shift to sustainability, initiated by the Brundtland Commission's report on sustainable development (World Commission on Environment and Development, 1987) is a useful start, or go back to the first Earth Day in 1970.

Stage 1 programmes could be those that focus on theoretical knowledge of tourism, sustainability and sustainable development principles.

Stage 2 adapting good practice through embedding transformative learning theory with sustainability and tourism.

Stage 3 seen as world leading in the area, would bring together a trans disciplinary approach to tourism education – highlighting the systemic nature of political values and ideology, social and cultural theory and practice, intergenerational theories and practice, and economics. Even stage 3 is not sufficient.

What would be your vision for a Stage 4? Returning to the work of TEFI and their call for 'a value-based approach to sustainable tourism that can help address the challenges facing the tourism industry' (Sheldon, Fesenmaier and Tribe, 2010). TEFIs 5 values that they hope all graduates will embody are ethics, stewardship, mutuality, professionalism and knowledge. Linking theory to practice, believing that they have the skills, knowledge, and attributes to make a difference in the tourism sector.

Portfolios, programmes, and projects

The 3P approach to developing and actioning strategy is explored below. The following is adapted from the APM Body of Knowledge (2016). The portfolio sets the general direction, values, and overall strategy for the organisation. The programmes are set up to deliver the benefits required by the portfolio. In higher education these are generally education, research, knowledge exchange, and outreach programmes.

In Higher Education, the Portfolio delivers the strategy direction of the university. In the UK many measures and tools enable students to choose which university to apply to. The National Student Survey, and other league tables add to the dataset. One could argue that these are helpful, but we could also argue that many of these surveys are fundamentally flawed.

Applying this to a typical UK University, the portfolio sets the direction, develops the values and instils the culture of the institution. In the case illustrated below: 'a community committed to making a difference, passionate about seeing individuals and communities flourish'. The portfolio, programme, and project model acts as the governance structure for the institution. How this filters down to faculties and individual programme strategies provides universities with their unique selling point. Universities are typical in that the different functions mirror that of other organisations. Professional services encompass marketing, operations, finance, technology, and human resources. The 3PM approach links these disciplines together to deliver the overarching and education strategy of the institution. We need to link strategic thinking of programmes to the delivery, which from this point will be referred to as the operations or value delivery of the University.

To embody a transformative and sustainability approach to tourism education, the following questions should be addressed.

1   What skills and capabilities do our educators need to provide transformative experiences, and challenging education?
2   What measures are appropriate? Remember the causality between performance measures and behaviour.
3   What systems and technologies do we need to support our education programmes?
4   What resources are available?
5   What are the business processes that underpin the value delivered?
6   Who builds up the RACI? Who is responsible, accountable, consulted, and informed?

Contribution to framework

Products

What are the 'products' offered?

In the educational context: a programme of study, a year of study within a programme, a semester or a module within a semester. Individual sessions can also be seen as products. How do we enable our educators and students to co-create sessions that will deliver the required skills, knowledge and attributes?

An example of this is the 'Whole Earth' exhibition curated by the photographer Mark Edwards. The series of banners are used to engage students (and staff) with the hard-hitting images of climate change, enabling educators to immerse their students in the themes and challenges (and successes) of linking quality education to climate action. Curated works such as 'whole earth' enable Universities to show the interconnectedness and multi-disciplinary approaches needed to equip our students to be leaders in the future. Tourism students are well placed to take a lead with sustainability education and ESD (education for sustainable development) as many tourist destinations are suffering from overtourism, exploitation, and the revenue from their endeavours flowing elsewhere.

Range offered

There are a number of considerations when identifying the range of programmes and modules offered.

The experience that our students have? In the field, in workshops, in lecture hall, placements

How are they supported? Online, face to face, mixed approaches, online, virtual reality, augmented reality

What sort of sessions do we run?

The guidelines that we give them for the work that's expected?

As educators we need to be there in the moment, co-creating the sessions with our students to ensure that we are providing them with an excellent, transformative programme, challenging and keeping them in flow.

The following factors enable the strategic development of educational programmes.

What makes this programme the clear choice for students? Is it accessibility? The challenge? The transformative nature?

Are the programmes contemporary and challenging, enabling students to be in flow?

Do they meet the specifications in the programme handbooks?

Are students satisfied with the education that they receive from an institution's perspective?

Designing strategic educational programmes

In this work, it is helpful to draw on good practice from innovators in this field, such as the innovative Danish KAOSPILOT Business School. Their approach to strategic development of education programmes draw on elements of design thinking, with an emphasis on connecting theoretical knowledge with experiential learning, ensuring theory and practice are intertwined in a challenging and stimulating way. The development of the 'whole' person is important, too often we build silos around our teaching, as a way of enabling our students to make sense of their discipline, however by doing this we put up barriers to learning, the interconnectedness of reality is sometimes lost. The practice ensures that students are educated for and IN real life and experiences. Problem-based learning is seen as helpful and crucial to developing students' attributes, knowledge, and skills to become reflective practitioners and global citizens in this area. The following dimensions are associated with transformative education:

5 PROCESS LEADERSHIP
6 DEVELOPING PEOPLE
7 HIGH PERFORMING TEAMS
8 INITIATING, DESIGNING, AND STARTING UP VENTURES
9 SEEING POSSIBILITIES AND RISKS
10 ACT IN ACCORDANCE WITH VALUES, BELIEFS, AND MOTIVATION
11 BELIEVE IN OWN CONVICTIONS
12 BE AGENTS OF CHANGE
13 LEADERS IN THEIR FIELD
14 CREATE SOLUTIONS IN RESPONSE TO 'WICKED ISSUES' (CAREFULLY DEFINED)
15 BEING ABLE TO COPE WITH AMBIGUITY, UNCERTAINTY, AND CHANGE

The overall aim is to build up knowledge bases, but to also gain the ability to act and react. Therefore, knowledge and capability building are needed for transformative education. Being challenged, developing responses, and becoming reflective practitioners is the goal.

A competency model has been developed which incorporates subject, relationship, change, and action competences. As you can imagine, this is a powerful combination. Enabling students to be challenged and transformed through their studies. Linking back to flow, enabling 'magic' to happen in terms of developing our students' understanding, skills, and attributes.

In terms of PEDAGOGY (the method of teaching and learning) this approach is systemic in nature, bringing together a heady mix of behaviours, skills, attitudes, values, knowledge, competencies, and learning that promote creative responses to problems and problematical situations. Bringing together the inner and outer world of theory and practice. As an aside this is transformative for the student AND the educator.

Distilling this further, the core principles of this approach include:

Action learning – projects provided by external clients, organisations and businesses. Making it real and live! **Grounded in practice** – using all of their senses to 'make sense' of situations and work to feasible solutions. **Mindful** – bringing the students' intent into play.

Intent – setting the goals and intent of the learning clearly. **Knowledge** – ensuring the knowledge base is contemporary, builds and benefits the body of knowledge in the discipline.

Reflective – developing students as 'reflective practitioners' builds the cycle of learning from pragmatism-action-theory-reflection to enable double loop learning to occur.

Experimental – enabling students to 'fail' and to learn from failure is a key strength of this approach and **Involving** – helping to develop strong high performing teams, and to ensure all are involved.

Suggested rubrics

The following competences could form the rubrics used in transformative tourism education.

Subject competence

Vocational vocabulary, knowledge of theoretical perspectives and the ability to place this competence into a context, for instance a tourism project.

Problem Solving, formulate the problems and solve these by applying the relevant theories, skills, and attitudes. Such as the possible causes for over-tourism and the potential solutions.

Research exploring, experimenting, selecting, and applying the appropriate knowledge, skills, processes and tools necessary to achieve the stated objectives. Exploring the lived experience of workers and visitors in the tourism sector.

Systems thinking, ability to see, understand, reflect, and interpret the tourism domain, from a systemic perspective and put it into an independent view and meaning – may it be societal, social, economic, cultural, and inter-personal relationships and contexts.

Relationship competence

To make *connections* and gain the *trust* of others.

Understanding and considering stakeholders needs.

Establishing cooperation and working together as high performing teams with projects, assignments and objectives.

Understanding communication channels and *social networks*.

Action competence

Ability to put one's knowledge, insight, experiences, visions, values, dreams and situational understanding into practical and goal-oriented action.

Leadership, follow through, tolerance of ambiguity, attitude towards risk, initiative, motivating oneself and others, ability to set goals, prioritise, and decide.

Change competence

Ability to challenges and think anew and outside the box in connection with understanding, framing and approaching a challenge.

Initiate inquiries with originality, innovation, and perceptiveness supported by informed critical analysis and judgement.

Ability to learn, to further existing competences or reject it and to connect competence from different disciplines.

Manage and integrate different perspectives, theories, complexity, and turbulence.

Structure and infrastructure

The **structure** is the hardware and **infrastructure** the software of the educational programme.

1   Structure – typical decisions to make:

Which tourism programmes and modules should be developed?
What learning activities should be done internally?
What could be outsourced? (e.g. hourly paid lectures, external suppliers, speakers, presenters, and outside organisations?
How should our physical and online space be utilised for transformative tourism education?
What types of technology do we have available?

2   Infrastructure – typical decisions to make:

How should the tourism and hospitality discipline function be organised?
What skills should be developed in our educators?
How should demand for our programmes be forecast and monitored?
How should our tourism programmes adjust our activity levels in response to demand?
How should we allocate resources?
How should we develop our external relationships with the tourism industry?
How should we measure success and failure?
How should we improve the overall offering for our transformative tourism education programmes?

In summary

Strategy, according to Slack and Brandon-Jones (2019), is the total pattern of decisions and actions that position the organisation and its environment, and are intended to achieve the organisation's long-term goals. Strategy concerns the pattern of strategic decisions and actions, and sets the role, objectives, and activities of the (educational) operation. It can be used to articulate a vision for the contribution to organisational success. Strategy has content and process. The content addresses specific decisions that are taken to achieve specific objectives. The process is the procedure that's used within an organisation to formulate its strategy. There are four key perspectives to strategy: top down, outside in, inside out, and bottom up. We have to

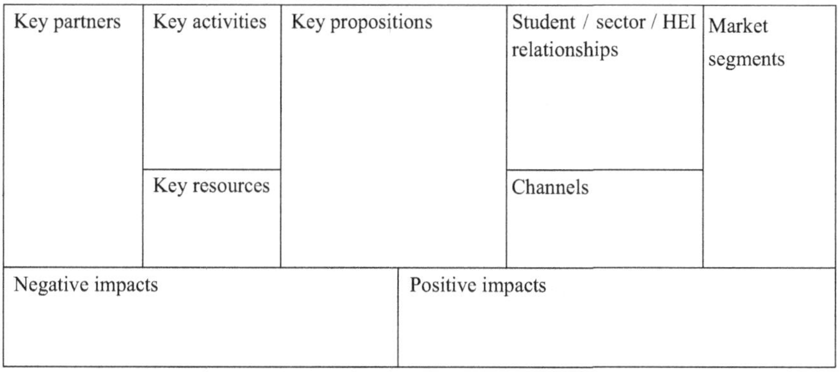

Key partners	Key activities	Key propositions	Student / sector / HEI relationships	Market segments
	Key resources		Channels	
Negative impacts			Positive impacts	

Figure 10.1 Transformative tourism education programme canvas.

remember to engage our full range of stakeholders, both within and outside of our institution.

The transformative tourism education programme canvas is offered as a road map and tool to develop these strategies at a programme level and has been developed from the business model canvas of Osterwalder et al. (2011). The canvas brings together the elements presented in the chapter (Figure 10.1).

The key proposition is the central part of the strategy, with the remaining elements showing the key activities, stakeholders, channels for delivery, market segments, and the perceived negative and positive impacts of tourism that are being explored.

Theory into practice

Designing strategic and transformative tourism education programmes and education strategies.

The purpose of the chapter is to answer the following:

1   How can we design strategic and transformative approaches to tourism education?
2   What good practice can we draw on?
3   What does our CANVAS (road map and framework) look like?
4   What are the paths through the roadmap?
5   What are the pitfalls? What are the delights?

The previous sections have covered questions 1 to 3. This section draws on literature to highlight the contemporary themes and topics that should be included in developing these strategies for tourism education.

Pathways through the canvas/roadmap

Weber (2017) distilled a series of cases analysed by a range of universities. From Baku to Cozumel, the great barrier reef to Soweto. The case studies showed the challenges facing the tourism industry, and therefore guide the response for universities providing the programmes to research, educate, and share knowledge with the future tourism leaders. A dominant theme shows core themes of over-burdened infrastructure, social impacts such as unaffordable housing, intolerance and inter-racial issues, and undesirable behaviour by visitors. Contextual factors were themed around facilities (lack of) sensitive ecosystems, social disparity, and high dependency on one sector. Of course the key findings are that challenges are individual and unique, and are strongly dependent on local contexts.

The contemporary issues that need to be weaved into the tapestry include the following: An appreciative inquiry approach to Tourism highlighting the positives of the sector, in balance with the challenges that need to be explored and addressed. The key challenges (which of course are location specific) include antitourism protests, lack of sustainability in tourism management, trexi (short for tourism exit), and overtourism (Seraphin, Sheeran and Pilato, 2018).

The positive movement of sustainability and sustainable development education has at its root – paraphrasing the UN and the Brundtland Commission – 'development that meets the needs of the present without compromising the ability of future generations to meet their own needs' (1987). The tourism industry is seen as having a positive and negative effect on the locality (Seraphin and Nolan, 2018). Future leaders and students will need to be able to navigate through these challenges. Visser's (2015) work on sustainable frontiers should form the core to tourism programmes and modules. Additional disciplines that should be embedded within tourism programmes include:

Systems and Design thinking, Ambidextrous management, Creativity and Flow, Green tourism, and the United Nations Sustainable Development Goals, Factory 4.0.

The UN Sustainable Development Goals 2 – Quality Education and 13 – Climate Action applied to the Tourism Sector (Table 10.2).

The strategic tourism choices and impacts should be assessed against the UN SDGs and ensure that when developing the strategies for transformative tourism, good practice from multiple disciplines are embedded. That programmes are challenging and ensure future leaders in tourism (students) are fully immersed in the learning outcomes and activities developed.

Transformative Education Theory calls for rapid, discontinuous, irreversible, and momentous modules and experiences. There are several approaches which could be used for this: problem based learning, assigning industry mentors and coaches, providing opportunities for industry shadowing, volunteering, and work experience which is challenging but is also

Table 10.2 UN Sustainable Development Goals 4 and 13 linked to tourist education

Goal 4 Quality Education https://www.un.org/sustainabledevelopment/education/ *By 2030...*	*Goal 13 Climate Action* https://www.un.org/sustainabledevelopment/climate-change/ accessed 29.02.2020
Tourism focused	**Tourism focused**
4.3 Ensure equal access for all to affordable and quality technical, vocational, and tertiary education, including university tourism programmes. **4.4** Substantially increase the number of youth and adults who have relevant tourism skills, including technical and vocational skills, for employment, decent jobs, and entrepreneurship in the sector. **4.5** Eliminate gender disparities in education and ensure equal access to all levels of education and vocational training for the vulnerable, including persons with disabilities, indigenous peoples, and children in vulnerable situations **4.7** Ensure that all learners acquire the knowledge and skills needed to promote sustainable development, including, among others, through education for sustainable development and sustainable lifestyles, human rights, gender equality, promotion of a culture of peace and non-violence, global citizenship, and appreciation of cultural diversity and of culture's contribution to sustainable development **4.A** Build upgrade education and tourist facilities that are child, disability, and gender sensitive and provide safe, nonviolent, and inclusive effective learning environments for all.	**13.1** Strengthen resilience and adaptive capacity to climate-related hazards and natural disasters in all countries through eco-tourism. **13.2** Integrate climate change measures into national policies, strategies, and planning for tourism. Advocating circular design and supply chains for providers of tourism products and services. **13.3** Improve education, awareness-raising, and human and institutional capacity on climate change mitigation, adaptation, impact reduction, and early warning. **13.B** Promote mechanisms for raising capacity for effective climate change-related planning and management in least developed countries and small island developing States, including focusing on women, youth, and local and marginalised communities. Embed ISO14000 to reduce carbon footprints of tourist operators.

held by the tutors and industry coaches with the understanding that students need to have time to download and assimilate the learning, which at times will be challenging. In the industrial landscape, Factory 4.0 is hailed as the next industrial revolution. The technologies that are part of this revolution include augmented reality, artificial intelligence, and the internet of things. In the tourism industry TOURISM 4.0 espouses 'big data, artificial intelligence and data mining are key to a sustainable and personalised tourism' (Curk, 2020). As Tourism Futures is about people, their exploration and aspirations. The landscape can be physical or virtual, it can be unknown and known. Digitalisation can benefit the tourism industry and the educators of future Tourism leaders, understanding the processes that underpin the industry, the ecosystem that must be protected, and the stakeholder needs, enables us as educators to use innovative approaches to promote innovation in the tourism industry, and to utilise big data to model impact (Peceny et al., 2019).

The chapter started with the aim of developing strategies with a focus on sustainability, developing transformative curriculum using good practice to enable 'flow', developing the governance themes to enable informed strategy development through Portfolios of work (strategies), programmes of work (tertiary education programmes) and individual projects linking the themes of sustainability, flow, and tourism education. The delights of developing approaches for a strategic and transformative approach is that educators and students will experience flow, and be able to challenge the status quo in a systematic way. The pitfalls of this approach may be the challenging environment that we are facing with climate change and COVID-19.

References

Camargo, B.A. and Gretzel, U. (2017). What do tourism students know about sustainability and sustainable tourism? An exploratory study of Latin American students. *Journal of Teaching in Travel & Tourism*, 17(2), 101–117.

Crane, F.G. (2004). The teaching of business ethics: An imperative at business schools. *Journal of Education for Business*, 79(3), 149–151.

Csikszentmihalyi, M. (2014). *Flow and the Foundations of Positive Psychology: The Collected Works of Mihaly Csikszentmihalyi*. Dordrecht: Springer.

Csikszentmihalyi, M. and Csikszentmihalyi, I. (Eds.), (1988). *Optimal Experience, Psychological Studies of Flow in Consciousness*. Cambridge: Cambridge University Press.

Curk, T. (2020). Faculty of Computer and Information Science, University of Ljubljana, https://tourism4-0.org/ (Accessed 3 April 2020).

Devis-Rozental, C., Eccles, S. and Mayer, M. (2017). Developing socio-emotional intelligence in first year HE students through one-to-one learning development tutorials. *Journal of Learning Development in Higher Education*, 12, 18–39.

Elias, D. (1997). It's time to change our minds: An introduction to transformative learning. *ReVision*, 20(1), 2+.

Hopkins, D. (2020). Sustainable mobility at the interface of transport and tourism: Introduction to the special issue on "Innovative approaches to the study and practice of sustainable transport, mobility and tourism." *Journal of Sustainable Tourism*, 28(2), 225–239. doi:10.1080/09669582.2019.1691800.

Joo, D., Woosnam, K.M., Strzelecka, M. and Boley, B. (2020). Knowledge, empowerment, and action: Testing the empowerment theory in a tourism context. *Journal of Sustainable Tourism*, 28(1), 69–85.

Kemper, J.A., Ballantine, P.W. and Hall, M. (2019). Combining the 'why' and 'how' of teaching sustainability: The case of business school academics. *Environmental Education Research*, 25(12), 1751–1774.

Kubler-Ross, E.K. (1969). *On Death and Dying*. New York: Touchstone.

Mezirow, J. (1997). Transformative learning: Theory to practice. *New Directions for Adult and Continuing Education*, 74, 5–12.

Moneta, G.B. and Csikszentmihalyi, M. (1996). The effect of perceived challenges and skills on the quality of subjective experience. *Journal of Personality*, 64(2), 275–310. doi:10.1111/jopy.1996.64.

Osterwalder, A., Pigneur, Y., Oliveira, M.A.Y. and Ferreira, J.J.P. (2011). Business model generation: A handbook for visionaries, game changers and challengers. *African Journal of Business Management*, 5(7), 22–30.

Peceny, U.S., Urbančič, J., Mokorel, S., Kuralt, V. and Ilijaš, T. (2019). *Tourism 4.0: Challenges in Marketing a Paradigm Shift. In Consumer Behavior and Marketing.* London: IntechOpen.

Pritchard, A., Morgan, N. and Ateljevic, I. (2011) Hopeful tourism: A new transformative perspective. *Annals of Tourism Research*, 38(3), 941–963.

Schott, C. (2015). Digital immersion for sustainable tourism education: A roadmap to virtual fieldtrips. In G. Moscardo and P. Benckendorff (Eds.), *Education for Sustainability in Tourism* (pp. 213–227). Berlin Heidelberg: Springer.

Seraphin, H. and Nolan, E. (2018). *Green Events and Green Tourism: An International Guide to Good Practice.* London: Routledge.

Seraphin, H., Sheeran, P. and Pilato, M. (2018). Over-tourism and the fall of Venice as a destination. *Journal of Destination Marketing & Management*, 9, 374–376.

Sheldon, P., Fesenmaier, D. and Tribe, J. (2010). The tourism education futures initiative (TEFI): Activating change in tourism education. *Journal of Teaching in Travel and Tourism*, 11(1), 2– 23. doi:10.1080/15313220.2011.548728.

Stone, G.A. and Duffy, L.N. (2015). Transformative learning theory: A systematic review of travel and tourism scholarship; *Journal of Teaching in Travel & Tourism*, 15(3), 204–224.

Visser, W. (2015). *Sustainable Frontiers. Unlocking Change through Business, Leadership and Innovation.* Sheffield: Greenleaf Publishing.

Walker, J. and Manyamba, V.N. (2019). Towards an emotion-focused, discomfort-embracing transformative tourism education. *Journal of Hospitality, Leisure, Sport & Tourism Education*, ahead-of-print, DOI:10.1016/j.jhlste.2019.100213

Weber, F. (2017). Overtourism. An analysis of contextual factors contributing to negative developments in overcrowded tourism destinations. *BEST EN Think Tank XVII: Innovation and Progress in Sustainable Tourism*, Conference Proceedings, 315–320.

Whitney, D. and Cooperrider, D. (2011). *Appreciative Inquiry: A Positive Revolution in Change.* ReadHowYouWant.com (accessed 4 May 2020).

Yacek, D.W. (2019). Should education be transformative? *Journal of Moral Education*, 49(2), 1–18. doi:10.1080/03057240.2019.1589434.

Conclusion

Hugues Séraphin and Anca C. Yallop

Education and its strategic impact on sustainability in tourism and cognate sectors

Tourism education has been given much consideration in the existing literature and suggested as a useful step towards preventing the problem of irresponsible tourism. However, it is crucial to look into tourism education from the perspectives of both formal and informal education. On one hand, formal education is the education provided in higher education institutions by way of professional courses or research conducted in the tourism domain. On the other hand, informal education through industry, business, and government initiatives aimed at informing and educating travellers is equally influential for stakeholders like tourists, locals, tour guides, travel agents, and local administrative staff involved in the tourism industry. While positive steps have been taken in academia to promote education concerning the negative ramifications of overtourism, another avenue for solving a collective action problem is to develop global rules and norms that promote sustainable tourism. Political aids and decisions become all the more important in this instance. Taking the example of the Principles for Responsible Management Education (PRME) that are voluntarily adhered to by some business schools worldwide, with the aim of improving education practices, such guidelines and principles could be enforced as required norms and standards. Although the aspect of (formal and informal) education is often overlooked in the study of tourism development and destination management, it has tremendous influence on how tourism is developed (its rate, scale, and form) and how a community will be able to respond to sustainable issues. Overall, this book suggests that tourism education has a positive impact on tourism destination performance in terms of nights spent, turnover, and added value, with a more prominent influence in the case of developing countries as it contributes to increase productivity and to maintain competitiveness. Tourism is a multi-disciplinary area of study that is deeply embedded in contemporary social and economic life. Tourism education can therefore contribute to understanding of (and dealing with) the broader societal challenges within the framework of the UN SDGs.

Tourism today and tomorrow: the need for a research agenda focused on young travellers

Focusing on young travellers is important for two main reasons: First, there is a dearth of academic research in tourism with children and young travellers (Canosa and Graham, 2016; Canosa, Graham and Wilson, 2018a, b; Khoo-Lattimore, 2015; Poria and Timothy, 2014; Seraphin and Yallop, 2019). For Canosa, Graham and Wilson (2018a, p. 520), 'the paucity of tourism and hospitality research involving children is rather disconcerting'. For instance, when some tourism studies are about consumers of the tourism industry, children are not systematically taken into consideration (Hertzman, Anderson and Rowley, 2008; Poria and Timothy, 2014; Seraphin and Yallop, 2019a, b). Indeed, 'tourism and hospitality research to date has focused almost exclusively on adult perspectives, often overlooking, if not neglecting, the views of children and young people' (Canosa, Graham and Wilson, 2018a, p. 519). Second, the current perception and practice of research with children and young travellers in tourism need to be reviewed and new approaches put forward, as many academics are supporting the fact that children are just as important as adults for academic research in tourism (Canosa, Graham and Wilson, 2018a; Khoo-Lattimore, 2015; Poria and Timothy, 2014; Radic, 2017).

Empowerment happens when a group (or an individual) attempts to gain control of its destiny and/or affairs by means of competencies development, which is the outcome of a learning process (Joo et al., 2020). For this reason, the term 'empowerment' is associated with other terms such as 'enabling', 'to make responsible', 'reengineering', 'mastery', and 'control' (Boella and Goss-Turner, 2020; Boley et al., 2014). Three types of empowerment have been identified in tourism (Boley et al., 2014; Strzelecka, Boley and Woosman, 2017): (1) Psychological empowerment (sense of pride); (2) social empowerment (development of social capital, and equilibrium within a group); and (3) political empowerment (involvement in decision-making). These different forms of empowerment come to fruition if appropriate practical strategies are put in place. Adams (2008) identified the following approach to empowerment as the most effective: Cathartic and facilitative (enable people to express their feelings), catalytic (enabling people to engage in self-discovery, self-directed living; problem-solving), supportive and catalytic (enabling people to build self-confidence), and finally self-advocacy (enabling people to speak for themselves). Involving children and young travellers in sustainability actions could contribute to their social and psychological empowerment, through self-advocacy and cathartic and facilitative strategies.

References

Adams, R. (2008). *Empowerment, participation, and social work* (4th edition). Basingstoke: Palgrave Macmillan.

Boella, J.M., & Goss-Turner, S. (2020). *Human resource management in the hospitality industry. A guide to best practice.* Abingdon: Routledge.

Boley, B.B., Gard McGehee, N., Perdue, R.R., & Long, P. (2014). Empowerment and resident attitudes toward tourism: Strengthening the theoretical foundation through a Weberian lens. *Annals of Tourism Research*, 49, 33–50.

Canosa, A., & Graham, A. (2016). Ethical tourism research involving children. *Annals of Tourism Research*, 61(15), 1–6.

Canosa, A., Graham, A., & Wilson, E. (2018a). Reflexivity and ethical mindfulness in participatory research with children: What does it really look like? *Childhood*, 25(3), 400–415.

Canosa, A., Graham, A., & Wilson, E. (2018b). Child-centred approaches in tourism and hospitality research: Methodological opportunities and ethical challenges. In R. Nunkoo (Ed.), *Handbook of Research Methods for Tourism and Hospitality Management.* Cheltenham: Edward Elgar Publishing.

Canosa, A., Graham, A., & Wilson, E. (2019). My over loved town: The challenges of growing up in a small coastal tourist destination (Byron Bay, Australia), In Milano, C., Cheer, J.M., & Novelli, M. (eds.), *Overtourism. Excesses, discontents and measures in travel and tourism* Wallingford: CABI, pp. 190–205.

Canosa, A., Wilson, E., & Graham, A. (2017). Empowering young people through participatory film: A post methodological approach. *Current Issues in Tourism*, 20(8), 894–907.

Hertzman, E., Anderson, D., & Rowley, S. (2008). Edutainment heritage tourist attractions: A portrait of visitors' experiences at storyeum. *Museum Management and Curatorship*, 23(2), 155–175.

Joo, D., Woosnam, K.M., Strzelecka, M., & Boley, B.B. (2020). Knowledge, empowerment, and action: Testing the empowerment theory in a tourism context. *Journal of sustainable tourism*, 28(1), 69–85.

Khoo-Lattimore, C., Prayag, G., & Cheah, B.L. (2015). Kids on board: Exploring the choice process and vacation needs of Asian Parents with young children in resort hotels. *Journal of Hospitality*, 24(5), 511–553.

Poria, Y., & Timothy, D. J. (2014). Where are the children in tourism research? *Annals of Tourism Research*, 47, 93–95.

Poris, M. (2006). Understanding what fun means to today's kids. *Young Consumers*, 7(1), 14–22.

Radic, A. (2017). Towards an understanding of a child's cruise experience. *Current Issues in Tourism*, 22, 237–252.

Séraphin, H., & Yallop, A. (2019a). Proposed framework for the management of resorts mini clubs: An ambidextrous approach. *Leisure Studies*, 38(4), 535–547.

Séraphin, H., & Yallop, A. (2019b). An analysis of children' play in resort miniclubs. Strategic implications for the hospitality and tourism industry. *World Leisure Journal,* doi:10.1080/16078055.2019.1669216.

Strzelecka, M., Boley, B.B., & Woosnam, K.M. (2017). Place attachment and empowerment: Do residents need to be attached to be empowered? *Annals of Tourism Research*, 66, 61–73.

Index

Note: **Bold** page numbers refer to tables, *italic* page numbers refer to figures and page numbers followed by "n" denote footnotes.

Printed in the United States
By Bookmasters